Sermons On The First Readings

Series I

Cycle B

Curtis Lewis
Richard E. Gribble, csc
Linda R. Forsberg
Timothy J. Smith
H. Alan Stewart

CSS Publishing Company, Inc., Lima, Ohio

Copyright © 2002 by
CSS Publishing Company, Inc.
Lima, Ohio

Scripture quotations marked (NRSV) are from the *New Revised Standard Version of the
Bible*, copyright 1989 by the Division of Christian Education of the National Council of
the Churches of Christ in the USA. Used by permission.

Library of Congress Cataloging-in-Publication Data

Sermons on the first readings : Series I, Cycle B / Curtis Lewis ... [et al.].
   p. cm.
Includes bibliographical references.
   ISBN 0-7880-1899-X (pbk. : alk. paper)
   1. Bible. O.T.—Sermons. 2. Sermons, American—21st century. 3. Church year sermons. I. Lewis, Curtis.
   BS1151.55 .S47 2002
   252'.6—dc21
                                               2002004241

For more information about CSS Publishing Company resources, visit our website at
www.csspub.com or e-mail us at custserv@csspub.com or call (800) 241-4056.

ISBN 0-7880-1899-X

Table Of Contents

Sermons For Sundays
After Pentecost (Last Third)
by H. Alan Stewart

Sermons On The First Readings

For Sundays In
Advent, Christmas,
And Epiphany

Curtis Lewis

These sermons are dedicated to the special people in my life:

My wife Patsy, who has been a source of encouragement and inspiration by her dedication to Jesus Christ.

Thanks, Carol P.

Kevin, Michelle, Lanissa, and Clay, who love Dad in spite of his "hyper-activity," and have always believed in him.

Marissa, Kiersten, and Baby Calvin, grandchildren who are the greatest!

Bob, a special friend who has been like a brother, with whom I have shared my heart.

Come On Down

One of the most popular television game shows is *The Price Is Right* hosted by long-time emcee Bob Barker. When you receive tickets to attend this highly-watched, fast-moving game show, you become automatically eligible to have your name drawn to become a participant. As the show opens, names are drawn, and an announcer exclaims, "Mary Jones, come on down!" Mary excitedly jumps from her seat and runs down to the front of the game show set to compete with other contestants for an opportunity to go on the platform to guess the price of various show cases. If Mary is lucky, she will beat out the other competitors by coming the closest to the price of a certain item or items. When this happens, she runs onto the platform to compete for various prizes and show cases. Competing on *The Price Is Right* all begins when the announcer calls a contestant's name and asks her to "Come on down!"

Isaiah in chapter 64:1-9 gives us a picture on this first Sunday of Advent of his desire for God to reveal himself once again to his people. For Isaiah, God must appear. The great Advent hymn reveals this desire of Isaiah and of people of all times for God to come down. The hymn echoes the heart cry of humankind:

> *O come, O come, Emmanuel,*
> *And ransom captive Israel,*
> *That mourns in lonely exile here*
> *Until the Son of God appears.*

This is Isaiah's desire, but it is also our desire: that God, during this Advent Season, would reveal himself to us anew.

Notice what the prophet does ...

He Petitions God

The prophet addresses a people who are powerless and oppressed. His address is in the form of a prayer which for us contains the hope of Advent. There are two distinct elements in this prayer, and they are a cry of desperation and a confidence in God who can intervene in the human situation.

Isaiah wants God to "come down." There is the suggestion that God is removed from the earth. In order for God to become actively involved in the affairs of humankind, he will, of necessity, have to rip open heaven so that he can become involved in the affairs of earth.

This petition of the prophet is a reminder that Advent is the cry for God to reveal himself. Elie Wiesel tells of an ancient story that has meaning for our time and helps us understand the prophet's cry.

A man is on a boat. He is not alone, but acts as if he were. One night — without warning — he suddenly begins to cut a hole under his seat. The other people on the boat shout and shriek at him: "What on earth are you doing? Have you gone mad? Do you want to sink us all? Are you trying to destroy us?" Calmly the man answers: "I don't understand what you want. What I'm doing is none of your business. I paid my way. I'm not cutting under your seat. Leave me alone!" What the fanatic (and the egotist) will not accept, but what you and I cannot forget, is that all of us are in the same boat.[1]

Wiesel was right; we are all in the same boat. Advent is our cry for God to come and do something before we sink.

Isaiah in his petition reminds God of how he came and helped in the past. He wants God to intrude once again in the life of the people. Is not the purpose of Advent to take us back to the beginning in the person of Jesus Christ and to remind us that Jesus Christ will come to consummate all history under his reign of love?

When we look at the pain and suffering of our dark world, the prophet's cry becomes our cry, for we want God to "come down" and right wrong and reveal his glory and majesty by his presence.

The prophet petitions God to "come down," but in order to attract God's attention, something must be done besides shouting. He then proceeds to ...

Confess The Nation's Guilt

The tone suddenly changes. As the prophet surveys the situation, he lowers his voice and confesses the guilt of the nation, for Israel has sinned and is unclean. What does the prophet do? He leads the entire nation in a confession of sin.

So often the church has viewed the Lenten season as the time of confession, repentance, and penitence. Is it possible that for the church really to experience Advent, there must be genuine confession and repentance? For all of us truly to prepare for the coming of Christ, there must always be confession and repentance. Confession is a clearing house for the church to seek the mercy of God. True confession washes away the arrogance of thinking that we can save ourselves.

W. E. Sangster, in his book *The Pure in Heart*, relates the story of an evangelistic preaching mission held in York near the end of the nineteenth century. One night at the conclusion of the sermon several people responded to the invitation. In the group that came forward was an elderly man. The speaker counseled with each one who had come forward, including this elderly man who quietly and meekly answered the questions he was asked. Later the evangelist learned that the elderly gentleman was David Hill, a saintly and distinguished Methodist missionary to China who happened to be home on furlough. Hill was soon to return to China, a country he dearly loved where he would die of typhus at Hankow. The evangelist sought David Hill out and made a stumbling apology for having treated him as a beginner in the Christian faith. David Hill responded very simply, "I thought it would do me good to kneel among the penitent."[2]

Advent comes each year to judge us and remind us that we are all sinners. Advent also answers the question, "How can we be saved?" The prophet reminds Israel and us that our own efforts to save ourselves leave us like a filthy rag, contaminated and impure, so awful that one dare not touch it. In our own strength we are like a fall leaf, faded and vulnerable, that will be blown away.

How can we be saved? It is only through true confession and repentance, which are echoed in the Kyrie Elesion, "Lord have mercy upon us."

From petition and confession the prophet moves to issue ...

A Plea To God

Suddenly, the emphasis of the prophet shifts from the past to the present. This is a present tense moment, and God for the first time is mentioned by name

Using powerful indicatives, God is reminded that:

> *You are our Father;*
> *You are our potter;*
> *We are all the work of your hand.*

It is almost as if the prophet has become a defense attorney making the final argument before a jury. As he proceeds with his argument, he acknowledges that God is the all-powerful, all-wise, all-loving one. In an emotional appeal, he begs God to look and see what has become of his people, the Holy City, and the Temple. His argument reaches its climax with the expression, "Yet, O Lord, you are our Father!" In other words, what God has started to fashion with his hands should be completed. It is a plea for God to break into their isolation and to destroy sin's gridlock. This plea is also the plea of Advent that God would come. Advent means coming, and in the person of Jesus the true Advent will come.

When the *Exxon Valdez* spilled thousands of gallons of crude oil along the beautiful Alaskan shoreline, accusations and finger pointing began immediately. In the midst of the fray, a suggestion was made that Exxon's president make a trip to see firsthand the horrible damage to the environment. His response was to imply that such a trip would be a waste of time. He could have gone, but chose not to. The response of people everywhere to this disaster

18

might have been different had the president of Exxon gone and gotten down in the muck, and cleaned and freed a few geese.

A Chinese Confucius scholar who was converted to Christ told this story:

> *A man fell into a dark, dirty, slimy pit. He tried to climb out of the pit, but he couldn't. Confucius came along. He saw the man in the pit and he said, "Poor fellow, if he'd listened to me, he never would have gotten there," and went on. Buddha came along. When he saw the man in the pit, he said, "Poor fellow, if he'll come up here, I'll help him," and he too went on. Then Jesus Christ came and he said, "Poor fellow!" and jumped into the pit and lifted him out.*[3]

Our plea at Advent is that God would come alongside us. The message from God is that he has come and that we are his people. We respond, "How do we know you have come?" He answers, "Look at Jesus beside you in the muck of your world and lives and know that I have come. I am down there with you."

---

1. Elie Wiesel, quoted in *Parade Magazine*, April 19, 1992.

2. W. E. Sangster, *The Pure in Heart* (Epworth Press, 1955), p. 161.

3. Gary Inrig, *Hearts of Iron, Feet of Clay* (Chicago: Moody Press, 1979), p. 285.

Advent 2
Isaiah 40:1-11

Getting Ready For Advent

Many Americans have become very familiar with courtroom settings. This familiarity has been made possible by the O. J. Simpson trial and such programs as *Judge Judy, Judge Brown,* and the popular Court TV Channel.

In a sense, Americans are afforded an opportunity to become involved in the legal and judicial profession simply by pushing the correct button on their remote control. Here they can listen to the evidence, predict the outcome of various trials, and practice law without a license.

Isaiah, the prophet in our Old Testament lesson for today, depicts a courtroom setting which is vastly different than what one usually pictures. This courtroom is a "heavenly courtroom." The people of God have been found guilty; they have been sentenced for their sins and are serving their prison term. Now something unusual happens in the "heavenly courtroom." God, the judge, meets with his council and issues a complete or full pardon because the people of God have paid what God has required them to pay. Their sentence is commuted. They are fully pardoned, and a new day is dawning.

How will God reveal to his people that their long nightmare has ended? What means will he use to reveal himself to a people who were deaf and blind? Isaiah helps us prepare for Advent ...

By Announcing Comfort

The "good news" of comfort comes to a people who have suffered moral degradation and mental humiliation. This word of

21

comfort reminds Israel that their long night of punishment has ended. These people had been dominated and beaten down so long that they remind one of a description given by Charles Colson who served a prison sentence because of his involvement in the Watergate Scandal. When Colson went to prison to serve his sentence, he noticed something that fascinated him. He described this fascination as the "prison shuffle"; people in prison trudging along, doing their time with bowed heads and slumped shoulders, shuffling along on lethargic legs.

Colson observed that those inmates who do the prison shuffle try their best just to blend into the woodwork or hide in the landscape. They do the prison shuffle.

Colson, in his book *Born Again*, describes it like this:

Federal Prison Camp ... Two hundred fifty men lived here, but watching them through the window was like watching a silent movie in slow motion. Droop-shouldered, stick-like figures of men were drifting aimlessly and slowly in the open area; others were propped up against the buildings and a few were sitting in small clusters on benches. The figures just seemed to be floating ever so slowly. I was soon to learn that no one walks fast in prison. [Everything was drab even] the expressions on the faces. Something strange here. Then it struck me — no one was smiling ... A chill swept over me.[1]

It is to a group of exiles that the message of comfort comes. This message of comfort simply states that God's people no longer have to do the "prison shuffle" because the period of their forced labor is ended, and they have more than paid for the sin of breaking off their personal relationship with God. Hence, God now speaks tenderly to their hearts inviting them to respond to his love.

This same comfort is at the heart of Advent. As the chapter 40 of Isaiah suggests, Advent offers us the good news that we can find this same comfort in the midst of our exile and estrangement from God. The expectation of such comfort can lead us to the Christ event which is the climax of Advent. It begins with the prophetic thunderings of judgment, but it moves to the fullness of time when hope emerges from the womb of Mary and our comfort is visible, physical, identifying with us because "the Word became flesh." Comfort is the message of Advent because this one who came from

Mary's womb is our Emmanuel who sets us free from the prison that incarcerates us. Because of "God with us," we no longer do "the prison shuffle." We understand that his comfort is "good news"!

From the "good news of comfort" Isaiah issues ...

A Command To Prepare For The Coming Of The Lord

The media that the prophet uses in issuing this command to prepare for the coming of the Lord is that of a human voice. This voice is used like an exclamation point. "Listen! Someone is calling out!"

In Isaiah's day when a reigning king decided to travel throughout his kingdom, workers were sent ahead of his chariot literally to clear the road on which the king had to travel. Isaiah knew what this entailed. Work crews had to go ahead of the king's entourage to level hilly places and fill in holes and ruts so that the king's journey would not be impeded. With this picture in mind, the prophet does something extraordinary. He pictures the living God marching before his people across the desert and hills that lie between Babylon and the homeland. All obstacles to God's coming are pushed out of the way as God moves out of the chaos and confusion of the wilderness.

As Advent is celebrated again this year, let us also be reminded that we too are to push any obstacles such as pride, prejudice, materialism, and selfishness out of our lives in preparation for the coming of the King who will bring structure and order to our chaotic and confused lives and world.

In the New Testament, John the Baptist picks up the role of herald. John does not proclaim that he is a prophet; rather he states that he is a voice. John, in the wilderness proclaims, "I am the voice of one crying out in the wilderness ... as the prophet Isaiah said" (John 1:23). The voice of Isaiah's herald is the voice of John in his own day. The old word of Isaiah now becomes the new word of John, and these words converge for a dramatic purpose. That purpose is to announce that Advent is coming.

Advent will simply mean that a new day will dawn with the birth of Jesus Christ. John the Baptizer brings together the word of promise from Isaiah and a new word of fulfillment. The essence of Advent brings "joy to all people."

In truth, what Isaiah and John both are saying is that Advent is the time to get ready; however, ready or not, the Messiah is coming. Do you remember playing Hide and Seek as a child? The person who was "It" hid his or her eyes and counted to one hundred by fives. When the magical number one hundred was reached, these words would be shouted, "Ready or not, here I come," and the search for those in hiding would ensue. Isaiah and John are warning us to get ready, to prepare for Advent, but whether we are prepared or not, "He is coming."

What will happen when he comes? Isaiah informs us that "the glory of the Lord will be revealed." With this expression, Isaiah reveals the universality of God's reign. Where God's glory is revealed and people acknowledge that glory, then and only then, will our crazy, angry world be changed.

That is the hope of Advent! Just before Yom Kippur 1997, eight-year-old Yuval Kavah was struck and killed by a car on a busy street in Tel Aviv. Yuval's parents rushed him to a hospital where coincidentally a little Palestinian girl, whose name was Rim Alija-roushiu, lay dying of heart failure. In a gesture that stretched across prejudice, hatred, and ethnic backgrounds, Yuval's parents offered their son's still beating heart to any child who needed it. After the organ was harvested from Yuval's chest, it was transplanted into Rim's chest. When the surgery was completed, an Israeli mother and Palestinian mother embraced, weeping tears of joy and grief, and a Jewish boy's heart beat inside a little Palestinian girl's breast.

When we hear and read of events like this, we pray and hope that the ancient cry of Advent will become our cry. "Prepare the way of the Lord. The glory of the Lord shall be revealed and all people shall see it together, for the mouth of the Lord has spoken" (Isaiah 40:3, 5).

From the preparation for Advent, there is now a ...

Cry Of Desperation

The prophet has been commanded to cry. He asks the question, "What shall I cry?" He is protesting the command. Because he does not know what to cry, he suddenly points to the fragility of human life. It is as if he shrugs his shoulders and says, "What's the use? There is nothing lasting in life!" In this statement the prophet is reflecting the resignation of the exiles to judgment and death. In his eyes everything is hopeless.

Suddenly, in verse 8 there is a response which overrides the objections and offers hope. Yes, humanity is like withering and fading flowers which quickly pass from the scene. However, in contrast to humanity, the word of God endures forever. Now the prophet no longer speaks his word; instead, he speaks the Word of God, and this word endures and becomes the very heart of his message.

Let's face it, we too can become very discouraged when we look at the human predicament, and we can find no reason to speak. When we remember the promise and hope of Advent, we discover the enduring word, and that word "will stand forever."

What then will be the word that we speak at Advent? It will be a word of hope. Mother Teresa related an encounter she had with an old man in Calcutta:

> *"Who is this Christ of Mother Teresa's?"*
> *"He's our Guru, old man, our Lord and our God."*
> *"What God is this?"*
> *"He's a God of love, old man. He loves all of us —*
> *me and you too!"*
> *"How could he love me, Mem Sahib? He doesn't even*
> *know me."*
> *"Oh, yes, he does! Didn't he reach out across the*
> *city for you? Didn't he send his Sisters to the slums of*
> *Motijhil to bring you here? Doesn't he love you then,*
> *old man?"*
> *After a pause the old man said: "Could I love him,*
> *do you think?"*
> *"Of course you could — it's easy to love him — we'll*
> *love him together, old man, but sleep now. We'll talk*
> *again in the morning. Sleep now old man."*[2]

Advent declares that human life may be transitory but that God's word "stands forever," and his word is a word of love.

Finally, the Herald completes his work by ...

Announcing God's Coming

There is only one place to proclaim the coming of God and that is a high mountain. This announcement is climactic: "Here is your God!" What an announcement of God's advent! Just as the Herald announces the coming of God to ancient Israel to take away fear and despondency, so the message of hope is announced by John the Baptizer. This cry of Advent is announced with the words, "Here is the Lamb of God who takes away the sin of the world" (John 1:29). What an Advent message! A battle has been fought, and the evil one has been confronted. In Christ his defeat is evident.

The God of Isaiah comes with might to protect his sheep and gather his lambs in his arms. This God was able to, and willing to, save Israel. She no longer needed to fear. Jesus is the Good Shepherd who will lead his people, and he will be the center of their lives bringing healing, reconciliation, and joy. Life without him is doomed to failure, confusion, futility, and the dread of death.

Advent informs us that our God is coming, and he will shepherd his people. "Here is your God!" "Here is the Lamb of God who takes away the sin of the world." This Advent announcement transforms the darkest tragedy into the most gracious blessing.

Advent comes to those who wait, whose sins God has forgiven in Christ. Let's get ready for him to come.

---

1. Charles Colson, *Born Again* (Fleming H. Revell Co., 1976), p. 266.

2. Mother Teresa, *In the Silence of the Heart: Meditations by Mother Teresa of Calcutta* (London: SPCK, 1983), p. 43.

Advent 3
Isaiah 61:1-4, 8-11

Good News!

For a period of time there was an emphasis on good news/bad news stories. In good news/bad news stories, details keep turning from triumph to tragedy and back again.

One such story which was related quite frequently was about two friends who were avid baseball fans. These two friends made a pact that whoever died first would come back and let the other know if there was baseball in heaven. The first one died and came back and contacted his friend and said, "Hey, man, I have great news for you! The good news is that there is baseball in heaven, but the bad news is that you're scheduled to pitch Friday."

Isaiah the prophet understood the good news/bad news concept. For a while it seemed that everything was bad news. The people of Judah had lived with bad news for so long that they wondered if there would ever be any good news. Suddenly, the prophet brings those who have been beaten down good news. This good news overcame all of the bad news which had been in place for so long. In words that bolster and strengthen, the prophet gives words of promise and deliverance. The people had confessed their inability to save themselves. God had intervened with grace and power and brought redemption and the reaffirmation of his everlasting covenant.

The prophet's good news is so good that the people know that the bad news has ended. This "good news" of the prophet Isaiah is also "good news" for the Church during Advent. The prophet announces to the people that ...

There Is Good News Over In Judah

The weary exiles had finally come home. As they glanced at the piles of rubble of their once-elegant city, all they could think of was what had been lost. Babylon and exile seemed in the far distant past. As they looked at the ashes of their holy city, as they stood in the midst of devastation, they grieved and mourned for a glory that was lost.

From out of nowhere, a prophet appeared on the scene in Judah with news — good news from God. This prophet was certain that he had been sent and joyfully announced: "The spirit of the Lord is upon me, because the Lord has anointed me; he has sent me to bring good news to the oppressed, to bind up the broken-hearted, to proclaim liberty to the captives, and release to the prisoners" (61:1).

The message of the prophet is simple, startling Good News! It is this: "God is faithful to his word and his promise. He keeps the covenant he makes. But there is more, much more; God is a God of salvation who brings relief and comfort to his people."

The prophet wants the returning exiles to understand that their cities will be restored, and they will be compensated for their loss.

These people, so beaten down, needed to be freed from their fears and have the joy of living restored. When we look at this lesson for the Third Sunday of Advent, it is as if we are seeing a woman dressed for a funeral. The symbols of ashes, the sound of weeping, and a faint spirit are apt descriptions of those in mourning. Judah suffered these symptoms because the people had lost all hope and felt they were doomed to death.

This lady who has received a death notice and is dressed for a funeral receives a message that a mistake has been made. Instead of receiving a death notice, she should have received an invitation to a wedding. What does this person do? Immediately, she washes the ashes of mourning from her face, changes from funeral clothes to clothing appropriate for a wedding, and then decorates her hair with a garland of flowers. The ashes of death have given way to a crown of joy.

The prophet Isaiah envisions this change of Jerusalem as a bride preparing for her wedding, flittering here and there with a blush on her cheeks, singing, humming, smiling, and laughing. The wedding dress of Jerusalem is the "garment of praise" which symbolizes the transformation of character. Jerusalem is now a beautiful bride dressed for her wedding and not a sad mourner headed for her funeral.

Something has happened to the people of God. They have been given a new name and a new status. The new name will remind them that they now have a new name which will offer them potential. They are now large trees with deep roots for the purpose of displaying God's glory.

The people will now be able to repossess the land that was destroyed and taken from them. All of their ruin and brokenness will be restored.

We have in these scriptures a picture of the hope of Advent. God will keep his word. Our redeemer will come and take away the funeral dirge from our lips. In its place he will give us a song of praise. Too many people are living dressed in the garment of death, but the good news of Advent is that there is one coming who will give us "life and that more abundantly."

The Good News over in Judah is the Good News of Advent, for you and for me. Not only was there Good News over in Judah, but Advent reminds us that ...

There Was Good News Down In Nazareth

Before the coming of Jesus Christ there was not a lot of joy in the world or in Nazareth. Poverty, slavery, superstition, and fear ruled the lives of people. They were dominated and controlled by a foreign power. There was no hope. God seemed remote and distant from the scene. One day a young man thirty years of age, a Jewish craftsman and the son of a craftsman in Nazareth, a despised village in a despised district, stood in a Sabbath service in the synagogue and was handed the Isaiah scroll to read. He read a portion of this lesson. To everyone's amazement, when he finished, he stated: "Today this scripture is fulfilled!" Who would have thought that God would appear in Nazareth, of all places? Who would have thought God would come down to dirty old Nazareth?

29

They didn't rejoice or celebrate when Jesus made that claim in Nazareth. He was just a hometown boy. Their response was to rush him out of the service and try to throw him off a cliff. The people of Nazareth were scandalized by the offer of unlimited grace and therefore did not receive the "good news." Jesus, the Son of God, was there in Nazareth! Salvation day had dawned, and God's promises were fulfilled. It was the dawning of a new day; a new age had started.

Advent is advance notice that our God is coming. The "good news" which was rejected down in Nazareth is now available to you and to me. Today, this day, the scripture is once again fulfilled in our hearing.

Yes, there was good news down in Nazareth, but the real news is that ...

The Good News Is Our News

God is breaking through. In the person of Jesus who is the hope of Advent, God is coming to our level where there is sorrow, sin, and guilt. Advent anticipates Jesus coming to meet us in our despair, sin, guilt, and death with the good news of forgiveness. This lesson reminds us that he will come to us when everything seems wrong, and we are wringing our hands in despair wondering if it will ever be right again. The great message of Advent is that when we are down, sick, and depleted, "Jesus is coming." We should not fear; he will make all the difference.

The story is told by Ian Macpherson of a tourist in Switzerland who spotted a beautiful mansion on the shore of a lovely lake. The tourist was deeply impressed by the large and well-manicured garden in which the mansion was set. Not a weed was to be seen anywhere. As the tourist was admiring the garden, he spotted one of the staff, the curator, and began to praise its beauty and order. He asked the curator, "How long have you worked here?"

"Twenty years," was the reply. In the ensuing conversation, it was disclosed that the owner of the mansion was absent most of the time.

"How often has the owner been in residence during your twenty years of service?"

30

"Four times," replied the curator.

The visitor was amazed. "To think," he exclaimed, "that for all these years you have kept this mansion and garden in such superb condition! Why, you look after them just as if you expected your master to come tomorrow!"

"No," corrected the curator, "I look after things as if I expected my master to come today!"

This is a picture of Advent people. They live each day as if the Savior is coming.[1]

Advent is like the preparation for a wedding. There is the moment of great expectation as the bridegroom anxiously awaits the bride. For Isaiah it is a picture of both the bride and the bridegroom clothed in special garments, which are the garments of salvation and the robe of righteousness. This is the same spirit of excitement that God wants his church to have at Advent, for God wants "praise to spring up before all nations."

There is good news over in Judah, good news down in Nazareth, but the best news is that the good news is for you and for me. Come, Lord Jesus!

---

1. Ian Macpherson, *News of the World to Come* (Prophetic Witness Publishing House, 1975), p. 296.

Yes, No, Someone Else

There is an old story about a beautiful emperor moth. This emperor moth was really not living, but was tucked away in a cocoon just waiting to be released. As this particular emperor moth was struggling to get through the narrow neck of the cocoon, a boy was intently observing it. As the moth struggled to release himself from the cocoon, the boy felt the moth would never make it out of the cocoon. As the struggle went on for several hours, the boy became increasingly impatient. He thought to himself, "Maybe there is something wrong." He decided to take matters into his own hands, and with a pair of scissors the boy gently snipped the threads around the opening of the cocoon to make it easier for the moth to emerge. As soon as the threads were snipped, the moth crawled out; however, as it did, it dropped behind it an ugly, distended, shriveled wing which was useless.

In the Old Testament lesson for today, David is much like the little boy who snipped away at the emperor moth's cocoon. For the first time since ascending the throne, David is in a position to snip the cocoon from which he had been emerging.

David is established in his new house and is secure from his notorious Philistine enemies. No doubt David has become bored and wants to emerge from the cocoon in which God has placed him. In so doing, he focuses on himself and his own insecurities. In this mind set, David decides that he must build God a house. In his own mind he has already said, "Yes," to his idea.

Yes

When King David says, "Yes," in himself, he decides that he will consult his pastor, Nathan the Prophet. Nathan, like most pastors, is thrilled and excited that such a distinguished person, the King of Israel, would seek his advice.

When David reveals to Nathan his thoughts concerning the building of the Temple, Nathan is enthusiastic. In simple parlance, he tells the King to "go for it." No wonder Nathan is excited; prophets aren't accustomed to kings offering to do something for God. This is a breath of fresh air for Pastor Prophet Nathan. Nathan is immediately inspired.

Pastor Nathan asks no questions; he gives no thought or reflection to the proposal. The prophet wholeheartedly endorses the king's idea. The king wants to build God a house. One does not have to think, pray, or reflect on this decision; nothing could be better than building God a house.

In the movie *Field of Dreams*, Iowa farmer Ray Kinella walks through his cornfield when he hears a voice. The voice is a whisper, but the words are clear and unmistakable: "If you build it, he will come." Kinella is filled with questions: Build what? Who will come? Who spoke to me? Then comes the revelation: Build a baseball field and Shoeless Joe Jackson, the great star of the Chicago White Sox, will come.

Kinella is deeply convinced that he is to build a ball field. He becomes obsessed with getting it built. A section of his cornfield is bulldozed, and a baseball diamond is constructed. He waits. One evening, out of the tall corn steps Shoeless Joe Jackson. Other White Sox players and members of the old New York Giants later join him. Every day the teams play each other, but they are only visible to the farmer, his family, and a social activist named Terrence Mann — people who have heard the voice and believe. The words of the voice become in a sense an invitation to the viewers: "If you build it, he will come."

Building God a house was David's Field of Dreams. God had never whispered to David, "Build me a house," nor had God ever revealed to David in any manner that he needed, wanted, or expected David to build him a house.

Both David and Nathan failed to realize that sometimes dreams and ideas are from God, and sometimes they are not. Even you and I often have friends who will encourage us to go for something which is our dream, our plan, our agenda, yet it may not be God's desire for us at all.

Advent comes to remind us that God had a plan for our world. This plan was divine, and God himself would dwell in a human temple, cradled in the arms of a mother, held by a nervous father, doted on by loving relatives. In God's plan, the "Word became flesh and lived among us."

God's plan was a divine "*yes*" based on his love for broken, hurting, estranged humanity. David's plan, to which Pastor Nathan gave positive assent, was based on human desire and false assumption. This "yes" was a human "yes" without divine consultation.

Maybe David crossed a line from being full of God to being full of himself. There is a clue found in 2 Samuel 7:2: "See now, I am living in a house of cedar, but the ark of God stays in a tent."

On this Fourth Sunday of Advent it would be well for each one to be reminded that God had a plan for our world. This plan was not conceived in the mind of man, but in the heart of God.

No

Nathan leaves David with a "green light" to go ahead with his dream to build a house for God. That night God got Pastor Nathan's attention. God didn't see David's intention in the same light that Nathan did. Early the next morning Nathan goes to the king and revokes his building permit. Pastor Nathan throws a wet blanket over the fire of David's desire. The message from God is, "No!"

This message from Pastor Nathan to King David is blunt, forthright, and final. "David, you are not going to build me a house, I am going to build you a house." God informed the king that God is doing the building, not David. God reminds the shepherd boy king of all that God had done for him. God does not want David calling attention to himself. Saul, Israel's first king, had been a dismal failure, and God didn't want David to follow in Saul's footsteps. God wants David to know that God is Sovereign and that David's kingship will witness to that sovereignty.

In his recital of all that he had done for David, God is the first-person subject of 23 action verbs. David, who thought he was going to do something for God, now has to listen to a detailed description of what God has done and will do for and in David.

The issue that David had forgotten was that God is a God of freedom and grace. God is simply saying to David, "Don't box me in. When did I ever state that I needed a house?" This free God reminds David that God and God alone is in control.

During the season of Advent we are reminded once again that God is sovereign, and in his sovereignty he decides what he will do for humankind. In reaching love he sent his Son Jesus to show us what he is like. Because of the coming of Jesus, we now check our plans and dreams with him so that our will is absorbed by his will. Sometimes God has to tell us "no," just as he did to David long years ago.

Someone Else

God makes very clear his purpose for David. That purpose was simply "that he was to be a king, not build a temple." God informs King David that he is not gifted for building a temple. David is a man of war, a soldier, a fighter, a military genius, but not a builder.

Then God, who is a God of great surprises, now opens the package of his grace and hands David a surprise package, wrapped in understanding and love. "Not you, David, someone else. Your son will build the temple. Yes, David, through your son your dream will find fulfillment."

God then moves to give David a promise and assurance. "Your house and your kingdom shall be made sure forever before me; your throne shall be established forever" (2 Samuel 7:16). Did God keep his word to David? Today there is no descendant of David sitting on a throne in the Middle East or anywhere else in the world. How does one interpret this promise and commitment made by God to David?

God is revealing to David a larger purpose, and the Christian Church has seen Jesus in the light of this promise. Jesus was born in the line of David and thus inherits this promise made by God to

36

David. The Gospel reading for today is the Annunciation to Mary (Luke 1:26-38) in which this promise given to David is reiterated and affirmed. The Incarnation is connected to David's promise. Advent each year offers the church the opportunity to wait again for the coming of the son of David and the Son of God.

Gabriel Garvin Marquez tells the story of a village where people are afflicted with a strange, contagious amnesia. This amnesia started with the oldest member of the village and began to work its way down to younger generations. The disease caused people to forget the names of common everyday objects. A young man who was still unaffected by the amnesia realized what was happening. He began to put labels on everything: "This is a window." "This is a cow which has to be milked every morning." On the main road leading into the town he erected two signs. One read: "The name of our village is Macondo." The other one in much larger print read: "God exists!"

This enduring promise to David was a promise that God existed, and David would not be forgotten. It also is an Advent promise to humankind that God has come to us in Jesus who is Emmanuel, "God with us." God reveals himself and his existence in Jesus. Advent informs us each year that God is not hidden from us.

When the emperor moth struggles to get out of the cocoon through the narrow opening, there is the hope that a thing of beauty and majesty will emerge. Advent is like the emperor moth. When allowed to fulfill its function in the church, it becomes a season of beauty and grandeur in which the promise of God for a Savior is fulfilled. This is always a thing of beauty and also of glory.

First Light

Have you ever seen the aurora borealis? That may not be a familiar term to you, and you may be asking yourself, "Is that a country?" "Is it some kind of strange animal that is nearly extinct that I have somehow missed?" Some of you already know what the aurora borealis is; for those who don't, they are called the northern lights. The northern lights occur in the far northern regions. Recently, while driving in an isolated northern area of the United States, I saw a brilliant display of colored lights that were lighting up the far north and extending for what seemed hundreds of miles. At first I had no idea what the brilliant display of lights was, but residents of a community I was visiting informed me that these lights were the aurora borealis, or northern lights. They illuminated the darkness of the vast northland for miles. It was indeed a spectacular sight.

The prophet Isaiah speaks of a "great light" which would illuminate the darkness of Galilee when the righteous reign of a coming King would begin. When Isaiah wrote to these people who were walking in darkness, they had not yet seen this light, but the coming of this light was so vivid and fixed in Isaiah's mind that he describes it as if this light had already dawned. Because of this light, the people will experience peace and blessing and a complete reversal of their present condition.

The question for us on this "holy night" is a simple one. Do we still see Isaiah's great light illuminating our dark, frightened, crippled world?

Let us examine this Old Testament prophecy to see if we can find our way from the darkness to the "light of Christmas." First of all, let us examine ...

The Significance Of This First Light

Isaiah writes about the "deep darkness" in which the people are living. This darkness was the darkness of anguish and spiritual death. However, there will come a great light that they will suddenly see which will shine upon them.

Why is this light significant? It is the light of a new life, the light of glorious hope. As we celebrate the Spirit of Christ, the United States is still grappling with the dismay and anguish of terrorist attacks on the World Trade Center and the Pentagon. It seems as if we have found ourselves as a nation in deep darkness. This darkness is the darkness of shock, of horror, and of questions. Why did nearly 3,500 people have to die? What was in the minds of those who were on their suicide mission? How could such evil be conceived in the minds of humankind?

Yet, in the midst of the darkness of grief and questioning, we are reminded, like Isaiah's audience, that the "light has come." Like people to whom he ministered, we can experience the increased joy, which is glorious and spontaneous. For Isaiah, this joy was like the rejoicing of people when the harvest was finished or like the joy experienced when they followed a retreating, defeated army who left behind essential supplies in their haste to find safety. This joy which we can know at this Christmas is a joy before our Lord which we have because God still showers his grace upon us.

On this night of light, we must remember that light permeates the whole of biblical revelation. In the creation account, light is described as victory over darkness. God himself is revealed as the "Light of light," who is the source of all life. Isaiah 10:17, describes him as the "Light of Israel." The whole idea of the coming of Jesus Christ is connected with light because Jesus is revealed as the light of the world (John 1:4; 8:12; 12:35). Paul writes that as believers our walk must be in the light of Jesus Christ so that all who confess Christ as Lord become a light for the world (Ephesians 5:8; Philippians 2:15).

40

The significance of Isaiah's light for us is that it has shined into our darkness and the greatness of this light has brought us "new life." In the Gospel of John 1:3-4, "... the life was the light of all people. The light shines in the darkness, and the darkness did not overcome it."

There is a custom among some of the people of Indonesia to place pearls, as symbolic of life, into the eyelids of deceased loved ones and friends to ensure that in the life beyond this world the departed person would "walk in the light." Christmas comes to remind us that "we can walk in light" now. For those of us in Christ, the light never goes out.

From the significance of this light Isaiah reveals ...

The Source Of This First Light

The source of this great light for Isaiah is the birth of a king. Scholars have divided opinions as to whether this is an earthly wise ruler or a messianic prophecy. The Church has seen in this ancient prophecy a messianic note that this future King of Isaiah would be the Messiah, the Christ.

Isaiah expresses the grace of the salvation to come in different ways. The people receive this grace with joy. Why? The burden of oppression by the Assyrians will be lifted. Israel no longer will be like an ox bearing the yoke of oppression. How will this come to be? This liberation will be the Lord's doing. At this Christmastime the Lord is still the great liberator who wants to lift the yoke of all that encumbers people and keeps them from knowing the true freedom which he came to provide on that first Christmas.

The prophet then gives a beautiful picture of what can happen when the true source of light is discovered. The weapons of war will be destroyed, but also the desire to use weapons of terror and mass destruction will be taken away. Oh, that this would happen!

How will this light come to the world? It will come through the birth of a baby who will establish the government of the Kingdom of God.

Years ago Bret Harte wrote a short story titled "The Luck of Roaring Camp." It is a story about a baby who made a difference.

Roaring Camp was supposedly the roughest mining camp in the West. It was notorious for its murderous fights, thefts, and drunkenness. The miners of Roaring Creek were a tough bunch. The only woman there was a Native American, Cherokee Sal, and she died in childbirth.

The baby survived and was quite healthy. The miners, however, were faced with quite a dilemma. What were they going to do with a baby? They made a crib out of an old box lined with dirty rags. The box was not good enough or clean enough to hold a baby. A cradle was purchased from a town 80 miles away, and they placed the baby in it. Beautiful blankets were brought in from Sacramento and placed in the cradle. The miners noticed that the shack where the baby was kept was filthy, so they washed the floor, walls, and ceiling. Nice curtains were installed on the windows. Life began to change in Roaring Creek. The brutality ceased. Every day the baby was taken to the entrance of the mine so that all the miners could watch the baby's growth. The miners decided the entrance to the mine was ugly, so they planted a beautiful garden there. These hardened men loved to pet and touch the baby, but their hands were dirty. Soon the general store sold out of soap. Life in Roaring Camp had completely changed because of a baby. These hardened miners had given up their nasty, profane ways — all for the love of a baby!

The good news of Christmas is that in a baby there is life-changing, redemptive power. Isaiah gives this child four titles and each title is comprised of two words.

1. *Wonderful Counselor:* In the original Hebrew "wonderful" means, "not of this world." A counselor was one who applied wisdom to all situations, even the government of the people. This son would apply the wisdom of God to the human situation. The Church has seen the wonderful counselor as Jesus, the Messiah. There is no counsel or counselor as great as he is.

2. *Mighty One:* This son whom Isaiah saw was a victorious hero who had defeated all enemies. The title Mighty God expresses his divine nature. He is truly "King of Kings

and Lord of Lords." It is this Mighty God who came in human form at Christmas in Jesus that we celebrate.

3. *Everlasting Father:* The term "father" has suffered in modern times because of many negative connotations brought on by abuse and abandonment. Isaiah's light is the "Everlasting Father," over all of his children, and his rule will be based on divine love and care.

4. *Prince of Peace:* Isaiah's concept of peace is so different from the frivolous way the word is thrown around today. It meant for Isaiah "wholeness, harmony, completion" and was not confined to the absence of hostility. For Isaiah "peace" offered people the hope that they could live in harmony with God, each other, and nature. In Jesus we can find true "shalom." He is the Prince of Peace.

The source of Isaiah's light was God himself. Isaiah however, moves to ...

The Song Of This First Light

Isaiah closes his depiction of "first light" with a song about this king. It is a song about the "True light."

First, Isaiah sings about an eternal king whose kingdom will not increase via the vehicles of war, but will grow through peace and the working of the Spirit of God in the hearts of humankind.

Second, this king, who is the "true light," will establish his kingdom through righteousness. The tyrants and dictators of the world have made their nations and kingdoms by oppression, brutality, fear, and tyranny. Isaiah's king will bring a righteous rule which people will joyfully obey forever.

Third, how will all of this be accomplished? Is this mere fantasy or wishful thinking? This vision is too wonderful to grasp. Is it possible that Isaiah's "first light" can fulfill everything Isaiah attributes to him? Yes, because the "zeal of the Lord of hosts will do this." Zeal expresses the thought of urgency, passion, jealousy. Has this happened? Yes, in Jesus Christ whose birth we celebrate on this night. John writes of Jesus the Messiah, "His disciples remembered that it was written, Zeal for your house will consume me" (John 2:17).

43

In Isaiah's view, God's good rule has been made flesh in the weakest of human creation, a baby. It is his birth and his Kingdom we celebrate on this eve of Christmas.

The story is told of an aspiring young author who was given the opportunity to read a fiction story he had written before a famous author. The plot of the young aspiring writer's story involved the only son of a poor widow who lived in a little cabin in Pennsylvania. The story went something like this: One day the son decided to go to New York to make his way in life. As he got ready to leave, his mother hugged him and said to him: "Son, if you ever get into trouble, come home, and as you come over the hill, look toward home. You will always find a light burning in the window, and I will be waiting to welcome you."

The young writer described what happened to the young man with words that produced images of the dark side of humanity. The young man went to prison, and upon his release decided to head home.

The boy hitchhiked his way back to Pennsylvania. As he climbed the final hill and started toward home, he saw the outline of a small cottage in the distance. He was filled with hope. But something was wrong, there was no light burning in the window! At this point, the renowned author jumped to his feet and shouted at the aspiring author, "You young upstart! Put that light back."[1]

The "light" which Isaiah wrote about has not and will not ever go out. For it is the light of God's glory, revealed in Jesus Christ. It is this "light" that we celebrate tonight! He is Isaiah's first light and our "Everlasting Light." Amen!

---

1. David H. C. Read, *I Am Persuaded* (New York: Charles Scribner's Sons, 1961).

Joy To The World

Open the hymnals. Pull out the stops on the organ, for we are going to sing a song. What song shall we sing? We could sing Martin Luther's hymn of the Reformation, "A Mighty Fortress Is Our God." Maybe a hymn by Charles Wesley, such as "And Can It Be," would express how we feel about our Christian faith. We might want to consider something on a little more feeling level like Joseph M. Scriven's "What A Friend We Have In Jesus," or Fanny J. Crosby's "To God Be The Glory."

No, let's not sing any of these. Instead, let's sing a song about Christmas. "Wait a minute! Did I hear you correctly? You want to sing a Christmas carol? Don't you realize that Christmas is over? Don't you think maybe it is time to put the carols away for another year?"

It's time to sing a Christmas carol. What carol should we sing? Shall we sing Phillips Brooks' "O Little Town Of Bethlehem," or Joseph Mohr's "Silent Night, Holy Night"? Maybe Edmund Hamilton Sears' "It Came Upon The Midnight Clear" would be appropriate. Perhaps Charles Wesley's "Hark, The Herald Angels Sing" is the Christmas carol we should be singing.

The Christmas carol that we need to sing on this Lord's Day is by Isaac Watts. It is "Joy To The World." "Why this carol?" you ask. It expresses the sentiment of the Old Testament lesson which is from Isaiah 61:10—62:3. This is a jubilant song of praise which is sung to give God glory for his redeeming grace. The dominant theme of this song is "joy." Hence, let's open our hymnals and sing to the top of our lungs:

Joy to the World!
The Savior reigns;
Let men their songs employ,
while fields and floods,
rocks, hills and plains
Repeat the sounding joy,
repeat the sounding joy,
repeat, repeat the sounding joy.

The prophet is so excited about what God has done that he cannot contain his joy. God has delivered his people, thus ...

The Prophet Shouts For Joy

The sad fact is that not everyone could celebrate. The children of Israel prior to this moment were in mourning. Doubt and despair had overwhelmed them. All of their social and religious activities were like attendance at a funeral. This will soon all be changed, for the children of Israel will celebrate a wedding rather than mourn at a funeral.

Why has the whole mood changed? It is because the people are now rejoicing in their God. Why is there so much joy when there had been doom and gloom everywhere? God has given his people a new status, which is highlighted by new clothing. God himself has put this new clothing on his people. God clothes the whole person — body, soul, and spirit — with the garments of salvation.

The story is told about Betty Hutton, a former movie star and box office attraction of the late '40s and '50s. Hutton fell on hard times and battled alcoholism and depression. A few years ago she encountered God and invited him into her life. God turned her life around and headed her in a different direction. She started on the trail to a comeback. Hutton joined the cast of the Broadway musical *Annie*, playing the role of Mrs. Hannigan. Those who were in attendance at the first performance noted the extensive biographical sketches of the members of the cast. However, under the picture of Betty Hutton there was no elaborate sketch. Instead, there appeared five words which Hutton had written herself. Those words were: "I'm back. Thanks to God."

46

The children of Israel were back in their own land, thanks to God, and this was cause for joy. This joy was expressed in the language of a wedding as the bride and bridegroom themselves are clothed in garments of salvation. It was true that Israel had sinned and broken her covenant relationship with God. Yet, God has forgiven her sin and cleansed her soul. This is the reason for Israel's joy.

The spirit conveyed in Isaiah 61:10-11 is the spirit of celebration, which God desires in his Church today. The Church is his bride, clothed in the garments of righteousness and radiant with his glory.

When the church is truly his bride, she can sing with Issac Watts:

> *He rules the world with truth and grace,*
> *and makes the nations prove*
> *the glories of his righteousness,*
> *and wonders of his love,*
> *and wonders of his love,*
> *And wonders, and wonders of his love.*

It's time for us to shout, "Joy to the World!" The prophet is also shouting because of ...

The Joy Of Restoration

A very close friend of mine made a nostalgic visit to his hometown, which is a county seat. When he was a boy, the downtown of this county seat came alive on Saturday. When the farmers had finished all of their chores, they came to town. From 4 o'clock in the afternoon until 8 p.m. the sidewalks and stores were packed with people laughing, talking, and shopping. Coming to town was a big deal on Saturday. Downtown was a place to share the latest stories, catch up on the news, and hear the latest gossip. It was downtown that one heard the news of a baby on its way or a person near the point of death. Engagements were announced downtown by the simple showing of a ring on a girl's hand. People sat on their cars, stood next to the stores, congregated in small eating establishments, or stood in the aisles of the stores to greet each other

47

and talk of life, death, and the future. Teenagers made definite plans to meet downtown on Saturday. Many courtships were carried out downtown. Neighbors would ask their friends during the week, "Are you going downtown Saturday?" A royal treat for a child was to get to go downtown.

On his visit, my friend went downtown and discovered that downtown now only existed in his memory. The stores and shops that he frequented are now closed and hardly anyone goes downtown anymore. The town has moved south, and everything revolves around small strip malls, K-Mart, Wal-Mart, and a Super Kroger. For all practical purposes, downtown is dead and buried. Not many people go downtown anymore.

There is something sad about a town becoming deserted. It's eerie! You can easily find a place to park. Buildings are empty, beckoning for someone to put them to use again and restore them to their original intention.

This is nothing compared to the destruction of Jerusalem. Jerusalem was deserted. The strong walls, which had held back invading armies for years, had been pulled down. The Holy Temple, the house of God, had been desecrated and was now only a shell. The Babylonians had razed the city and carted off the citizens to a distant land.

After years in exile, the people were returning home to a land that was devastated. They were resolved to begin the task of rebuilding. Soon cracks of doubt became evident because of the perception that God was indifferent. The people wondered if all the talk about God coming as redeemer was accurate. What the people needed was a fresh vision of a glorious future.

In chapter 62:1-3, we suddenly hear God's voice. God is no longer silent and these three verses are a sign of fresh resolve on God's part. God will remain active and engaged until Jerusalem has been vindicated and rescued from oppression.

The message of Christmas is that God has not remained silent, for in Jesus Christ the silence has been broken. With the coming of Christ there is the promise of restoration and renewal. This causes us to respond, "Joy to the World, the Lord has come." Just as our Sovereign Lord came to those surveying the ruins of their land as

48

they returned from exile, so he comes to us who are estranged and exiled from him. It is his desire to make us whole and complete and to bring us joy which is a product of his coming.

Just as God desired to restore the joy of those ancient exiles, so he desires to restore our joy which has been stolen by Satan who is totally committed to our joylessness. C. S. Lewis, in *The Screwtape Letters*, depicts for us the devil's view of joy. *The Screwtape Letters* are a series of letters from senior devil Screwtape to Wormwood, his nephew who is a demon in training. Screwtape offers a wide range of advice from how to distract people from coming to Christ and how to keep those who come to Christ from being effective and productive.

In one letter to Wormwood, Screwtape writes about joy. (In his letters, "the Enemy" always means God). He writes to Wormwood:

> *Fun is closely related to joy — a sort of emotional froth arising from the play instinct. It is of little use to us. It can sometimes be used, of course, to deviate humans from something else which the enemy should like them to be feeling or doing; but in itself it has wholly undesirable tendencies; it promotes charity, courage, contentment, and many other evils.*

After discussing some other issues, Screwtape gets around to joy:

> *You will see Joy among friends and lovers reunited at the eve of a holiday. Among adults some pretext in the way of jokes is usually provided, but the facility with which even the smallest witticisms produce laughter at such times shows that they are not the real cause. What the real cause is we do not know. Something like it is expressed in much of that detestable art which the humans call music, and something like it occurs in Heaven — a meaningless acceleration in the rhythm of celestial experience, quite opaque to us. Laughter of this kind does us no good and should always be discouraged. Besides, the phenomenon is of itself disgusting*

and a direct insult to the realism, dignity, and austerity of Hell.[1]

God speaks to his joyless people and reminds them that they are not nonpersons and their future has changed. Suddenly the ruins and destruction become an ornament in God's hand, and Jerusalem itself is a glorious crown, a sparkling diadem, a treasure and a delight which honors God. These returned exiles will be a sign that he is King. When you and I come back from our exile in the far country of sin, we too are a sign that he is King. Then, and only then, can we sing:

> *Joy to the world,*
> *the Lord has come.*
> *Let earth receive her King.*

Like those ancient exiles, we have been redeemed, renewed, and restored because God is full of joy and Jesus is full of joy and this joy is for you and me.

---

1. C. S. Lewis, *The Screwtape Letters* (New York: Macmillan Publishing, 1977), p. 50.

A Song, A Dance, A Savior

Simon Wiesenthal in his book, *The Sunflower*, relates a discussion that took place at the Mauthausen Concentration Camp when he was a young Jewish prisoner.

Wiesenthal was sound asleep one night when Arthur, another young prisoner, a sort of dreamy skeptic, grabbed him by the shoulder and began to shake him awake.

"Simon, do you hear?"

"Yes," he stammered, "I hear."

"I hope you are listening; you really must hear what the old woman said."

"What could she have said?"

"She said ...'God was on leave.' What do you think of that Simon? God is on leave."

"Let me sleep. Tell me when he gets back." When Simon awakened he began to reflect about the conversation with Arthur and walked to find him. When he found Arthur, he questioned him, "What were you talking about last night?" Arthur replied that Josef, an honorable prisoner whom Wiesenthal highly respected, had asked an old woman if she had any news. The woman simply looked up to heaven and prayed, "Oh, God Almighty, come back from your leave and look at thy earth again."

That statement got Wiesenthal's attention and as he reflected on what the old woman had said, he wrote: "One really begins to think that God is on leave. Otherwise the present state of things wouldn't be possible. God must be on leave. And he has no deputy."[1]

Exiled, Israel at times felt that God had taken a leave of absence and that they were left to the wicked design of their Babylonian masters. Yes, they had been disobedient. Admittedly, Israel had forsaken God; now she languished in a foreign country, hoping beyond hope that God would somehow come back from his leave of absence and remember, redeem, and restore his people. It is Jeremiah the prophet who will bring to those exiles a message of hope. For forty long years he has foretold of doom and destruction which has earned him the nickname, "Old death and destruction." With the beginning of chapter 30, the mood of the prophet shifts, and he begins to write of a gracious God who has not forgotten his people, but who will bring comfort in the form of deliverance from exile and restoration of their homeland. Chapters 30 through 32 are often called "The Book of Comfort." They are powerful statements of hope.

In Jeremiah 31:7-14, there is an exuberance, a joy, and optimism that only God can give to the restored, returning exiles. The passages not only speak of an historical event in the life of Israel, but they speak also words of hope, encouragement, and comfort to those of us who feel like exiles and need somehow to find our way back to God.

Notice what Jeremiah does ...

He Leads Us In A Song

It seems very strange to hear the words of a song coming from the lips of Jeremiah. His words up to this point have been harsh, condemning, and critical of the nation's faithlessness. He describes Jerusalem as a harlot, and Israel's leaders as a voice without prayer, empty cupboards, wells without water. His themes are violence, grief, judgment, and punishment. Suddenly, Jeremiah has become a choir director, and he invites the whole nation to join him in praise (v. 7). The prophet uses the following expression to summon the nation to join his choir, "Sing aloud, raise shouts, proclaim, give praise, sing!" This is a song of celebrative declaration for God's rescue of the people. God has gathered his people from the farthest points of the world, and God alone, has gathered his

52

people. Displaced people are coming home! The weak, the vulnerable, the lame, the blind, and pregnant. Jeremiah wants the choir to sing because God is faithful, and he is leading his people into the promised joy of their Lord. The Christmas carol "Here We Come A-Caroling" describes the song of Jeremiah when it states, "Love and Joy come to you." Jeremiah leads in a song of "love and joy." We need Jeremiah's song today to counterbalance the weeping and gloom of our broken, despairing world of exile so that we, like Jeremiah's Israel, might be led into the promised joy of our Lord.

Ronald Barclay Allen in his book *When Song Is New* describes an event which illustrates the song of Jeremiah:

> *A year ago I was ministering in a church in southwest Minnesota. I learned that a little boy from a farm across the border in Iowa had wandered into the fields of corn that encircled his house. A massive search began that was to last for three days and was to involve thousands of people. They searched for him Thursday, Friday, and Saturday.*
>
> *Night came on that Saturday. With it came a prevailing sense of gloom. The boy's parents stood on their back porch and thanked the people who had worked so hard. They had searched six miles square. The fields nearest the house had been searched five or six times each. But little Justin, only two-and-a-half, had not been found. The parents thanked the people for their prayers on behalf of their little boy. Then they commended their child to God and told the people not to return the next day. The search was off.*
>
> *But one farmer kept on looking. After all others had stopped, he continued to search. Forty-five minutes after the search had been canceled, this intrepid farmer found Justin. The little boy was frightened and whimpering. He was dehydrated and covered with mosquito bites. He was taken to the hospital and was found to be sound and was released, sucking on a popsicle for moisture.*
>
> *The next morning a film crew from the local television station filmed the morning worship service where the family gave praise to God in their community of faith.*

And did they sing! And in their joy in the work of the
King in their midst, all who saw that broadcast later in
the same day joined in the song. Song was made new in
our hearts as we witnessed the grace of God in response
to countless prayers on behalf of a lost little boy.[2]

Jeremiah the choir director led the nation in a song of praise and thanksgiving because of God's faithfulness, but he also wants the people to ...

Dance A Dance Of Praise

Dancing a dance of praise was part of Israel's heritage. Many scholars feel that the real beginning of Israel's history is not found in Genesis, but in the exodus from Egypt. When the people of God were safe from Pharaoh's army, they sang, but they also danced. Miriam, the sister of Moses who was a prophetess, danced a dance of joy for God's mighty deliverance. As she danced, other women joined her in a dance of praise to celebrate the saving acts of God. The Old Testament is punctuated with the praise dances of those who encountered the God of steadfast love.

Jeremiah imagines all of the exiles journeying together in one great homecoming parade led by God himself. When the exiles arrive home, they find a land that is well-watered, crops that are fruitful, and animals which are flourishing, and there will be no more drought. God has made abundant living possible. Newness abounds because God has ransomed Israel and redeemed his people.

The idea of redemption found in this passage reminds us that in Jesus Christ we have our redemption. Redemption is a family matter. According to Old Testament law, a redeemer had to be a near-kinsman. Jesus became our near-kinsman on the first Christmas. His purpose in coming was to redeem humankind from the curse of sin.

The mood of those returning from exile has changed. God has taken away the mourning and sorrow which was characteristic of the exile, and replaced them with dancing and merriment and comfort.

Even the priests who have been in opposition to Jeremiah and gave him so much grief and who received of the offered sacrifices have an abundance. Everyone will be satisfied with God's goodness.

What a time for dancing a dance of praise. We dance the dance of praise to the God who has power to transform and has promised to do so.

Jeremiah led in a song about God's faithfulness, he has called for a dance of praise, but he also wants to ...

Remind Us Of A Savior's Care

Jeremiah uses two metaphors to remind us of God's care. He uses the words, "lead," "brooks of water," and "straight paths," which bring to mind the picture of a good shepherd who seeks those who are lost in order to bring them home (v. 9). There is also a reference to the "first born," the one who is loved and valued and who received God's special protection, care, and gifts. The shepherd who is the protector is also the Father who values. This shepherd had scattered his flock but now he gathers them home from exile. It is the shepherd who seeks and saves the lost ones. This is a picture of God's care and concern, not only for Israel, but of his concern for you and me. God wants those who have wandered into exile in any generation to be gathered to him. It is his desire that all exiles will come home to his joy.

This Old Testament story of song, dance, and Savior finds more obvious fulfillment in the opening chapters of Luke's Gospel. Here Jeremiah's hopes are realized. Young Mary and Priest Zachariah burst forth in eloquent praise to God who cares and is concerned about his people.

It is old Simeon who realizes that in the baby who is brought to the Temple by his parents is the fulfillment of Israel's hope and the answer of God to the lostness of humankind. Simeon reminds us that God cares and is concerned for his people because God's great promise has come true. Emmanuel, "God with us," has come in Jesus Christ who shows us how much God cares. He is our Savior.

In Charles Dickens' "A Christmas Carol," it is the "Ghost of Christmas Yet to Come" that deeply disturbs Ebenezer Scrooge. Dickens describes the scene:

The Ghost of Christmas Yet to Come conveyed him ... into a churchyard.

The Spirit strove among the graves and pointed down to one.

Scrooge crept towards it, trembling as he went; and following the finger, read upon the stone of the neglected grave his own name, Ebenezer Scrooge. Scrooge was scared into changing his life and performing acts of kindness and goodwill.

The doom and gloom prophecies of Jeremiah could not frighten Israel into being the people of God. The country was overcome by foreign armies, and the leaders were carried into exile. During Jeremiah's lifetime the story ended in death and destruction. It looked as if God had gone on leave and left no one in his place. That was not the last word, for Jeremiah believing in God's goodness wrote:

He who scattered Israel will gather him and will keep him as a shepherd keeps his flock.

I will turn their mourning into joy.

I will comfort them and give them gladness for sorrow (Jeremiah 31:10b, 13b).

Jeremiah invites us to join him in a song, a dance, and celebrating a Savior who cares about his people. The song is God's love song. It is our love song. So let us dance the dance of praise, for our God reigns and he cares.

Amen! Amen! Amen!

---

1. Simon Wiesenthal, *The Sunflower* (New York: Shocken Books, 1976), p. 13ff.

2. Allen Barclay Ronald, *When Song Is New* (Nashville: Thomas Nelson, 1983), pp. 236-237.

**Epiphany 1
(Baptism Of The Lord)
Genesis 1:1-5**

Morning Has Broken

Some years ago, popular singer Cat Stevens (who has become a convert to Islam and now spends his time in meditation) popularized Eleanor Farjeon's hymn, "Morning Has Broken." Pop stations played Steven's rendition all over the United States. People found themselves fascinated by the tune and also by the words. The hymn aptly depicts Genesis 1:1-5. Farjeon wrote:

> *Morning has broken*
> *Like the first morning*
> *Blackbird has spoken*
> *Like the first bird.*
> *Praise for the singing!*
> *Praise for the morning!*
> *Praise for them spinning*
> *Fresh from the Word!*

Every time the hymn was hummed, played, or sung, the Creation story was being revisited. This hymn simply affirms that in a sense every day recapitulates the dynamics of Genesis 1:1-5. Each day offers us the opportunity to be awakened to the first dawn, the dawn of Creation.

The Bible begins with the simple affirmation that the "creation" sprang from the Word. There are all kinds of questions and issues that can be raised in the twenty-first century regarding the Creation, but the Creation story does not offer answers to the questions that are so often asked. We need to be reminded continually that Genesis 1:1-5 is not a scientific treatise, but that it is a theological picture in narrative form. The simplicity of this passage states that "God did it, and God commanded it."

How does this narrative relate to us today? Is there any meaning or message that we can glean from this Old Testament Lesson. Together, let us see what lessons there might be for us in the twenty-first century from five simple, yet beautiful verses of scripture. The narration informs us that ...

God Brought Creation Out Of Chaos

Chaos is a word that Americans perhaps understand in a way that they have never understood before. In the past few years we have discovered what real chaos is. In horror we have witnessed the bombing of the Murrah Federal Building in Oklahoma City and the chaos which followed. Images of Paducah and Columbine will be forever etched in the soul of America.

September 11, 2001, is a date that, to use the words of Franklin Roosevelt, will "live in infamy." The pictures of airplanes deliberately crashing into the World Trade Center and the Pentagon will be etched upon the psyche of the United States for years to come. When someone speaks of anthrax, small pox, e. coli, and nuclear warheads, immediately the picture is of the chaos bio-terrorism might bring.

At times it seems we are living in the chaos before God spoke in Genesis 1:1-5. The chaos of our world at the present time can be understood by the story of a couple who had two boys, ages eight and ten. These little guys were very mischievous and were always getting into trouble. The parents knew that if any mischief occurred in their community, these boys were probably involved. They were at wits' end as to what could be done to help the two little rascals. The boys' mother was informed of a pastor who lived nearby who had been successful in helping with the discipline of hard-to-manage children. She contacted the pastor and asked if he would speak to her boys. The pastor agreed, and he visited first with the eight-year-old in the morning and planned to see the ten-year-old in the afternoon. When the younger boy walked into the clergyman's office, he was seated. The pastor who had a booming voice asked him sternly, "Where is God?" The little guy's mouth dropped open, but he was so frightened he could not respond. The question was repeated a second time by the pastor in a louder, sterner voice, "Where is God?" The boy made no attempt to answer; therefore, the pastor raised his voice even louder and shook his finger in the boy's face and bellowed, "Where is God?" Frightened out of his wits, the boy screamed and ran from the room straight home and upstairs to his room. He dove into his closet, slamming the door behind him. His older brother discovered him in the closet and asked, "What happened?" The younger brother, gasping for breath answered, "We are in *big* trouble this time, Bud. God is missing, and they think *we* did it!"

We live in a time of chaos when people are asking, "Where is God?" Did we somehow lose God along the way, and in his place there is now chaos? Our God is a God who brings order and meaning out of chaos. That is the essence of creation which simply confirms that, even in chaos and the way life is, it can be claimed and redeemed by God. Creation out of chaos must be understood as an ongoing work God has begun and continues. It began in the creative mind of God and continues even now as the Creator God works to bring meaning and order out of our chaotic world and lives that can be used by God for his grand purposes. Any time God enters chaos, it is a creative moment that brings the breaking of a new day and offers grace for all that would threaten and destroy his creation.

God brings creation out of chaos, but he also brings ...

Order Out Of Disorder

We read in the Creation narrative that "darkness covered the face of the deep." "How was God to deal with the darkness?" The scripture informs us that "a wind from God swept over the face of the waters." The Hebrew verb which is translated "swept" in the NRSV is elsewhere translated "hovered," as an eagle hovers over its prey. It is a picture of God as a divine observer preparing to do a creative act. This creative act will bring order out of disorder.

How does God propose to bring order out of disorder? He does it by bringing "light out of darkness." The first step that God took

59

then was to create light. Light is absolutely essential to any kind of life. Without light there can be no essential life.

From where does this light come? The only answer can be that this light is from God. In scripture, Light is a symbol for God.

There are various levels of light. Physical light is light which fills a room and enables one to see another person or objects which cannot be seen in the dark. Light can also refer to knowledge or truth. If someone asks you "to shed some light on an issue," they are asking you to explain something to them. Light on the subject occurs on the mental or emotional level, but there is also a third and deeper level of meaning, the spiritual level. On this level we deal with the nature and character of God. The Apostle John helps us understand the nature and character of God as light when he writes in his prologue (John 1) of the "true light coming into the world." In his first epistle, John states that "God is light and in him there is no darkness at all" (1 John 1:5b). Thus, when the Genesis account speaks of light, there is a spiritual meaning that enables us to understand that out of disorder God brings order.

A friend of mine who was attending college had to work late one Christmas Eve and after work was planning to drive with a classmate some 350 miles in order to be home for Christmas. Both individuals were anxious and excited about getting home to celebrate Christmas with their families. Driving through the long night they encountered a sudden snowstorm which caused the roads to be treacherous. Suddenly, the car spun out of control and sped down an embankment. No one was hurt and the car was not damaged, but there was no way they could get the car out of the ditch without help. It was cold, dark, and desolate at 2 a.m. in the morning. There was no light anywhere. My friend and his companion decided to walk the road hoping to find a house from which they could make a phone call for assistance. Struggling in the cold darkness, they walked several miles but could not find a house or see a light. As they rounded a curve in the road, they spotted a glimmer of light in the distant woods. Eventually, they came to a gravel road and followed it to a barn, shed, and house. In the shed were several men who were busy restoring an old car. They warmed themselves by a fire and told the men of their predicament. The men offered assistance by using a truck to pull their car out of the ditch and start them on their way toward home again. The light in the distance which they saw enabled them to bring order out of the disorder which had been caused by inclement weather.

Our Creator God seeks continually to bring order to the disorder of his world that has been caused by sin and rebellion. He is always in the business of separating the light from the darkness. When God, in love, removes the darkness of sin from our lives, morning breaks anew, and we can sing as a new creation, "Morning has broken   "

The text has informed us of how God, the Creator, brought creation out of chaos, brought order out of disorder, but it also reminds us that God moved from ...

Creation To Evaluation

God has created and now steps back to evaluate that which has been created. When God evaluates his creative act of bringing light, the text states, "And God saw that the light was good" (Genesis 1:4). God then proceeds to separate the light from the darkness, defining the light as Day and darkness as Night.

God's evaluation is not one of finality but of an ongoing process within which it is possible to improve. "Good" here does not mean perfect but that what has happened has achieved his divine intentions. The use of "good" also implies that God remains involved with his creation. The Creator sees what he has created and is affected by what is he sees.

God's use of the word "good" to evaluate what he has done begs the question: "What have we done with God's good creation?" Sad to say, humankind, created in God's image, has left his good world an ecological mess by our misuse of natural resources, despoiling of nature, and polluting of our air and water. Our Old Testament text reminds us that God evaluated his creation as good, something to be improved continually. We by our selfishness and greed have made that which God called "good" ugly and useless, almost returning God's creation to a chaotic state.

61

We have done the same with our own bodies by our gluttony, substance abuse, and misuse of his good things.

Also, because of sexual abuse, child abuse, verbal abuse, and emotional abuse, humankind has distorted God's good plan for life lived in relationship to him and to others. Because of this, that which was good has been diminished and destroyed.

Is there any hope for planet earth? Can God's evaluation of his Creation ever be called good again? Yes, it can, and there is hope; however, it will take a reclamation of creation. This reclamation for humankind came when "the Word became flesh." Jesus Christ is the answer for humankind's deepest needs.

Reclamation for our world will ultimately and finally come when God establishes his Kingdom forever. The Revelation speaks of this:

> *And I saw a new heaven and a new earth; for the first heaven and the first earth had passed away ... And I saw the holy city, the New Jerusalem, coming down out of heaven from God, prepared as a bride adorned for her husband.*
>
> *And the one who was seated on the throne said, "See, I am making all things new."*
> — Revelation 21:1-2, 5

Then creation will be "good" again, and true morning will break.

Epiphany 2
Ordinary Time 2
1 Samuel 3:1-10 (11-20)

I'll Be Somewhere Listening

Children are very perceptive. When our friend's daughter was small, if she was talking to her father or her mother and she felt that they were not quite tuned in to what she was saying, she would adamantly inform them that they were not listening to her. Sometimes she would take a different approach, especially if they were seated in a chair or on the couch. She would be talking away and realize that they were not giving her their undivided attention. Her approach to handling their inattentiveness was to climb into their laps, cup their faces in her hands, get close to their eyes and inform them in no uncertain terms that they were not listening to her. What she was simply saying by her action was that she wanted their undivided attention. She wanted them to listen to what she had to say.

Admittedly, at times all of us have trouble listening. You are watching your favorite football team on Monday night, and your wife is talking to you about something important that happened to her. As she talks, you mumble, "Uh huh." Finally, in exasperation, she says with tension in her voice, "You are not listening to what I am saying."

When God speaks, do we listen to him? As a boy growing up, my mother taught me an old spiritual that went something like this:

> *When the Savior calls I will listen*
> *When the Savior calls I will listen*
> *When the Savior calls I will listen*
> *I'll be somewhere listening for my name.*

I'll be somewhere listening
I'll be somewhere listening
I'll be somewhere listening for my name.

In our Old Testament Lesson for today, we have some examples of the powerful benefit of listening. This can be seen first of all by ...

The Relinquishment Of Eli

God is present in human history. He is in the beginning and the ending of human affairs. When one looks closely at this story, it is evident that it is a story of endings. Judgment has fallen upon the household of Eli, the priest, because of the conduct of his sons. He will lose everything. How will Eli handle God's judgment upon his life and family?

Eli handles the ending of his career as a national figure with a spirit of relinquishment. His is not fatal resignation to "what will be will be." Instead, his relinquishment is with piety and acquiescence. The relinquishment of Eli is that of obedience to God's greater plan and good. He is a model of faith in the midst of very difficult circumstances. Eli gave up his interests to trust the will of God.

This Old Testament text speaks to us at the very heart of our faith. God's will and purpose in our lives is very often a call to relinquish our plans and our dreams for a higher good. Doing God's will often means the giving up or the laying down of something we wanted to grasp or control.

A pastor friend of mine tells the story of his church organist who was very accomplished. An organist moved to the community from another area of the country and was asked to play the offertory. The guest organist was magnificent. After the worship hour concluded, the regular church organist asked for an appointment with the pastor. When they met together, the organist handed the pastor her resignation. The pastor was shocked and asked her, "Why?" She informed him that the guest organist would be attending the church regularly and that she was a much better organist and would do a better job. The pastor tried to encourage the organist to reconsider. She informed him that her mind was made up because someone else could do the job better. She also advised the pastor that she would now sing in the choir on a regular basis and play the organ as a substitute if needed. There was no bitterness, rancor, or self-serving. She had only a spirit of relinquishment.

Yes, Eli had weaknesses. In spite of these weaknesses, he teaches the Church that much can be accomplished when in faith we relinquish ourselves fully and completely to God. Sometimes God asks us to make very difficult choices. Can we, will we, have Eli's spirit of relinquishment? May it be so.

Eli had a spirit of relinquishment, but it is to Samuel that we must look to see ...

The Availability Of Samuel

When one reads the Call Narrative of Samuel, it appears that Samuel is a sort of passive person who seems very content to remain in the background. By the conclusion of 1 Samuel 3, he will emerge as a prominent figure on the national scene. How does Samuel move from the shadows into the spotlight? He does it by being available to God.

Samuel was being trained to perform priestly duties, to carry out the rituals of temple worship; however, God interrupted Samuel's function in priestly duties and called him to be a prophet. Samuel, as a prophet, functioned not so much as a foreteller of future events, but as a forth-teller of God's purpose and direction for his people.

As the future prophet sleeps near the Ark of God, he is awakened by God calling his name, "Samuel! Samuel!" Samuel responds, "Here I am," and runs off to Eli, assuming that his mentor needed him. Eli informs his young protege that he did not call him. This scene is repeated twice again.

Eli is perceptive enough to recognize that God was issuing a call to Samuel. The old priest gives young Samuel specific instruction on how he should respond if he hears the voice calling him again. Our Old Testament lesson informs us of Samuel's positive response to the voice of God. Samuel, by responding positively to the voice of God, is making himself available to be used by God for God's greater purpose and glory.

Samuel's story begs the questions, "Does God still speak today? " "What vehicles of communication does God use?" My response to those two questions is, "Yes, God still speaks today." When one says that God speaks to someone it simply means that God is directing his or her thoughts toward something. God speaks today through his Word, the Church, our friends, and the Holy Spirit. God may use only one of these means to communicate to us, or he may choose to reveal his will to us by using all. The fact is, God still speaks! Too often when God speaks, we remain ignorant of the fact that this thought is coming from God, and our response is negative. When God sends us a message, are we available to do what he wants?

There is a story that comes out of the Civil War about General Stonewall Jackson. He was at his camp with his troops, miles from the headquarters of General Robert E. Lee, Commander-in-Chief of the Confederate forces. A messenger informed Jackson that General Lee wished to see him. In the message that Lee sent to Jackson, he told Jackson he could come at his leisure since the matter was not of great importance. As soon as Stonewall Jackson received the message, he had his horse saddled and rushed to General Lee's Headquarters. General Jackson had to ride through a terrible freezing rain. The road was icy and muddy. He arrived at Lee's camp just as he was finishing breakfast. Lee looked out of his tent and spotted Jackson riding through the ice and snow. He hurried out to meet Jackson exclaiming, "Man, I told you it was not a matter of great importance!" Jackson replied, "When my general wishes to see me, my general's wish is my command."

We must make ourselves, like Samuel of old, available to God. Our response must be the response of Samuel: "Speak for your servant is listening." As we make ourselves available to God, we move from passivity to action. In so doing, we honor God, for God is not passive.

It is good for us to pause at times and ask God this question, "Do you have anything for me to do?" Then we must listen for God to speak. If he speaks to us, we must be available like Samuel of old to do as he tells us. If God does not speak to us as we have requested, we must then do what seems to be wisest. The issue for Samuel and for us is that we must always be available for God. The old spiritual gives us good advice when it states, "I'll be somewhere listening for my name." When God calls our name, our response must be the same as Samuel's, "Speak, for your servant is listening." Samuel was available to God, are you? Am I?

From Samuel's availability the text invites us to explore ...

The Resolve Of God

God is a God of beginnings. In the narrative, God asserts that the beginning of Samuel the Prophet's ministry, is a new thing. This new beginning of God is not the figment of an overactive religious imagination on the part of Samuel. The narrative opens with an absence of God's Word and revelation (3:9), but it concludes with Samuel as the proclaimer of God's Word and the revealer of God's new thing.

God is always the God of new beginnings. He is resolved that there will always be new possibilities in spite of failure. God, in his resolve for Israel and for us, gives us the power to dream again.

You remember the cartoon character Popeye the Sailor Man? When old Popeye became frustrated or wasn't certain exactly what to do, he would simply exclaim, "I yam what I yam." Popeye was a simple seafaring man who loved Olive Oyl. He was unpretentious, and yet his story belonged to him. "I yam what I yam."

When you look closely at Popeye, it seems he is saying, "Don't get your hopes up; don't expect too much. I yam what I yam, and that's all." Ancient Israel could say before Samuel, "I yam what I yam." God did not want Israel to remain as she was. Thus, through Samuel, God called Israel to a new resolve, a new beginning. This new beginning was to be characterized by God's Word as it came to Samuel. It became the Word of God for the nation.

God is still a God of resolve who desires to bring to his people a "new thing." God's "new thing" was made available to everyone "when the word became flesh and lived among us" (John 1:14). In his resolve God desired to reveal to us what God was like. In order

67

to do that, he laid aside that which was his right and came to serve, redeem, and love humankind. One day God laid aside his majesty and came knocking on our door. God came for you and for me.

In his resolve, God still calls. I wonder if you are "somewhere listening for your name."

The Gospel According To Jonah

Have you ever encountered a real "Scrooge"? I'm speaking about a negative, critical, carping, demanding, selfish person who cannot stand to see other people happy and enjoying life. You remember that the original Scrooge was a figment of the imagination of Charles Dickens, the great English author. Out of the imaginative mind of Dickens comes "A Christmas Carol" whose main character is one, Ebenezer Scrooge, whom Dickens calls, "a squeezing, wrenching, grasping, scraping, clutching, covetous old sinner!"

As Dickens unfolds the story of Scrooge, we see him at various stages of his life: Christmas Past, Christmas Present, Christmas Future. Eventually, old Ebenezer came to his senses and was marvelously converted and became a man of good works.

I believe there were other "Scrooges" long before Dickens' Scrooge. As I read the story of Jonah, I would label him a "Scrooge." Yes, I realize he was a prophet of God, but he seems to me to be the ultimate Scrooge. Why? When God told him to take "good news" to Nineveh, he instead hopped in a boat and headed in the opposite direction to Tarshish, which is about as far away from Nineveh as one can get.

A storm came up, and eventually Jonah confessed that he was the cause of the problem. He urged the ship's crew to throw him overboard. Finally, they threw him into the sea where Jonah was immediately swallowed by a great fish. The prophet cried out to God and the fish vomited him on dry land. God finally got old Scrooge's attention, and miracle of miracles, there is ...

A Second Time Around

As the scene opens, old Jonah is sitting on a Mediterranean beach, probably all shook up by his recent fish encounter. Suddenly the same word from God came to him a second time saying, "Get up; go to Nineveh, that great city; and proclaim to it the message I tell you" (v. 2).

Jonah carried out his assignment with very little enthusiasm. In his "Scrooginess" he only went part way into the city. Why was he such a reluctant prophet? One reason was that he was called to preach to a nation other than Israel, and this went against his "religion." Good Jewish prophets didn't preach to other nations. There was to be a strict separation from other nations. Also, Jonah believed that other nations were out to annihilate Israel.

Not only was he to preach to a people outside of Israel, but the particular city to which he was being sent was Nineveh. It was the capital of Assyria, a nation which in its day had set a standard of dread and terror. For Jonah, preaching to Nineveh would be like going to Baghdad in modern Iraq for you and me. For Jonah, the thought of preaching in Nineveh was out of the question. There was no way Jonah was going to preach to that gang of cutthroats. You can bet Jonah didn't sing the old gospel song which states: "Trust and obey, for there's no other way to be happy in Jesus, than to trust and obey." Jonah surely wouldn't have written a song like that, nor would he sing it.

As Jonah sat on the beach, stewing in his own juice, God called him a second time, and he responded as a prophet is expected to respond. So Jonah set out and went to Nineveh, that great city.

Jonah went to the city of Nineveh with a message of ...

Bad News Which Became Good News

Jonah walked toward the city of Nineveh, called by God a "great city." He was not a happy prophet. He did not even do what he was told. Jonah stopped short of going across the city of Nineveh. His sermon was not a homiletical masterpiece, for in the Hebrew it consisted of only eight words: "Yet forty days and Nineveh will be overthrown." Not much of a sermon! It does not take great oratorical ability to deliver that kind of message.

70

Surprisingly, Jonah's sermon was successful, and the response of the people was amazing. They accepted the message, believed it, trusted God, called for a fast, and dressed themselves in the clothes of mourning. Jonah was called to preach bad news to his enemies. This was Jonah's gospel, but Jesus, who is our Gospel, was called to die for his enemies. Jonah was unwilling to go until he was forced to go. Jesus, however, came to do the "will of his father." Jonah spent three days in the stomach of a great fish because of his disobedience. Jesus spent three days in a tomb of earth and death as an act of obedient love.

Not only did the people of Nineveh repent, but the king also repented and joined his subjects by putting on mourning clothes and sitting in ashes. The king then called for a fast and admonished all of his subjects to turn from their evil and wickedness.

How did God react to all of this? God saw the repentance of Nineveh's citizens, and he called off the intended destruction. The prophet's "Bad News" was heard, and the people repented. Destruction was called off, and that was "Good News." Yes, the "Bad News" of Jonah became the "Good News" of God for Nineveh. In the story of Jonah there is something more that is essential, and it is this ...

God Is A God Who Cares

While Jonah acted like a "Scrooge," God revealed that He is a God who cares. Jonah certainly did not care for the city of Nineveh. Who cares? God does, and God goes to great effort to see that a prophet was sent to the city. The New Testament reveals the extent of God's caring love in a single verse: "For God so loved the world, that he gave his only Son, so that everyone who believes in him may not perish but have eternal life" (John 3:16). One might go so far as to say that "God so loved Nineveh that he sent Jonah to preach to them."

Paul Yongi Cho pastors what is believed to be the largest church in the world. This Korean pastor has been used by God to impact the world. When his ministry began to receive international acclaim, Cho informed God that he would go anywhere to preach the gospel except Japan. Cho could not forget what the Japanese had done to Korea and her people, as well as members of his own family. Eventually an invitation came for Cho to preach in Japan. He accepted the invitation but with bitterness.

His first speaking assignment was to address a pastors' conference with a thousand Japanese pastors. When he stood to speak, these words came out of his mouth: "I hate you, I hate you. I hate you." Cho broke down and wept. His hatred had gotten the best of him.

One Japanese pastor, then another, until all one thousand stood up. One by one these Japanese walked up to Yongi Cho, knelt in front of him, and asked forgiveness for what their people had done to Cho and his people. As these pastors humbly sought Cho's forgiveness, Cho found himself saying to each one, not, "I hate you," but, "I love you." The Japanese were Paul Yongi Cho's Ninevites. Who are your Ninevites?

Who really cares? God does! What does the story of Jonah then mean for the Church? It asks those of us within the body of Christ to examine our attitudes toward those who are outsiders. This story warns us of a "Scrooge" attitude which conveys the message, "We are on the inside, and you are on the outside, so stay on the outside because we insiders don't want anything to do with outsiders." The story of Jonah reminds us that we exist for the sake of the people of our world. Who cares? God does, and God's people should.

The story of Jonah ends with a question mark. This "Scrooge" doesn't have a heart for the people. So here's the question for you and me: If Jesus came to save the people of Kabul, New York, London, Tokyo, and all people everywhere, what kind of love should we show others if we claim to experience God's love?

God asks Jonah this question; "And should I not be concerned about Nineveh, that great city, in which there are more than a hundred and twenty thousand persons who do not know their right hand from their left, and also many animals?" (Jonah 4:11). Amazingly, Jonah's response is not given. Jesus ends his ministry, not with a question, but a command, "Go therefore and make disciples of all nations, baptizing them in the name of the Father, and of the Son, and of the Holy Spirit, and teaching them to obey everything that I have commanded you. And remember, I am with you always, to the end of the age" (Matthew 28:19-20).

The gospel of Jonah just doesn't measure up, but the Gospel of Jesus, now that's a gospel for all people everywhere.

Epiphany 4
Ordinary Time 4
Deuteronomy 18:15-20

How To Recognize A Prophet

In his autobiography, *Up From Slavery*, Booker T. Washington tells of being awakened every morning in the slave quarters long before daylight by an old rooster crowing. The sound of the crowing rooster was the sign for the slaves to hit the floor and move out to the field to begin a day of hard work. According to Washington, when President Abraham Lincoln signed the Emancipation Proclamation and the slaves realized they had been freed, something changed in the Washington shanty. He recalls awakening the morning afterwards not to the sound of a rooster crowing, but his mother chasing that rooster around the barnyard with an axe. According to Mr. Washington, the Emancipation Proclamation was hard on roosters all across the South. That day the Booker T Washington family tried and ate their alarm clock for lunch. Before the signing of the Emancipation Proclamation, the Washington family's day was dictated by the ritual crowing of the rooster. Now Booker T. Washington's family knew the true meaning of freedom. Young Booker T. discovered that the first day he didn't have to get out of bed was the first day he really desired to get up and start living for his own reasons. He realized a purpose for living and a passionate call to serve others.

The book of Deuteronomy recognizes that the people of God will be faced with crowing roosters who will stifle and harm the purpose and passion of the nation. Our scripture for this Lord's Day focuses on the function of the prophet in the life of the nation. The prophet of the Old Testament did not serve as has often been depicted as some sort of spiritual rooster continually crowing to

73

remind the people of Israel of their obligation to God. The fear of Moses was that there would be various prophetic roosters crowing and stating, "This is God's way," or, "That is God's way." It is to the issue of what a true prophet is that Deuteronomy 18:15-20 speaks. The question that confronted the children of Israel is the question that confronts us today. How do you recognize a prophet? Deuteronomy helps us answer that question by informing us of ...

The Prophetic Initiative

How does one know the will of God? Where does one go to discover God's will for the Church? Those are very interesting questions. Ours is not the first generation to ask those questions. As a matter of fact, the Children of Israel were asking those very same questions as they made their way from Egypt to the land of promise.

One of the haunting questions that the Children of Israel had to deal with was, "How do we discern God's will for the community?" Resources for supposedly discerning God's will were readily available in the Near East. You could discover God's plan by examining the life of an animal, studying the flight pattern of a bird, or speaking to the dead through a medium. (That sounds very familiar, doesn't it?) Trying to discern the will of God by such means is condemned in the book of Deuteronomy. If these customary means of discovering God's will are rejected, how then will the people know or discern what God is up to?

The answer is very clear and forthright: "The Lord your God will raise up for you a prophet ..." (v. 15). Israel is not to use the means to discover God's will that other nations have devised. God's will is part of the divine initiative which is set over against all the devices concocted by human schemes. Notice how the divine initiative unfolds, "I will raise up for them a prophet ... I will put my words in the mouth of the prophet, who shall speak to them everything that I command" (v. 18). It is through the prophet that the will of God will be made known.

In our sophisticated age without the prophetic voice, how can we be assured that God still speaks? What means does God use to reveal himself to us today? Just as God spoke through his Word in

74

the time of Moses, God speaks today by the Holy Spirit through the scriptures. The Holy Spirit uses the Word of God to reveal to us the things of God.

God not only speaks today through his Word (scripture), but God also speaks to us through prayer. Prayer is a relationship which is a two-way street. We speak to God and God speaks to us. Sometimes we are so busy doing the talking that we forget to do the listening. God speaks by the Holy Spirit to his people through prayer.

God reveals his will for us in scripture and by prayer, but also God speaks by the Holy Spirit through our circumstances. God reveals himself oftentimes by giving us his perspective in the midst of circumstances. When we acknowledge God's love and sovereignty, then we can allow God to show us his will in various situations.

Finally, God reveals his will by the Holy Spirit through the Church. The Church functions at its best when all of its members are able to sense and share what they believe God's will is. One of the great purposes of the Church is, through the Holy Spirit, to direct us in doing God's will.

In relationship to the community of believers, we can depend on others in the body of Christ to help us understand God's will. God still takes the divine initiative and speaks to us through the Holy Spirit via scripture, prayer, circumstances, and the Church God is not in the business of hiding his will and purpose for any of us. From the prophetic initiative the scripture invites us to look at ...

The Prophetic Model

In Deuteronomy 18:15-20, Moses becomes the model for any prophet who will follow. He is portrayed as the greatest of all prophets (34:10-12). As a prophet, Moses possesses certain characteristics which will be the test for other prophets. Moses is a wounded healer; he is a teacher and also an intercessor. These same characteristics are to be found in the life and work of future prophets. As important as these characteristics are, there is a distinguishing function that makes Moses the ideal prophet. Moses' primary function is as the proclaimer of the Word of God. This function is given to

Moses by the people and by God. An undergirding principle of the book of Deuteronomy is the relationship of prophecy with the communication of God's Word. Moses stands out as prophet above prophets; not because of the miracles he performed by God's power, but because he faithfully proclaimed the word and will of God to the people.

How did Moses become the prophetic model? It all began when God made an appearance on Mount Sinai. It was such an awesome and terrifying sight that the people begged Moses not to require them to come near the mountain. They implored Moses to serve as their mediator, stand before God, and convey God's words to them.

Recently, a friend of mine was in the Dallas/Fort Worth area when a tornado hit downtown Fort Worth, Arlington, and other areas of the Metroplex. Those who witnessed the tornadoes said they had never seen or heard anything like it. On a television news program several people said they hoped they would never experience anything like it again. It was a terrifying experience. Think of what it must have been like to witness God's presence on Mount Sinai. The children of Israel had never seen anything like this before nor did they want to see it again. They begged Moses to become the mediator of God's will on their behalf. Because of his role as the mediator of God's will, Moses became the prophetic model for future prophets of Israel.

Moses is also an excellent model for ministry in our time for both laity and clergy. Those who minister within the congregation effectively need to be wounded healers, teachers, and intercessors who continually bring people into the presence of God.

From the prophetic model the scripture invites us to look at ...

The Prophetic Message

The message that the true prophet will proclaim is God's message. This prophet will speak everything that God commands him. How will the people know who the true prophet is if there are several voices claiming to proclaim truth? Israel continually faced the problem of distinguishing false prophets from true prophets. There were two characteristics that distinguished the message of the true prophet from false prophets. First, the false prophet spoke in the names of other gods. Second, if what a prophet declared failed to happen, he was a false prophet. The whole purpose of the prophet's message was to communicate God's will.

The prophets did not stand around gazing into a crystal ball. Instead, they looked at the life of Israel in the present time. If that life conformed to salvation, history, and the great commandment, then everything would be fine. If not, the future would be one of doom and destruction.

A few years ago, a televangelist informed his audience that God had told him he would die if he did not raise a million dollars for one of his institutions. Who knows if he raised the million dollars or not, but he is still alive.

When the Gulf War began, books on prophesy were rushed to religious bookstores warning that the end was coming and that the ancient Babylonian Empire would rise again, ushering in the end time. A few months after the Gulf war ended copies of these books could be found at drastically reduced prices on clearance racks. God's message is never incompatible with the Christian story!

There will come a prophet who is like Moses. He will be the ultimate prophet. This prophet will be a suffering servant, an intercessor, and a teacher. The early Church believed this prophet "like Moses" was none other than Jesus Christ (Acts 3:23-26). In his own ministry, Jesus was referred to as a prophet. When Jesus raised the widow of Nain's son, the cry of the crowd that observed the resurrection of the son expressed their fear and appreciation and voiced the faith generated by Jesus, "A great prophet has arisen among us!" (Luke 8:16:6). Luke uses this expression as descriptive of Jesus whose ministry was reminiscent of that of the prophets, notably Elijah and Elisha.

In our rush to remind people that Jesus is the promised Messiah, we ignore the rich tradition of the prophet in Israel. The prophet was God's spokesperson and brought to bear, by word and deed, the Word of God to the life of the people. Some of the contemporaries of Jesus taught that the age of prophecy had closed, but the crowds around Jesus announced that God had reopened it. "A great prophet has arisen among us!" echoes Deuteronomy 18:18: "I will raise up for them a prophet like you from among their own people."

What will the message of Jesus Christ, the Messiah, the ultimate prophet be? It will simply be that "When you see him, you see God, and he has come to bring *life*." Jesus, the ultimate prophet, has been "raised up" by God and is the Lord's servant.

As the film *Schindler's List* moves toward its conclusion, Oskar Schindler is seen lamenting the fact that he still owns a gold Nazi lapel pin. He tears it from his coat and cries painfully, "With this pin I could have ransomed two more Jewish lives." He stares at the pin in his hand and weeps! Itzhak Stern has observed this display of emotion. Stern touches Schindler and gives him a little piece of paper on which is written a Jewish proverb: "He who saves one life, saves the world in time!" The whole purpose of the message of the "ultimate prophet" was to save the world in time. The true prophet is Jesus Christ our Lord. Not only was he prophet, but he is Priest, and he is King. How do we recognize a prophet? The prophet is recognized by the redemptive scars he bears so that he might "save the world in time."

Lord Of All

A question that is often asked by parents of small children is: "How big are you?" Children are so cute, and generally they give the same answer as they stand on tiptoe and spread their little arms to illustrate how big they are. With arms outstretched and spread wide, they inform their inquiring parent that they are "soooo big!" What children are saying is: "I'm huge. Can't you see how large I am?" When parents ask their children this question, they do so because they want them to realize they are growing.

The exiles who once lived in Judah now dwelt as captives along the banks of the Euphrates River, surrounded by Babylonians who worshiped Marduk, Nebo, and other gods. These gods were part of the pantheon of Babylonian gods. If you had asked the exiles the question, "How big is your God?" the answer might have surprised you. Many of those in captivity felt that they were in this predicament because of the powerlessness of their God to secure the safety of the nation. Because of this, the Jewish community was in danger of losing its spiritual identity.

It is into this setting that Second Isaiah, the prophet of exile and comfort, steps. Nothing is known of the personal life of the prophet. His whole purpose as a prophet was to present God as the God who is active and present in the midst of human history. It was his job to call the people back to God and to remind them that the God of Abraham, Isaac, and Jacob was not a figment of humankind's mind but was Lord of all.

Like those ancient exiles, we too live in a culture that has run amuck, a world that has tried to make God in its own image. In a time such as ours, we need the ancient prophet to remind us in no uncertain terms that God, the true God, is Lord of all.

Just as Second Isaiah reminded his people, we need to have our minds renewed to the fact that God is ...

Lord Over All Rulers

In order to show that God is over all earthly rulers, the prophet begins with a series of staccato-like questions. There is a sense of exasperation, for the prophet cannot believe that the people have so completely forgotten who God is. In language that is regal, God is depicted as sitting on top of the earth, high and lifted up. In the exalted position, those who inhabit the earth are seen as small insects. What is God doing in all of his splendor? He is engaged in creative activity, forming and stretching the heavens.

God is also engaged in another activity, and that is of observing the political activities of the rulers of the earth. He becomes involved in the political issues which confront those in exile in Babylon.

There are kings who are in power, but God in his sovereignty can destabilize and dislodge them from their thrones. Before him they are helpless. The prophet pictures God as blowing upon these earthly rules, and when he does so, they are helpless.

William Willimon tells the story of an acquaintance of his who visited Russia in the late '70s when the Cold War was at its peak. The man was sent as part of a delegation from the World Council of Churches to investigate and bring back a report on the state of the Christian Church under an atheistic regime. He was not impressed. He informed Willimon in a condescending manner that "the church is just a bunch of little old ladies praying." Willimon told the story in the early '90s when the statues of Lenin and Stalin were being removed or destroyed. Yes, little old ladies were praying, but God was observing, and he is Lord over all rulers.[1]

Alan Jacobs, in an article published in 1996, notes that one thing that Joseph Stalin, the ruthless Soviet leader, could not tolerate was laughter. In his paranoia he felt that people might be laughing at him. The very empire he created was dark, dingy, and grim. Even his parties and celebrations were dark and laughterless affairs.[2]

80

The good news for us on this Lord's Day is that our God reigns and is in control. He is Lord of presidents and kings, prime ministers, and sultans. He is over all rulers. This gives the people of God a reason to celebrate. It is time for joy. Joy is deep, belly-shaking laughter. God is over all the kingdoms of this world. Rejoice, because our God reigns. Break out in the songs and laughter of joy.

Are there any lessons for us so far removed from these ancient exiles and this ancient text? Yes, for the message of Epiphany is that God has disclosed himself in the world. These scriptures invite the church once again to reflect on God's goodness and his greatness. When the Church really focuses on Epiphany, she can become "God intoxicated" so that the life of the Church is ordered by joy which breaks forth in the doxology, "How great thou art!"

God is Lord over all nations and rulers; however, he is also ...

Lord Over All Gods

There were detractors in Isaiah's day who maintained that God did not see, care, or hear. These detractors proclaimed loudly that God was not interested in each individual. The problem with these detractors was that they were looking for magic, a genie in a bottle. They were seeking an immediate fix, a magical potion. Because of this, they became involved in the worship of idols.

This is a picture in miniature of people in our age. Fortunetellers, psychic readers, astrology charts, and horoscopes have become a way of life for many. When Ronald Reagan was president, his wife Nancy created quite a stir when the news media reported that Mrs. Reagan regularly consulted an astrologer for advice, not only on a personal level, but also on world matters. People become fascinated with other gods when the creation is worshiped rather than the Creator.

A group of clergy attending a meeting had a good laugh when it was reported that the Psychic Television Network had declared bankruptcy. One person in the group with tongue in cheek exclaimed, "With all of their supposed psychic powers, you would have thought someone would have been able to foretell the coming bankruptcy."

81

The Creator wants his creation to look up to him and remember by his power he created. God is letting the Jews in exile and us know that he is the transcendent and the "Holy One" who is Lord of all.

God is Lord of all rulers and gods but also God is ...

Lord Over All

The exiles have been fearful about returning to Jerusalem, but God comes to allay their fears by promising them that he will give them his power for their weakness, and they will have his strength for their weariness. God is preparing the hearts of his people for his entrance. God does this by revealing his oneness and uniqueness.

In the spring of 1998, a series of tornadoes ripped through the southeastern part of the United States, spreading death and destruction. The day after one of the deadly tornadoes hit, the National Public Radio program *All Things Considered* aired a story about the Church of the Open Door, whose building had been destroyed by the storm. The children's choir was rehearsing when the storm hit. The pastor saw the tornado coming and hurriedly gathered the children into the main hallway of the church. Terrified, they huddled while the winds destroyed their church. In an effort to calm the children's fears, the pastor led them in singing, "Jesus Loves the Little Children." Some of the children were injured but miraculously none were killed. A deeply moving part of the broadcast was the report of a little girl who said, "While we were singing, I saw angels holding up the hallway. But the winds were so strong that the angels shouted out 'We need help!' and some more angels came and helped them." This is quite a story! That little girl will never forget what she saw. She will always believe that there were angels watching over all those children that day.

You and I may have trouble accepting what the little girl reportedly saw. Yet, when we reflect that our God is Lord over all, the story seems very plausible. The Lord who created all is the Lord who rules overall — even nature.

When people realize their own powerlessness, it is then that they will be open to the power that saves — God's power. Kierkegaard's statement, "The purity of heart is to will one thing," reminds us that

82

there must be no distraction in the human heart. The human heart, when it has divided loyalties, is confused and chaotic. Out of his own experience Augustine reminds us: "Thou hast made us for Thyself and our hearts are restless till they rest in Thee." God, like a forceful wind, sweeps away all obstacles to his Lordship. This forceful wind which is the Divine Breath fills the heart that is purified with hope and love.

This Old Testament lesson reminds us that quick fixes, magical cures, and false gods do not get the job done. But to those who surrender their lives completely to God, the prophet has a word of deep encouragement. It is this: God is the one who does not faint or grow weary, but God gives power to the faint and strength to the powerless.

The God of Second Isaiah is our God, and God is Lord over all. God will renew and restore his people around his Lordship.

---

1. William H. Willimon, *Peculiar Speech: Preaching to the Baptized* (William B. Eerdmans Publishing Company: Grand Rapids, Michigan, 1992) p. 20.

2. "The Man Who Heard Voices," Alan Jacobs, *Books and Culture* (January/ February 1996), p. 25.

Epiphany 6
Ordinary Time 6
2 Kings 5:1-14

Going Down To Look Up

Our story opens with Naaman, the military Chief of Staff of the Aramean army. Naaman is a very great man who has received the favor of the King of Aram, Syria, because of his victory over Israel. Anytime Israel lost a battle or a war, the disaster was felt to be the hand of God at work. In the theology of ancient Israel, no foreign army could be victorious over Israel unless it was God's will.

As we read this story in 2 Kings 5, we come to the conclusion that Israel's defeat is in accordance with the will of God. This defeat at the hands of the Arameans would result in the conversion, for God's glory, of a Gentile military genius, Naaman. In spite of defeat and tragedy, good can still be achieved.

Naaman, the Aram general, was a great warrior who was brave and strong. Josephus believed he was the nameless archer who shot the arrow that resulted in the death of King Ahab (Antiquities 15:5).

As great as Naaman was portrayed to be, there was something wrong. What was it that caused Naaman, who had everything, such deep concern? Let us try to discover the source of Naaman's consternation.

The scripture informs us that ...

Naaman Had A Problem

Naaman the Commander, the great man, one who was held in the highest esteem, had a problem. His problem is introduced with the three-letter conjunction "but." That small word changes everything. In spite of all his accomplishments, his power, and his

85

prestige, there was something controlling and defining his life. Naaman was a leper.

A few years ago Christopher Reeve, the talented movie star who played Superman, was injured in a horse riding accident which left him a paraplegic. Adored by fans and depicted by the movies he made as a man of steel, Reeves now is confined to a wheelchair and breathes with the help of a pulmonary device. Nothing can change that fact.

Naaman was a leper and leprosy was the AIDS of his day. His leprosy was probably not the most serious form, but it was a skin disease which carried with it certain social stigma. He was now Leper, Chief of Staff, Naaman, and nothing could change that. This meant for Naaman that he was an outcast, a person to be avoided, one who would be devoid of all human touch. Naaman would be treated as an object of disgust.

In the household of Naaman, there was a girl who had been taken captive from the land of Israel. This girl was a servant to the wife of General Naaman. Instead of being bitter and thinking to herself, "Let him die; he's getting exactly what he deserves," this captive girl informed her mistress that there was a prophet in Samaria who could cure Naaman of his leprosy. This good news from the girl set wheels in motion. The King of Aram sent a letter which was to be given to the King of Israel via a diplomatic courier. Naaman would follow with an entourage of "stuff," which is highly valuable. When the King of Israel received the letter he went into a "tizzy" thinking that Naaman was coming to start a war. The King was paranoid and tore his clothes as if he were in mourning. He saw only the impossibility of the situation. Contrast the king's attitude with the attitude of the captive girl in Syria who saw only the possibility of the situation. In spite of captivity, she perceived hope for Naaman. The King of Israel was throwing his hands up in despair.

In a sense, many of us are like Naaman. We are crippled by some hurt, some pain, a memory from our past, or a lingering illness. We too need someone who will reach out and touch us, who will love us, who will see our pain and tell us where we can find help.

This captive girl reminds us of what the church is about. The church must be a place where people are encouraged to find healing and wholeness. Also, the church must offer to all who are in need a resource which is the result of faith. All of Naaman's wagons loaded with finery from Aram would do him no good. Naaman had a problem, and a captive girl pointed him in faith to someone who could offer him help. Where would Naaman find his health and hope? It would be found in a prophet whose name was Elisha, which leads us to look at ...

Elisha's Prescription

Elisha sends a message to the King of Israel: "Why have you torn your clothes? Let him [Naaman] come to me, that he may learn there is a prophet in Israel" (v. 8b).

Naaman would have to go to Samaria, which was an armpit of a nation. If ever there was a second-rate country, Samaria was one. Naaman went trekking off to Elisha's house in Samaria.

General Naaman came with his wagons and his assistants. They arrived at the abode of Elisha the prophet. One wonders what Naaman expected to find. What kind of greeting did he expect? Was he looking for Elisha to come out and bow before him and acknowledge what a great man he was? If this is what Naaman expected, he was in for a rude awakening. He was in for a surprise. Instead of the prophet Elisha, the servant of Elisha showed up at the door with a prescription for Naaman's cure.

The general was livid. He was a bigshot in Aram. He expected a welcoming committee when he arrived at Elisha's remote home. He wanted the red carpet treatment and instant healing by the wave of prophet Elisha's hand. There is a lesson in this for us, and it is this: God does not always do things the way we want. God often chooses the unexpected to accomplish his purpose for our lives.

Naaman was angry because Elisha did not greet him at the door. It seems the prophet had misplaced his book on protocol. Elisha then added insult to injury as Naaman was given the prescription for healing through Gehazi his servant. This prescription was bizarre: "Go, wash in the Jordan seven times, and your flesh shall be restored, and you shall be clean" (2 Kings 5:10). Naaman couldn't believe it. Seven dips in dirty Jordan. There were far cleaner and better rivers back home. The issue for Naaman was not the river Jordan, but obedience to God. His problem is our problem. We would rather do it our way than God's way. Thus, we miss the great blessing God has in store for us.

Naaman almost rejected his opportunity for healing by becoming angry. We, too, by our anger at God for not acting on our behalf in the ways we demand of him, can miss our opportunity to see God work in his way, on his own time schedule, for his glory and our good.

What is going to happen to Naaman? Will he get Elisha's prescription filled and become whole, or will his pride keep him from taking his medicine? What about you and me? Will we let our pride stand in the way of God's miracle by not getting our spiritual prescription filled?

This leads us to the next phase in the story of Naaman, which is ...

The Servant's Persuasion

Naaman's servants persuaded him to heed the command of Elisha to go and dip in the Jordan seven times. Their argument was simple but persuasive. They simply argued that this was not difficult. If Elisha had asked him to do something difficult, he would have done it. So the servants asked what the big deal about dipping seven times in the Jordan was if it meant wholeness.

Naaman had to descend into the Jordan to receive healing. So must you and I. When God speaks to us, we must be compliant toward his instructions. God will meet us at our point of need when we bow humbly before him.

What did Naaman finally do? He humbled himself in complete obedience to God's instructions. In so doing he experienced a healing that did not fit his expectations. He was healed, and his flesh was restored like "that of a young boy" (2 Kings 5:14).

Naaman experienced the grace of God and he was physically healed. The story does not end with his healing. In verse 15, which is not in our Old Testament lesson for today, we learn that Naaman became a believer in God. This was a defining moment. Naaman felt God's touch and was changed. Have you received God's touch and been changed? If we are honest, all of us need the changing touch of God. God does not deal with all of us the same way, and we must be open to his unique way of working with us.

Don Snyder has written a fascinating book titled *Cliff Walker*. It is a story about being a non-tenured literature professor at Colgate University. He was terminated because of budget cuts. Snyder had been a very popular professor with the students. When he received the notice that his contract would not be renewed, he was devastated. Snyder's book is about transformation from a college professor to a construction worker and painter. He relates the decision to rid himself of the library he used as a professor. When Snyder made this decision, he broke with the old way and chose a new life. Here is how he describes what happened: "I got some trash bags from the kitchen and began going through all my books, separating the ones that I'd written in. But soon I decided to put them all in trash bags, along with more than a dozen spiral notebooks that contained the notes for my lectures." Then he went to the town dump with the trunk of his car full of books. "I was the first car there, waiting outside the gates when they opened." "Whatcha got there?" the toothless man in charge of the landfill asked. "An old life," I said.[1]

Naaman had a choice to stay a leper or to become whole. He chose to become a whole person. In so doing he dropped his old life. Naaman's choice is ours. It is the choice of being obedient or disobedient. That is always the choice, isn't it? The choice is that of humbling ourselves before God so that God can touch us. This choice might mean washing ourselves in a dirty river just because God says so. When we obey God, we see God. Naaman had to go down to look up. When he did, he discovered "grace." When you and I go down to look up, we too will discover "grace."

---

1. Don Snyder, *Cliff Walker* (New York: Little Brown, 1998).

Sometimes It's Okay
To Be Absentminded

All of us have heard of the absent-minded professor. I have a friend who is the full embodiment of the absent-minded professor. On one occasion he became so absorbed in a chess game that he failed to show up for his Contemporary Theology class. This professor's wife told of asking him to get her a couple of aspirin because of a splitting headache. He left to go retrieve the aspirin and water so she could find relief. When he returned a few minutes later, she inquired as to the aspirin and water. According to the story, the professor took the aspirin and drank the water. Story after story has been told about my friend's absentmindedness.

All of us at some time or another find ourselves bearing the burden of absentmindedness.

Isaiah, in our lesson for today, gives us a picture of God which at first glance is not flattering. God is asking his people to be absentminded. This memory lapse was to take place in the midst of international uncertainty which threatened to obliterate the people of God.

Suddenly, God seems to contradict himself and in the midst of asking his people to forget, God suddenly wants them to ...

Remember

The story is told of a man who had experienced horrible tragedies in his life. One night when he was alone in his room, he prayed that God would completely erase his memory. When the man's prayer was finished, an angel appeared and informed the man that God had heard his prayer and was granting his request.

There was, however, a downside to the granting of the request. It was that the man would have the power to destroy every person's memory that he contacted. After a while the man realized that for some odd reason he was creating distress and unhappiness in the lives of people. One day it dawned upon the man that he was miserable and making everyone he came into contact with miserable. The man began to pray and asked God to restore him to his original state. The story concludes with the man's memory, as well as the memory of all the people he had contacted, being restored. The story simply ends with the man praying this prayer, "Oh, God, keep my memory green!"

God wants the memory of his people to be kept green. God asks the people to remember God's mighty acts in their past. This was a call to relive the Exodus. They were to remind themselves of God bringing them out of Egypt, his destruction of Pharaoh's army, and his faithfulness in leading them through the wilderness and making of them a community. They were to remember, for memory would remind them in the midst of their decades of despair that "God was there."

We, too, are called by God to remember: to remember our Exodus from the far country of disobedience and rebellion. God wants us to remember that in the midst of our loneliness, rootlessness, and sin, he is there. It is God's purpose to remind us that he experienced God-forsakenness, and for us he died. Like ancient Israel, we are to remember and believe.

God speaks again and informs the people that they are to ...

Remember To Forget

It is as if God contradicts himself. God has told his people to remember his mighty acts, and now in the next breath God informs the people that he wants them to forget what he told them to remember.

What are they to forget? Forget God's creative acts? Forget God's redemptive acts, like the Exodus? Forget the rebellion and waywardness which brought destruction to Israel? Isaiah is simply saying, "Forget all of what's past."

In order for the people to be open to God, they must experience forgetfulness. The forgetfulness that God called for was a forgetfulness of things past, both the good and the bad.

The Apostle Paul had a sense of the meaning of Isaiah 43:18 when he wrote: "Forgetting what lies behind and striving forward to what lies ahead, I press on toward the goal" (Philippians 3:13b-14a).

God is saying the same thing to us today: "Forget those things that are behind you. Do not let the sins of yesterday haunt you. Also, forget your good deeds as well." What God wants us to do is not to brood over past victories or recent failures. He does not want our past to control the present or diminish the future.

God's greatest act was the new Exodus which he brought forth in Jesus Christ. Those who receive the new Exodus are those who have fallen out of love with their own history. In Christ's day those who were caught up with their own history and the business of remembering were the scribes and chief priests. Because of this, they were not able to discern what God in Christ was doing before their very eyes.

Isaiah is not calling us to absentmindedness, but he is warning us not to tie God down to the past. The Jesus who walked on to the pages of history 2,000 years ago was resurrected from the dead. The tomb is empty. Christ is risen. We must look and see what God in Christ is doing right now, this very moment.

In one of the late Charles Schulz' *Peanuts* comic strips, Lucy and Linus are getting ready to go to church for the annual Christmas program. This conversation ensues:

> *Lucy: "Linus, are you sure you know your piece for the Christmas program?"*
>
> *Linus: "I know it backwards and forwards and sideways and upside down! I could say it in my sleep!"*
>
> *Lucy: "Yeah, well, I remember last year, how you forgot and how you almost goofed the whole program."*
>
> *Linus: "Well, this is this year, and this year, I won't forget. Listen to this: And the angel said unto them, 'Fear not — for behold, I bring you good tidings of great joy which shall be to all people ...' "*

Lucy: "Say, that's pretty good."

Linus: "I told you I know it. I've got it nailed this year. I now have a memory like the proverbial elephant! Well, I'm going ahead to the church. I'll see you there."

Linus walks along the sidewalk in the snow rehearsing his part over and over again! " 'For behold, I bring you good tidings of great joy which shall be to all people ...' Perfect. What a memory I have!"

The scene changes, and it shows Linus coming in the front door of his home. Lucy says, "Linus? What in the world? I thought you just left!"

Linus responds, "I did, but I came back. I forgot where the church is."[1]

Like Linus, the Church and God's people in all ages have remembered what they deemed essential. In the process of remembering, the tendency has been to forget God's presence. When this happens, the Church forgets that it is located in a world that desperately needs to see God's presence. Instead of focusing on the God who is present and active in the now, the emphasis has been on God's activity in the past. There are some things we need to remember to forget, but there is one thing the Church must continually guard against and that is of remembering the past to the neglect of locating God in the present. God's presence is never limited to the past. God is active in the everyday events that shape our lives. Let us not overlay our faith with non-essentials, but let us remember those things that are essential.

God has told his people to "remember to forget" and now God gives to them ...

A Faithful Reminder

God informs the people by way of a wonderful reminder that he is "about to do a new thing." God is going to make a way through the desert. God is going to send the exiles home — back home to Jerusalem. They are not to worry about the journey even though they will have to cross the desert, for God will provide water, a veritable river in the desert.

94

Isaiah sees God providing a new exodus, a way out, a new salvation, a homecoming, freedom from the bondage of the Babylonians.

In a sense, the whole world was in exile wrapped in the grip of sin, death, and hell. Jesus our Savior came in the fullness of time to set God's captives free. God has done his new thing in Jesus Christ, and it never grows old and is always springing forth anew.

What do you need? Do you need to be set free from a past that haunts you with memories of your sin and failures? God has provided a way out in Jesus Christ. God wants to release you today from those things that have hindered you in order to release you for his service.

What do you need for God to do for you? Are you afraid of death? Jesus Christ died for you so that you may live. God in Christ has provided life for you now and forever more.

What do you need? Do you want God to set you free from the spectrum of hell which haunts you and causes you to walk in darkness? God is victor over all darkness which threatens to destroy you. He triumphed over all evil to give you victory.

What is the need of the Church? The greatest need of the Church is to be set free from crusty, worn-out, unworkable tradition. When this happens, the Church will return to its first love and God will do new and wonderful things greater than we can perceive.

What is the need of our world? The greatest need of the world is to remember that God has created us and that God wants to recreate us in his image. When God does his "new thing," all will sing his praises. Birds and animals, humankind, all creation will praise God for his greatness and goodness. Creation will someday recognize the new thing that God has done in Christ.

Right now you can begin to praise God for his "new thing"! Forget about past praises and be reminded of what God is doing now, right at this moment. Praise God anew and keep on praising him as he extends his forgiving grace to all of us. In order for us to see God's "new thing," we must remember that all absentmindedness isn't a bad thing. Sometimes it's okay to be absentminded.

---

1. Charles Schulz, *You Don't Look 35, Charlie Brown* (New York: Holt, Rinehart, and Winston, 1985).

Epiphany 8
Ordinary Time 8
Hosea 2:14-20

The House Of Hope

A friend of mine lives in a remote area of the United States which has a very low emotional quotient. Because of this, alcoholism is rampant, incest is above average, and spousal abuse is prevalent. One of the dominating social ills is the abuse suffered by teenagers. In a recent study released by the state where my friend resides, a survey revealed that one out of every three teenagers has been abused sexually.

In order to help these teens who have suffered mentally, emotionally, and physically because of sexual abuse, the communities, with the help of the state, have opened a facility called "The House of Hope." This house offers counseling, as well as long-term housing, for those who are trying to find healing from the indignities perpetrated upon them. It is the feeling of the small communities involved in this caring venture that many teens will find hope and help which will enable them to overcome the horrific damage and pain they have encountered. The House of Hope is a lighthouse in the darkness in which many young sexually-abused victims find themselves trapped.

Hosea the prophet found himself in darkness due to the unfaithfulness of his wife Gomer, who left him to engage sexually with multiple partners. He was heartbroken and had to be the caregiver for their bewildered children who cried nightly for their mother. The prophet's brokenheartedness over his wife's unfaithfulness is a picture of a faithful God who is heartbroken over the unfaithfulness of his people Israel.

Out of the prophet's dilemma, God gives a picture of a "House of Hope" which is the story of Gomer's return and restoration. Also, this is a picture of God wooing his people back from their infidelity and restoring the marriage relationship which had existed between himself and Israel.

Just as Hosea will woo Gomer and bring her back to his "House of Hope," so God will seek after unfaithful Israel to bring her back to his "House of Hope." This House of Hope which Hosea speaks of will be ...

A Place Of Grace

This Old Testament lesson begins with "therefore." This is not the first time that "therefore" has been used in Hosea 2. The two previous "therefores" were succeeded by two announcements of punishment. However, this third "therefore" does not have any announcement of punishment. Instead, it opens with grace abounding. This grace is unconditional, and it is God who does the changing and reveals the "House of Hope" as a place of grace.

God does this in the language of courtship, "I will allure ..." (v. 14). The future of Israel is not of destruction, disaster, and death, but it is a future of life. In his grace, God will do four things: God will allure, God will bring, God will speak, and God will give. These words are words which speak to the joys of courtship and its happiness. They bring the hope of a new beginning.

When old Madison Square Garden was constructed in 1890, a statue of the Greek goddess Diana crowned New York's first indoor arena. Diana, in Greek mythology, was a goddess of the woods who later was depicted as a huntress and patron of women. The sculptor who fashioned the statue of Diana found a lovely girl to serve as a model for the statue. After the statue was finished, and it was placed on the top of Madison Square Garden, it became a huge success. Because of the artistic beauty of the sculpture, the model became famous. Her beauty was stunning, and everywhere she went, people recognized her as the model for Diana. Fame is fleeting, and personal tragedies caused the world of the lovely model to collapse. Eventually she became a derelict and a recluse.

Years later a broken, homeless woman made her way into a Salvation Army kitchen in a seedy New York neighborhood. This woman begged for something to eat. As she quickly gulped down her food, the Salvation Army officer who was on duty observed her. Something about her seemed familiar to the officer. He approached the woman and asked her name. To his amazement he discovered who she was. He exclaimed, "You are Diana!" She smiled a crooked smile which revealed missing teeth. She was pleased that someone remembered and recognized her. Yet, she was ashamed of what she had become. She quietly responded, "I was Diana."

This Salvation Army officer was able to look beyond what this woman had become. He did not see a bedraggled, care-worn recluse. Instead he saw the beautiful Diana. What this man did was a picture of grace. He looked at her and saw not her ugliness, but the beauty hidden beneath her ragged edges.

The grace of God will erase the unpleasant memories of the past. Hosea mentions the Valley of Achor, which has always been associated with failure and trouble. Achan was disobedient and took a valuable robe, 200 shekels of silver, and a gold bar. He hid them under his tent. Not knowing any of this, Joshua led the army of Israel in an attack on a place called Ai. Instead of the anticipated easy victory, the army of Israel was repulsed. God revealed to Joshua the reason for the defeat, and Achan and his family were executed for their disobedience. This judgment took place in a valley which was subsequently named the Valley of Achor, or "trouble." It was a place of terrible failure. The people of God in the eighth century were in their Valley of Achor because of their corruption, idolatry, and rejection of God. In spite of Israel's forgetting God, God now, in an act of grace, states that he will transform Israel's repetition of the sin of Achan into a place of grace.

God's promise to ancient Israel has deep personal meaning for us. We all have memories of sin and failure. The good news of grace is that the One who offered a door of hope to Israel came in Jesus Christ to be that door. When we enter into a relationship with Jesus Christ, the cross and resurrection became our "House of Hope," a place of grace.

A Place Where Broken Relationships Are Restored

Israel had broken her relationship with God, and in the breaking of that relationship, worship had disintegrated to the point that the name of God (Yahweh) and Baal were being used interchangeably. Worship in Israel reached its lowest point when God was worshiped as Baal. When the broken relationship between God and his people was restored, Israel called her God, "My Husband." This is the language of endearment and intimacy. It is language which has the implication of ownership and lordship which God's people lavished and squandered on the Baals.

God, in restoring the broken relationship between himself and Israel, will take the name of the Baals from Israel's mouth and memory. A restored relationship will result in total transformation and a new inner nature. Israel will no longer be distracted from her devotion to God. Can this happen? Is it possible for human nature to be changed? Is liberation from false gods possible? Yes, by the transforming power of redemption — a redemption that includes a place called Golgotha, an empty tomb, and a Savior who is alive. The miracle is that God in Christ gives us the gift of faith to accept his love and forgiveness.

Josh McDowell in his book, *Evidence That Demands a Verdict*, writes of this love and forgiveness. He states that his father "epitomized everything I hated ... He was the town drunk. My high school friends would make jokes about him making a fool of himself around town. Sometimes when we had company, I would tie Dad up in the barn and tell them he had to go on an important call." When McDowell became a Christian, God's grace was able to transform his hatred for his father into love. Shortly after his conversion to Christ, McDowell was injured in an automobile accident. His father came to visit him in his hospital room. At one point as they were talking together, he broke down and said, "Josh, I've been the worst kind of father to you. How can you love a man like me?" "Dad," said McDowell, "six months ago I couldn't. But now, through Jesus Christ, I can love you." He explained to his father the meaning of God's grace in his life. Before leaving that hospital room, Josh McDowell's father had committed his life to Jesus Christ. He was a changed man! Scores of people who saw the change

100

in his life also came to know Jesus Christ. A year later this changed man died at peace with God and at peace with his son.[1]

God is a faithful God who seeks to restore broken relationships which is part of the structure of "The House of Hope."

The House of Hope is a place of grace, a place where broken relationships are restored, but it also is ...

A Place For The Renewal Of Wedding Vows

Hosea has wooed Gomer and renewed their wedding vows. The prophet sees in his renewed relationship with Gomer a picture of God renewing his marriage vows with Israel. It is a portrayal of the bride and groom standing before the minister. The days of courtship and wooing have come to an end. The bride and groom will renew their vows and their marriage will be legal, binding, and irrevocable. The renewal of the marriage vows begins with the formal vow, "I will take you for my wife forever" (v. 18). This vow is repeated three times. It is not a period of engagement, but of marriage, for this vow is "forever."

As the groom stands with his bride to renew their wedding vows, he knows that he can expect nothing from the bride. As they stand together at the altar, the bride is asked to promise nothing. Only the groom makes promises. The promises of the groom are fantastic, unconditional, and anchored firmly in God's unchanging nature. The vows of renewal contain some of the greatest themes of scripture. Righteousness is that aspect of the wedding vow which is the foundation on which the "House of Hope" is built. God fulfills the vows he has made. Justice is the next aspect of the vow renewal. This defines how people live in relationship to God and each other. These vows celebrate God's loving kindness. God acts to maintain the relationship he has established. God's love is reliable. God also vows to be faithful. He will be constant in word and deed toward his bride, his beloved Israel. God is simply stating, "This is what I am like and what you can depend on me to be to you."

Finally, the ceremony has ended, and the vows have been renewed. The greatly anticipated moment has arrived, and the bride and groom will honeymoon. On the honeymoon they will know the joys of a renewed wedding night in which "they will know each other." We too must know God. A true sign of our knowledge of God is that we are able to express righteousness, justice, loving kindness, and mercy. This all begins with the personal acknowledgment of God's reign over all and our devotion to him. God's wedding gifts of righteousness, justice, loving kindness, and mercy come to us through faith in Jesus Christ. Singing is heard because of the recommitment of a husband and a wife to their original wedding vows.

Nelson Mandela was imprisoned for 27 years by the South African government. While he languished in prison he never lost his hope for a new South Africa. As the day for his release drew near, Mandela's only daughter was allowed to come and see him. When his daughter came to visit her father, she carried in her arms the granddaughter Mandela had never seen. She wanted her daughter's grandfather to name her. "I don't think a man was ever happier to hold a baby than I was that day," he wrote in his memoirs. The name Mandela gave his granddaughter was Zaziwe, an African word for hope. He called her Hope, he said, because "during all of my years in prison, hope never left me — and now it never would." Nelson Mandela had built a "House of Hope."[2]

God is our bridegroom and will help us build, out of the ruins and wreckage of our waywardness, a "House of Hope." The only true hope we have is in God and God alone.

---

1. Josh McDowell, *Evidence That Demands a Verdict* (Arrowhead Springs, California: Campus Crusade for Christ, 1972), p. 374.

2. Adapted from Lewis Smedes, *Standing on the Promises* (Nashville: Thomas Nelson, 1998), p. 39.

**Transfiguration Of The Lord
(Last Sunday After Epiphany)
2 Kings 2:1-12**

Going, Going, Gone

Recently, a friend of mine went to Wrigley Field in Chicago to watch an afternoon baseball game. For my friend, an afternoon at Wrigley Field is the ultimate in baseball. Those who attend an afternoon game at Wrigley Field still sing enthusiastically during the seventh inning stretch, "Take Me Out To The Ball Game." When a player drives a ball deep into left field towards the bleachers, and it looks as if the ball will make it into the bleachers, you will hear a familiar cry from the faithful at Wrigley, "It's going; it's going; it's gone!" The crowd goes wild. Whether the Cubs win or lose is not the issue. This is baseball at its best, and Chicago loves its Cubs. It is worth the hassle, bustle, and bother to see a home run at Wrigley and hear the joyous expression, "It's going; it's going; it's gone!"

Elisha, the successor to Elijah the Prophet had no knowledge or understanding of modern day baseball, nor the parlance that surrounds baseball. He could, however, understand "Going, going, gone," for he would watch the man who had been his spiritual mentor for ten years suddenly taken from him by supernatural means. Elisha, the prophet, understudy to Elijah, could shout, "He's going; he's going; he's gone!"

On this Lord's Day when the Church reflects on our Lord's Transfiguration, are there any lessons that can be gleaned from the Elisha/Elijah narrative? Are there any truths which can help the Community of Faith remember the significance of the Transfiguration of our Lord Jesus Christ? As the Church reflects on the Transfiguration, she remembers ...

103

The Legacy Of Elijah

The Prophet Elijah's story begins as Elijah, a solitary figure, emerges out of nowhere and confronts the wicked King Ahab. As the life of this solitary figure is reviewed, we watch him as he stands on Mount Carmel confronting the prophets of Baal, calling down fire from heaven. As his story continues, he can be seen as a lonely figure on top of Mount Horeb, bemoaning his plight and complaining: "I, even I only, am left."

It is in this final scene of the old prophet's life that we begin to discover his legacy. His greatest victory is not that he leaves the earth in a whirlwind. His final victory, his eternal legacy, is that he left some schools of prophets plus a well-trained assistant to carry on his work.

The thing that is the most impressive about the life of Elijah is that he invested himself in others so that his ministry might be multiplied. It could be said that Elijah was a person who used his influence to promote godliness.

Elijah trained Elisha, who in turn trained the various schools of prophets who then became equipped to teach the people. These prophets were men who spoke to men the "word of the Lord."

F. B. Meyer has stated that the original word for "prophet" meant "bubbling over." Elijah was a "bubbling over" mouthpiece for God, and as such, he activated others to be the same.

His ministry began with his testimony before Ahab where he affirmed the very meaning of his name, "The Lord, he is God." With God's help, he triumphed over Baal's prophets, and the people applauded and shouted, "The Lord, he is God." His greatest success, however, lies in the fact that he trained others who would now "bubble over" with the proclamation, "The Lord, he is God."

On this Lord's Day when we celebrate the Transfiguration of our Lord, we reflect once again on his eternal legacy. We are reminded that he trained a small band of men who, after Pentecost, would "bubble over" with this expression which would revolutionize the world forever, "Jesus is Lord."

Lou Holtz, former Notre Dame head football coach and now head coach of the University of South Carolina, is an entertaining and humorous speaker. Holtz tells the story of a man who accidentally ran his car off the road and into a ditch. The man was not injured, but his car was stuck. He asked an old farmer for help. The farmer responded by getting his old mule named Dusty and hooking him up to the car. When everything was ready, the farmer snapped the reins and shouted, "Pull, Jack! Pull, Joe! Pull, Tom! Pull, Dusty!"

With relative ease the old mule pulled the car out of the ditch. The car owner was deeply gratified and thanked the farmer over and over again. He finally said to the farmer, "I want to know something. Why did you call Dusty by four different names?" The farmer responded: "Well, it's like this. Dusty's eyesight is about gone, and if he thought for a second that he was the only one pulling, he wouldn't have tried at all!"

When Elijah established his seminary for prophets, he realized he would not have to pull by himself. In so doing, he left the Church a legacy that the "good news" is better announced by many than by the few as loners. From Elijah's legacy we see that ...

The Leadership Is Passed To Elisha

For ten long years Elisha has worked in the shadow of the ministry of Elijah, and now it is time for Elijah to be taken up to heaven. It is interesting that Elijah tried three times to get away from Elisha. Three times Elijah told Elisha, "Stay here for I am going to go to the next town." Elisha refused to obey him. Why did Elijah not want Elisha, his successor, to go with him on his farewell journey? That is a hard question. It seems to me that Elijah, who was a loner, wanted to be alone and spend some time alone before he met the living God face-to-face. No matter what the reason was, Elisha stuck with him. For ten years Elisha had been referred to as Elijah's servant, and he resolved to remain Elijah's faithful servant to the end.

There is a problem area in this narrative in regards to the "double portion" that Elisha requested of his master. It must be understood that Elisha is not asking to be twice as powerful as Elijah. His request relates to a custom which in Deuteronomy 21:17 informs us the firstborn son was entitled to a double share of the father's estate, while the younger sons would get only a single share. Elisha is requesting that he be designated as Elijah's rightful heir, receiving double what the other prophets would receive which would indicate to the various schools of prophets that Elisha would now be the "lead prophet."

Elijah informed his understudy that this would be a very difficult request to grant. If however, God permitted Elisha to see Elijah when he was taken up, that would be a sign that God had granted Elisha's request, and then he would become the successor to Elijah (vv. 10-11). Verse 12 tells us that "Elisha saw it." Because of the many miracles associated with the life of Elisha, it is safe to assume that he did receive the double portion he had requested. Elijah's departure was spectacular. Not only was there the whirlwind, which was anticipated, but there also were the chariot and horses of fire, which apparently were a surprise. The prophet Elijah left behind his mantle and a double portion of his spirit. Elisha takes the mantle and returns to the Jordan River and strikes the waters with this invocation, "Where is the Lord God of Elijah?" The answer which is implied by the miraculous opening up of the river is, "God has not abandoned us; he is now with Elisha as he was with Elijah."

Elisha picks up the mantle of the prophetic office and turns the word of God loose on another generation. The Church in each generation must pick up the mantle by retelling the stories of God's mighty acts, thus releasing God's word on a new generation so that they can be empowered for mission.

Elijah has passed his leadership to Elisha, but there are still ...

Lessons Which The Church Can Learn

During the time of Christ, there was an expectation that Elijah would return. Even today as our Jewish friends celebrate Passover, a cup is placed at each table for the prophet Elijah in case he should choose to visit. In a sense, John the Baptizer picked up the mantle of Elijah with his ministry. Jesus himself called John "Elijah," which simply meant that John carried the same mantle.

Elijah appeared on the earth one more time, on the Mount of Transfiguration. There with Moses they talked with Jesus while

106

the disciples, in awe and fear, ran around trying to start a building program.

What did Elijah and Jesus talk about? Could it be that Elijah encouraged our Lord as he moved towards his impending sacrifice of love? We don't know, but I like to think so. What we do know is that Elijah was given an encore on the Mount of Transfiguration, which simply reminds us that God uses ordinary people and kisses them with a destiny.

It's strange, isn't it, that God used Elijah, who was a person "just like you and me." His life wasn't perfect, and there is no mention of him in Hebrews 11, the great faith chapter. God remembered him and gave him to us as an example. There is only one prayer of Elijah's that God never answered, and that prayer was that God would take his life.

In the midst of a high profile career, Charles Colson, who had access to power and enormous influence, found himself headed for prison because of the Watergate Scandal. Colson thought his life was over, and life for him as he once knew it was over. Yet, life for Colson was just beginning. He would be called to serve humanity through his gifts and his brokenness. Reflecting on his life, Colson stated: "The real legacy of my life was my biggest failure — that I was an ex-convict. My great humiliation — being sent to prison — was the beginning of God's greatest use of my life; God chose the one experience in which I could not glory for his glory."

Just as God used Charles Colson and Elijah, so he wants to use you and me. We are not spare parts; we are on a mission for God.

Elisha looked up, and Elijah was going, going, gone! What a way to go!

Sermons On The First Readings

For Sundays In
Lent And Easter

Richard E. Gribble, csc

The Christian journey from reconciliation to resurrection requires us to understand the powerlessness of the human condition and our absolute need for God to transform us in every way to a higher level of understanding. I have learned how better to walk this road of faith through the assistance of my friend and fellow Holy Cross religious, Father Joseph Carey, CSC, who has served as mentor, priest, and confidant. It is to him that this collection of reflections on the journey of Lent and Easter is dedicated.

Introduction

A few years ago a young and very successful business executive named Josh was driving a bit fast through a Chicago neighborhood in his sleek, black, sixteen-cylinder Jaguar XKE, which was only two months off the showroom floor. He was watching for children who darted in and out of parked cars along the street. All of a sudden Josh heard and felt a thump on the side of the car. A brick had been hurled at the Jag's shiny side door. Josh hit the brakes, threw the car into reverse, attempting to stop at the location from which he thought the brick had come.

He jumped out of the car, inspected the damage, a slight dent in the door, and began to search for the culprit. He saw a young boy, and, assuming this was the one, pushed him against a parked car and began to scream at him: "What do you think you're doing? That is a brand new Jag and that brick you threw is going to cost you plenty. Why did you throw it?" "Please, mister," came the response, "I'm sorry about your car, but I did not know what else to do. I threw the brick because no one would stop." Tears were dripping down the boy's chin as he pointed to a young lad lying on the ground. "That's my brother, mister. He fell out of his wheelchair and I can't lift him up." Sobbing the boy asked the executive, "Would you help me put him in his wheelchair?" Stunned to the bone, Josh desperately tried to swallow a rapidly swelling lump in his throat. He helped the boy right the wheelchair and then together they lifted the boy back into the chair.

It was a long ride back home in that sleek, shiny, black, sixteen-cylinder Jaguar XKE. As the story goes, Josh never fixed the dent in the car door because he wanted always to be reminded that there is a need to slow down, seek reconciliation, and find conversion to a new way of thinking in one's life.[1]

111

This little story illustrates the journey the Christian community takes during the seasons of Lent and Easter, a journey from reconciliation to resurrection, from seeing our need to change to being converted to a new and higher understanding of God's call and presence in our life. This annual excursion provides numerous opportunities for the person of faith. If we open ourselves fully and allow the seasons to engage us, the benefits will be abundant.

The season of Lent, inaugurated on Ash Wednesday, is a time when the church traditionally asks us to reflect upon our need to pray, fast, and give alms. We may dedicate more time to personal prayer or find new ways to speak and listen to God. We may abstain from some food or drink item that is our favorite, or we may, as the prophet suggests, "loose the bonds of injustice, undo the thongs of the yoke, [and] let the oppressed go free" (Isaiah 58:6). Lent encourages us to be more thoughtful in our use of the world's goods. We who live in the first world need to be conscious that we have an obligation to others. Thus, giving alms is a basic requirement of the Christian journey of life.

Lent is a season when we reflect upon prayer, fasting, and almsgiving, but more generically it is a time of reconciliation. We need to be, as the parable of the prodigal son so aptly demonstrates, a reconciliation people. We need to forgive ourselves of any past problems, cut our ties to past hurts, and move forward. Next, we must seek to be reconciled with our peers, our brothers and sisters, those who have hurt us and those whom we may have injured in some way. Finally, we need to be reconciled to God.

The reconciliation we need and begin in the season of Lent is completed through the transformation that the resurrection of Christ, celebrated during the Easter season, brings to each and every human person. As the Acts of the Apostles so powerfully demonstrate in the case of Saint Peter, transformation through belief in the resurrection is possible. Christ's triumph over death transformed Peter from a person who could not understand and denied the Lord three times into a man who fearlessly proclaimed Jesus' message, healed cripples in his name, and refused to be cowed by threats of imprisonment or bodily harm. It was necessary for Peter and the other disciples of Jesus to experience Good Friday and their need

112

for reconciliation before the power of the resurrection could be fully felt. The apostles needed to be laid low, to encounter their personal failure, before they could be reinvigorated, namely transformed, by the power of the resurrection which the great Easter mystery provides.

We, like Peter and his compatriots, seek to travel the road from reconciliation to resurrection as we celebrate Lent and Easter. In her wisdom, the Church has chosen scripture passages which powerfully illustrate many important ideas associated with this significant annual pilgrimage. The sermons contained in this volume represent my personal journey of forgiveness to conversion, reconciliation to resurrection. Each person will find different nuggets of gold imbedded in the scriptures, wonders that provide inspiration for reflection and prayer. It is my hope that the words contained in this volume will provide food for thought and give you additional insight to God's word. The spiritual journey is by its nature highly personal, yet the Christian community collectively must move from reconciliation to resurrection if it is to make a difference in a world which is increasingly less open to its message as first preached by Jesus. I sincerely hope that these sermons can inspire individuals to gain personal confidence in their call as we join together in the common endeavor of building God's Kingdom, day by day, brick by brick. It is a journey from reconciliation to resurrection; the goal is eternal life.

Richard Gribble, CSC

Ash Wednesday
Joel 2:1-2, 12-17

Preparing For Our Homecoming

The idea of going home is experienced by various people in different ways, depending on circumstances, time, past history, and many other important factors. When we are young, the experience of returning home is generally very pleasant, not troublesome, and most often an opportunity which we all welcome. If we were away from our home visiting grandparents or a friend, or even the day-to-day return home from school, it was nice to know that we had returned. Home was a place of safety; it was the location of all our possessions. We were glad to return home and re-enter our zone of comfortableness. Even when we got a little older, the idea of coming home was for most of us a pleasant experience. The first time we went back to our high school after graduation, especially our first homecoming football game and dance, was a great event. We had the opportunity to share with all of our friends our recent experiences and exploits and to hear what was going on with them. In a similar way we may have had great joy in returning to a former place of employment, seeing all of our former associates, and sharing with them what has happened since the time we departed. In all these cases the need for preparation was minimal and the intensity of emotions was subdued. While some consternation might be present out of fear that we might encounter a person from the past with whom we had trouble, generally our fears were few. We went home with joy; our homecoming was an event of great delight.

When we become older, homecomings become more complicated. If we are returning home to the place of our birth or the setting in which we were raised, there is much preparation that is necessary. First, we have to find the time to leave our present routine in order to travel and physically go to another location. There is a need to calculate the cost of this event, not only monetarily, but more importantly emotionally. If it has been a long time since we have returned home, there may be some wounds, hurts, misunderstandings, and general pain from the past that must be negotiated in order to make the trip. Some people might be able simply to pick up the phone and say, "I am coming for a visit," and the rest of their preparation simply falls into place, but most people, I believe, must make rather extensive preparations for a return home, whether that is to our family, past work colleagues, the homecoming event at high school or college alma maters, or the revisiting of a past situation that must be resolved. In the latter cases, there is much that must be done, for time, distance, environment, and extenuating circumstances generally complicate our plans. We are uncertain what we will find and how people will react to us. These concerns raise fears and often keep us from actually following through with our plans. There is an absolute need for most people to plan their homecomings in life properly.

The Hebrew people were very familiar with homecomings; they experienced significant ones over the course of their history. The first major homecoming was led by the great deliverer Moses who brought the Hebrews back to their original "promised" land after 430 years in Egypt. While Moses had petitioned Pharaoh on numerous occasions to let the Hebrew people go, he had always been frustrated in his efforts. Thus, after the last plague and the death of all the firstborn in Egypt, Moses was not ready for the journey back to Israel. The Israelite community was forced to leave Egypt immediately with even the bread they brought not having sufficient time to rise. Lack of preparation and disfavor with God led the people to wander in the desert for forty years on their return home. Even when they arrived they had to fight for every inch of ground that would be their home.

Many centuries later the Hebrews again were in a situation of a homecoming. Transgressions of the covenant led God to exile the people to Babylon. There for fifty years the people had the opportunity to plan their return home. Prophets such as Isaiah,

116

Ezekiel, and Baruch proclaimed God's message to the people, telling them that they had not been abandoned and that one day they would be led home. When that special day arrived, the people were better prepared than their ancestors and were able to reestablish their community, rebuild the Temple, and regain some of their status among the peoples of the Near East.

The Hebrew people also experienced many minor homecomings that came from the challenges presented by the prophets sent to them by God. The Hebrew Scriptures are filled with episodes of how God's people rejected the Law and the covenant with disastrous consequences for the people. The punishment for these failures may have been defeat in battle by a rival army, such as the Philistines, or the sending of some natural disaster, such as a plague or drought. In each case, the prophet invited the people to return home to God, to accept the Lord's commandments and love. The invitation was to renew the people's relationship with God, both individually and communally.

The prophet Joel, read in today's lesson, proclaimed God's message to the Hebrews in Judah in the fourth century B.C.E., after the infamous Babylonian exile. He describes a terrible plague of locusts that has come to Israel in punishment for their transgressions. The plague is an eschatological sign that the people need to return to God; it is a heaven-sent warning that God is displeased with the people. Yahweh wishes the Hebrews to hold a holy fear of his power and presence in the world. Thus, the prophet in today's reading is pleading that the people must return to God; they must begin the process of homecoming anew. First, the prophet calls the people to repentance (vv. 12-14) and then speaks of the need for lamentation (vv. 15-19). Joel calls the people to more than a cultic or external return; the cosmetic approach will not be sufficient. The prophet expects the people to change their personal conduct. Joel is confident that God will hear the prayer of the people because God is "slow to anger," "rich in kindness," and "relenting in punishment," but the people must pray. They cannot expect God to act on their behalf without some outward sign that they are changed. In other words, the prophet is suggesting that the people must prepare themselves spiritually for their homecoming with God.

The season of Lent is a special period of the liturgical year when the Christian people have the opportunity to prepare themselves for a special homecoming, their return to a closer relationship with the Lord. The traditional forty days of Lent prepare us for the most important events in the history of Christendom, the paschal mystery — the passion, death, and resurrection of Jesus. It is a time to be reconciled with ourselves, others, and God.

Like all homecomings, the great events of Holy Week necessitate preparation on our part. The Church has traditionally focused on three special actions — fasting, prayer, and almsgiving. We can prepare ourselves for the renewal of our relationship with God by making the conscious decision to eat less and to avoid certain things that we might especially like. One might also consider abstaining from some habitual pleasure that is harmful to us, such as drinking or smoking, during this holy season of homecoming preparation. We can also prepare by greater devotion to prayer. This may manifest itself through a daily reading and reflection upon the scriptures, periodic visits to our local parish church, gathering with family and friends and sharing prayer, or an extension or new innovation in our daily personal prayer. Lent is also a time when our thoughts may turn to those less privileged than ourselves. The season provides the opportunity to move beyond what we normally do and reach out in a special way to those who may need us. This can manifest itself in visits to those who are sick, at home, in hospitals, or in nursing homes, volunteering time at a soup kitchen or other social service agency that provides direct service to the poor, or donating our time and/or expertise to assist an individual or a group. We should make every effort to share not simply from our excess, but rather from our own needs. In this way, we are truly in solidarity with those whom we wish to assist. Our sacrifice makes our preparation more meaningful, personal, and challenging.

In our society, people are constantly in a state of preparation. In our youth we prepare through education to enter the adult life and the working community. As adults we are constantly preparing, whether it is for a change of jobs, geographic location, or state in life. Many of the places we wish to go, especially the many homecomings of our life, necessitate that we make the time to prepare adequately. If we enter upon some endeavor or project without the proper preparation, the results will not be what we expect. We may not fail completely, but we will be dissatisfied with ourselves and our efforts. Thus, we must do what is necessary to assure that we are prepared so that the results we seek will be a reality.

Lent asks a lot of the Christian people, but if we seek to follow in the footsteps of the crucified we cannot expect our burden to be any lighter than that which Christ carried. We cannot arrive at the Resurrection, the great celebration of Jesus' triumph over the grave, without first passing through the Good Friday experience. The message of the prophets in the Hebrew Scriptures, the need to get straight with God and return to the Lord, was not an easy one for the people to digest. The challenges of God are often not easy. We must, however, see the great merit in seeking the road less traveled, the path that Jesus walked and in the process brought the possibility of eternal life to all who believe. The famous British essayist and novelist, Gilbert Keith (G.K.) Chesterton, expressed the Christian challenge so aptly: "The Christian ideal has not been tried and found wanting. It has been found difficult, and left untried." The cross was an instrument of torture and pain, but it was the vehicle by which salvation came to the world. Thus, the Christian people must not run or hide from the cross, but rather it must, in a paradoxical way, be embraced. We remember Jesus' challenge in the Gospels, "If any want to become my followers, let them deny themselves and take up their cross and follow me. For those who save their life will lose it, and those who lose their life for my sake will find it" (Matthew 16:24-25). Jesus did not walk to Calvary in handcuffs and leg irons; he went voluntarily. If we are to follow him, then we must be willing participants in his life, passion, and death.

Ash Wednesday is the beginning of a special journey that assists us in obtaining a more complete and closer relationship with God; it is the period of preparation for our annual homecoming. Like all homecomings, our journey to Holy Week requires concerted and active preparation; we simply will never arrive at our destination with the proper attitude and vigor if we do little or nothing to prepare ourselves for the great events we anticipate. The prophet Joel proclaimed a clear and challenging message to the Hebrews of their need to get right with God in order to remove the Lord's wrath as manifest through a plague of locusts. We must hear a similar challenge in our need to prepare for the paschal mystery. Let us be inspired by the prophet who alerted the people to their need to prepare and do similarly for the great events of our faith. Along the road we will draw closer to God and be that much better prepared for our ultimate goal and God's great gift to us — eternal life.

The Challenge Of God
Brings Hope

Carlo Rienzi, an attorney with no prior mission or court case, had never been tested. He was fearful and apprehensive, because he had never been challenged in his chosen profession. He did not want the trial that would test his will and challenge his skill, but he knew it must eventually come. When the case came, it seemed an impossible task for him. A young woman had shot the mayor of a small village without provocation, at least so it seemed on the surface. Carlo was assigned by the court as the woman's legal defense. Everything seemed to be against him; the evidence was overwhelming. The people in the town had loved their mayor; they could see no reason why he should be killed. The whole town was against Carlo and his client. Although it was the woman who faced the jury, the trial for Carlo may have been greater. It was a test of his character. Could he perform as he had been trained; would he hold up under the pressure; could he meet this great challenge? The trial was a test of his will as well. In the face of overwhelming adversity, could he remain with his client and give her a fair and complete defense?

Although the evidence was against his client, Carlo's perseverance would win the day. The trial took place in a small court room in the village where the crime had been committed. Carlo went to the place of the trial in order to find himself. In his investigation Carlo Rienzi discovered a reason for the young woman's actions. He learned that the mayor was not the kind and gentle man whom most people in the village knew; he had a mysterious past. In the end Carlo's client was convicted, but she received the least sentence possible for the crime. Carlo Rienzi as a lawyer had been tried and found worthy of his vocation.

Morris West's novel *Daughter of Silence* tells the story of the testing of a man and how he found himself and discovered great hope through that experience. Lent is a time when we are tested and challenged to find ourselves, experience our faith in greater and fuller ways, and discover the hope and joy that only the Lord can give. Today our lesson from the book of Genesis speaks of the great test given the world by God, a test that all failed, save Noah and his family. Because of the faithfulness to the test of one family, however, God's promise will be present for all people for all time.

Scripture scholars tell us the great flood narrative in the Book of Genesis signifies important events in world history. According to the Priestly tradition of the Old Testament, the great flood, a story which most exegetes believe arose from the famous Babylonian epic "Gilgamesh," signals the end of the first great epoch of world history. The second epoch, marked by the covenant with Noah, presupposes the theological disorder caused by sin and introduces as normative those adverse conditions of life, namely the many tests, challenges and vicissitudes of our daily journey, that the average person encounters.

Today's lesson is, as we know, the end of a longer story. God, dissatisfied with the actions and attitudes of the peoples of the world, sent a great flood to destroy humankind. The peoples of the world failed God's test and challenge to live in harmony and to demonstrate love to each other. There were members of one family, however, Noah, his wife, children, and their spouses, who passed God's test and were found upright in their actions. Thus, the Lord presented Noah with another test, to build an ark in order to provide safe passage for his family and the animals of the earth. Again Noah responded positively to the call and challenge of God.

The book of Genesis clearly says that God was disappointed with the peoples of the world and wanted to start again, but the faithfulness of only one family in its acceptance and completion of God's test and challenge allowed God to demonstrate the great hope that comes to those who successfully negotiate the tests of life. Carlo Rienzi accepted a great test and found himself and his professional vocation in the process. Noah's ability to meet the challenge of the Lord brought the permanent and unfailing protection of God to the world. Without imposing any obligations or special conditions on the human race, God provides solicitude and divine blessings, symbolized by the rainbow in the heavens. It is further a sign of divine faithfulness that gives the world a sense of security and stability. The reading, especially its beautiful promise from God of faithfulness, allows the story of God's wrath sent upon the peoples of the world to end on a very positive note. We are able to find through this scripture passage the courage to meet the challenges and tests the world brings our way, for we can have full confidence that God's faithfulness and promise of divine blessing will always be present for those who demonstrate complete devotion to God's ways.

The story of the great flood, which exhibited the faithfulness of Noah and his family, and God's promise of complete devotion as manifest through the sign of the rainbow, is only one of numerous lessons from the Sacred Scriptures that describe great tests and challenges that people of faith endured. We recall the great test given by God to the first patriarch Abraham. After being promised progeny as numerous as the stars in the sky, Abraham's great faith was tested by God when he was asked to sacrifice his only son, Isaac, the very promise of future generations. Abraham passed the test and, thus, the hope and promise of God were granted to him. We remember as well the test given to many of the judges and prophets, men and women called to lead Israel and to proclaim God's word, although they may have felt unqualified, to often hostile and unreceptive communities. Yet, these people too responded to the challenge presented them and God's promise was once again demonstrated by Israel's victory in battle and the return of the people to a closer relationship with God. Finally, on this First Sunday in Lent we are reminded of Jesus' great trial in the desert, when, after forty days and forty nights of fasting and prayer, his personal Lent that prepared him for his ministry, the Lord was challenged by Satan with the three great challenges of today's society — power, wealth, and prestige. Conquering this challenge, Jesus shows us the way and brings us hope and promise through his public ministry in Israel.

Tests, challenges, and trials are part of everyday life; they simply cannot be avoided. When these opportunities for growth come our way we have several options for our response. We can run away, hide, and pretend as if the challenge never arose. We can in so many words place our head in the sand, like the ostrich, and hope that all will pass us by and we simply won't have to deal with life and the challenges it brings. There are times when we are tested that we recognize the need for action but delegate our response to another person. We might ask others to make the decisions that should rightly be ours; we may delay our response hoping that the situation might change and the required action not be necessary. We can, however, fully engage the challenges and tests that the world brings our way and see them as opportunities for personal and possibly communal growth. Challenge is almost never easy, but for those who can muster the courage to meet the test head on and engage its possibilities for growth, then the promise of God, as exemplified by Carlo Rienzi's discovery of self and the covenant rainbow in the sky, will be manifest.

While it is probably not readily recognized nor appreciated, possibly the best way we grow, in every aspect of our lives, is through tests and challenges. The intellectual dimension of our lives is best exercised through challenge. During our days of formal schooling most have found that the courses and instructors that challenged us the most are the ones we remember and those from which we learned the most. Sometimes students tackle more difficult subjects, knowing that the course will stretch their ability and possibly their purview as well. Working hard as opposed to "waltzing through" a class will pay benefits in the end. The challenges to our intellectual selves must be continued throughout life. If we fail to read or reject new ideas simply because we cannot be bothered or don't want to negotiate another intellectual hurdle, then we will mentally stagnate. Sometimes we hear people say, "The first day I stop learning places one foot in the grave."

We must challenge ourselves socially as well. People have different personalities, but generally speaking we classify ourselves as introverts or extroverts. The introvert needs to be challenged to move out, at least somewhat, from his/her comfort zone. Daily tasks at work, ministries we perform, and interaction with people become challenges to those who are shy, but they are also opportunities to grow and discover gifts that might have lain hidden, possibly talents never discovered. Extroverts can be challenged by their need to discover the quiet side of who they are. Having the courage to look on the inside and take time in personal reflection is a great challenge to the person with a more exuberant personality, but such an endeavor will provide much grace and growth for the one open to such possibilities. It is only through the challenge or test to be more open to discovering the other side of our personality that we find the promise of God.

We need to challenge ourselves physically as well. When we drive through town, we often see people jogging along the road; we observe a similar scene when we enjoy a picnic with family and friends in a local park. Such observations ought to motivate us to ask what we could do to get into better physical shape. Most of us lead rather sedentary lives and thus we need to make the extra effort to exercise. It will take time, time we might not have in the busy lives we lead, but God's hope and promise will be found at the end of this endeavor also. We have heard the expression, "No pain, no gain." We need to challenge ourselves to become more physically active, to the extent that our environment and life conditions will allow. When we are in better shape, we will feel better, possess more energy, and be better prepared for the challenges that will come our way.

Unquestionably the most important aspect of our lives is the spiritual dimension, and this area too needs to be tested and challenged. Our faith is tested on many occasions in varied ways. We periodically come across other members of the faith community who disagree with our opinion or theological understanding. Decisions are sometimes made with which we have difficulty, disagree, or simply do not understand. These challenges to our faith are ones we must engage, although it is not easy to navigate safely around such troubled waters. Other tests of our faith come when things happen, especially when people we know and love become sick, are the victims of accidents or crime, or die, especially unexpectedly. We generally ask, "Why?"; sometimes we become angry with God. These tests of faith are more difficult to avoid, but even in these cases we can find ways to avoid the challenge. The cruel reality is, however, that until we negotiate these challenges to our faith development, we will be stunted in our progress to God, the common goal toward which all people of faith strive.

Lent is the great period in the liturgical year when we have the special opportunity to be challenged in our faith development. The Christian community is on a journey that leads us home to God. Lent is the special season of grace provided by the Church that, if used well, allows us to prepare ourselves more fully, not only for Easter, but for our eventual return to the Father. Lent, prayerfully engaged and lived, asks us to challenge and test ourselves. We need to ask: What is it that I need to do or rid myself of in order to be sufficiently free to celebrate fully the joy of Easter? What inhibits our growth and holds us back from furthering our relationship with God? What can we do during Lent to challenge ourselves sufficiently to move beyond our present zone of spiritual comfortableness and attain a closer or more fulfilling relationship with the Lord? What good works, special prayers, and other outward means can we wisely use this season and thus gain the hope and promise which God's promise assures us is at the end of the rainbow?

Challenges and tests are endemic to human existence, and they come, most often, when we find them totally inconvenient. The natural tendency is to run, hide, or simply ignore these challenges. The physical and psychic energy plus mental fortitude necessary at times to engage these tests fully often appear to be too great. But when we find ourselves with such an attitude, we must remember that it was never easy for the great people of faith to meet their challenges. They did so, nonetheless, because they were confident of the divine blessing, unfailing protection, and benevolent promise of hope that God would, through such trials, provide great things for us. Jesus, we must recall, was the one who accepted the greatest trial of faith, but his faithfulness to the will of his Father brought us hope. In a totally paradoxical way, the cross of Christ became the only hope of salvation for those who believe.

126

Let us during this Lenten season do our best to meet squarely the challenges and tests of faith that come to us. Our encounters might not be easy; many may be quite difficult. But if we negotiate the hurdles, we will be better prepared for our return home, not only at Easter, but more importantly at the eternal banquet, when we will share the joy of all the saints in beholding the face of God forever.

Have We Kept
Our Contract With God?

One day a man went to his son's room and knocked on the door: "John, wake up, it is time for you to go to school!" From inside the answer came back, "I don't want to go to school, Dad." The father was persistent, knocked again, and said, "You must go to school." The answer again came back, "I don't want to go to school!" "Why not?" asked the father. "There are three reasons," came the reply. "First, I find school boring; second, the kids tease me terribly. Third, I simply hate school." Then the father responded, "You have given me three reasons for not going to school. I will give you three that say you must attend. First, it is your duty; second, you are 45 years old; and third, you are the principal!"

This story, found in Jesuit Father Anthony de Mello's book *Awareness*, suggests the problem we ofttimes have with meeting our commitments — to others, to work, and even to God. Sometimes we are too busy and on other occasions we are too tired to meet our commitments. There are times as well, if we are honest, when we simply are lazy or see no value in what we are asked to do. There are even those occasions when people are hostile to their responsibilities and openly reject their duties. We are asked to do many things — tasks and responsibilities — which in some ways are contractual. These duties may be formal or informal, written or verbal, understood and acknowledged or assumed, but when they are not completed, there are generally consequences to pay.

We are all familiar with contracts. A contract is an agreement between at least two different parties in which each person or group agrees to perform a certain task, pay a certain amount of money, or provide a certain service that is needed by the other party. Contracts come in many different forms, but the most formal kind is a written document. Most of us have a contract for the place we live — a mortgage or a rental agreement. We agree to pay a certain amount of money each month and in return the contractor of the home or the apartment owner is to provide a residence. We use contracts when we purchase most high-priced items, including cars and electronic equipment. Most of us have a contract or two with certain credit card companies.

There is another form of contract which is more subtle but certainly more common and generally more important than any written agreement. Verbal contracts are made all the time, whether we realize it or not, and these are very significant, for they are used every day of our lives. Married people live under a contract made the day they professed their vows to each other. Couples promise fidelity, love, honor, and companionship until the day they die. Each time we promise to pick someone up, meet a person at a designated spot, run an errand, or visit a sick relative or friend, we have made a verbal contract. We usually do not think of these daily occurrences as contracts, but most assuredly they are agreements where at least two parties are counting on each other.

Contracts that work well service all concerns, but those that are broken are problematic for those involved. The consequences for failure in contracts differ depending on the nature of the agreement. If we fail to make our house or car payment, there may be a period of grace, but ultimately the item upon which we owe money will be taken away, repossessed, and we will lose both the item and our investment. Because the consequences of failure in written contracts are high, people are generally faithful to these agreements. The consequences of failure in a verbal agreement do not on the surface appear to be that great and, thus, the incidents of non-compliance are high. If we fail a friend or family member, the result may be some frustration, anger, or even a temporary parting of company, but somehow the severity of what we have done does not register with us; the consequences do not appear to be problematic.

On this Second Sunday in Lent, our First lesson describes the special contract or covenant made between God and Abraham, an agreement that was basis of a relationship between the Lord and the Hebrew people. The book of Genesis actually presents two versions of the covenant (as we recall it does with the creation story), written by two of what scripture scholars call the four Old Testament written traditions, namely the Yahwist and Priestly traditions. In chapter 15 of Genesis we read the Yahwist version of the great covenant, written (most probably) in the tenth century B.C. and emphasizing the role of the tribe of Judah in the Hebrew community. In this version Abram, while being warned of the future bondage of his people in a strange land (prediction of the community's trial in Egypt), is promised descendants as numerous as the stars in the sky.

Today's lesson, the second of the great covenant stories, comes from the Priestly tradition of the Hebrew Scriptures, written about 500 B.C. and emphasizing the Hebrew tradition in well-ordered prose. Abram, as in the earlier covenant version, is promised multiple generations as a unilateral pact between God and God's people. Here God extends the promise to succeeding generations and the patriarch seals the agreement with the promise of circumcision for all male descendants. The Priestly author also adds the important detail that both Abram and Sarai have their names changed after the covenant is made. Scholars suggest that this signifies a change in life and/or function for the bearer. It also indicated a turning point in one's life. The relationship between God and God's people, the Hebrews, was from hence forward different. Each party had agreed to be faithful to the other; each was to uphold its end of the agreement. We know by faith and history that God was and is ever faithful on his part, but unfortunately the same could not be said of Israel, nor for that matter of the Gentiles, the inheritors of the great promise. Lent should be a time to revisit and reevaluate our commitments, promises, and contracts in all aspects of our lives.

The Christian community, collectively and individually, has made a significant contract with God through the sacrament of baptism. This contract was sealed when, for most of us, our parents and godparents, speaking on our behalf, told the minister or priest who administered the sacrament that we believed in God, the Father, Son, and Holy Spirit, and in the life and mission of the

131

Christian community, the church. As children we might not have known of this special contract, but as we mature and gain knowledge it becomes incumbent on the Christian to learn the nature of the pact made between the individual and God and make certain our half of the agreement is fulfilled.

God and the Christian community have always been faithful in upholding their end of the contract. God is ever present in our lives, patiently listening, leading, guiding, and sometimes challenging and cajoling us in an effort to push us toward the goal of our eternal reward with the Lord. We at times may think that God is not listening, uncaring, or asleep on the job, but such can never be the case. We remember well the prophet's words, "Can a woman forget her nursing child, or show no compassion for the child of her womb? Even these may forget, yet I will not forget you" (Isaiah 49:15). God provides the leadership and points the way, through the church, and we are asked to follow. The Christian community provides us with the sacraments as moments of God's grace and special presence in our lives. We have the wonderful gift of the community's proximity in our lives, supporting, assisting, and, yes, at times challenging us to be all we can be in the eyes of the Lord. God and the community of the faithful have met their commitments to us; have we been as faithful to God and the church?

The Christian life gives us many privileges, but there are significant responsibilities that we must meet in order to uphold our end of the contract with God. The most basic element of our agreement with God is something I suspect most of us don't think much about. We are all called to be holy; we have a common vocation to holiness. Members of the Christian community participate in many varied and generally multiple vocations. Some are called to the vocation of the married state, others to the single life, and others still, in the Roman Catholic tradition, to the celibate religious life. This, however, is only the most basic avenue of our life vocation; there are many other sub-vocations in which we participate. Many people are called to the vocation of parenthood. All of us have some occupation, the daily work we do. In this light we may have the vocation of professional service as a physician, attorney, engineer, or teacher; we may have the vocation of greater direct service

132

in sales, ministry in the church, or outreach to the poor and destitute of our world. Some people are called to more individual vocations in offices as clerical workers, writers, and computer operators and programmers. Regardless of our state in life or the day-to-day work we perform, all Christians are called to lives of holiness; it is our basic and common vocation and one we can never let slide. When we forget or disregard this most basic element of our relationship with God, we have failed in fulfilling our end of the contract with the consequence that we become estranged from God and the faith community. The contract will be broken and its benefits for both parties can be lost.

Our contract with God goes beyond the basic requirement for holiness; we are called to hear the Lord's voice and respond to his call to "Follow me." Discipleship is the second step in the common response of God's people to the One who first loved us. We simply cannot bury our heads in the sand like the proverbial ostrich and think that God will not see us or that the Christian community will not miss our presence. Discipleship is not an option; it is a requirement of our contract, our baptismal promise made to God. Being a true follower of Jesus is not a passive endeavor, but rather requires our active participation. We often wish to place limits or attach special requirements to our active discipleship, but the famous Lutheran pastor, theologian, and writer, Dietrich Bonhoeffer, told us in his book *The Cost of Discipleship* that being a true follower of Jesus Christ will cost us everything, even our life. We cannot make compromises with the Lord and say, "I will be your disciple tomorrow, but I am too busy or not of the right mind today." Such an attitude suggests an on-again, off-again agreement with God, but this cannot be for the true and loyal disciple. God, as Francis Thompson's immortal poem, "The Hound of Heaven" suggests, never ceases to be our advocate and will leave no stone unturned in searching for our soul. We, therefore, cannot take an attitude of partial participation. We can either follow Jesus all the way or leave the road somewhere along the journey; the choice is ours. Yet, we know, because we have been promised, where the journey will end. Saint Paul reminds us, "What no eye has seen, nor ear heard, nor the human heart conceived, what God has prepared for those who love him" (1 Corinthians 2:9).

The requirements of discipleship are multiple and can be subsumed under the idea of faithfulness, but during the great season of Lent, the concept of service to God's people might well be emphasized. We are called to minister to God's people in little and great ways. If we have the time, energy, and opportunity to serve the poor in some sort of volunteer service, such as at a soup kitchen, homeless shelter, or free clinic, this would be a great response to the call of discipleship and certainly would make great strides in upholding our end of the contract with God. We may have the opportunity to visit a sick neighbor or relative or possibly assist a needy person next door with some routine household task. Our service need not be pointed outward but might be even more needed within our own families. Sometimes we become so wrapped up in the needs of others, we forget or at least gloss over our duty of service to those we know and love most. Children can do lots to help out around the house; parents can make special efforts to spend more time with children. Families in general can spend greater quantity and quality time together. This might not seem like service; it might even appear to be self-serving, but how can we muster sufficient strength and fortitude to be good disciples and ministers to others if we cannot gain strength from the most basic unit of our common human experience? Strengthening family life and fostering its membership is internal service and most certainly is appreciated by God.

The holy season of Lent provides the Christian community with the opportunity to renew and strengthen the many contracts we have made with people. In most all cases these are verbal agreements and thus the ones that might slip because the ramifications of our failures in such contracts will not result in the repossession of a material item or the loss of our job. Yet, our verbal contracts, especially those made to God, are the most important, because they are signed, not on paper, but on our hearts and are, thus, of great significance. Lent is a time for spouses to re-commit themselves to each other. Marriage is a verbal contract of commitment and love that needs to be fostered and renewed on a regular basis. Those who have chosen the married vocation and family have the obligation to revitalize this most basic human unit. We can also take the time to reflect upon how we can re-commit ourselves in our place of work. At times our day-to-day job may become so routine and dull that we don't want to continue. We need to ask ourselves what we can do to put more spark into these daily tasks so that we will faithfully and completely maintain our end of the agreement we made with our employer.

The most important contract renewal we must make is our agreement with God and God's people. Living our baptismal commitment fully, as holy and committed people, following Jesus as true disciples is absolutely necessary; it is not an option. Through the traditional Lenten practices of prayer, fasting, and almsgiving we have the opportunity to renew and strengthen our contract with the Lord.

We at times, like the man in Anthony de Mello's story, may not feel like meeting our commitments; we may even feel like running away. But such an attitude is inconsistent with our Christian life and demonstrates no trust in God who is ever faithful, always present, and ready to renew his side of the bargain. As members of the Christian community, we have responsibilities that are in many ways contractual, but they are not in written form. As God made a contract with Abram, sealing it with a change of name to Abraham and the practice of circumcision, so we have a contract with the Lord, sealed with our baptismal commitments to live holy lives as disciples. During this Lenten season let us renew our relationships with the many people with whom we have contracts, within our family, place of work, and most especially with God and God's people, the church. Let us be faithful to what we proclaim. It is Jesus' kingdom we preach, build, and await; it is the Lord's life of holiness and faith we seek to emulate, today and to life eternal.

Follow The Signs
To God And Eternal Life

"Red, right, returning." "Even red nuns have odd black cans." To the mariner entering harbor from sea these expressions keep ships, their occupants, and cargo "out of harm's way." Remember the expressions and follow the signs and you will navigate safely home.

Navigation, the art or science of moving precisely from one location to a second, has been practiced by humans since the dawn of civilization. With increasing sophistication men and women travelers have used various navigational aids, all of which are signs, to arrive at their destinations successfully. When travel was by foot, cart, wagon, or beast of burden, points of land served as the principle signs. It might have been a mountain peak, a river, or some rock formation. Each navigational aid told the traveler direction and distance to the desired location. Today planes, trains, and automobiles use more sophisticated methods, but they all have one purpose — to get the traveler safely to a specific destination.

Although every form of travel necessitates navigational aids, signs provided to mariners seem to be the best illustration. For centuries sailors have been using visible signs to navigate safely to far and distant lands. At sea the position of the stars and planets on any particular night helps fix a vessel's position. Closer to shore there are many landmarks that can be used, such as a jetty, harbor, or inland mountain peak.

Two of the more important navigational aids for mariners are lighthouses and buoys. Each lighthouse is different, not only in its construction, but, more importantly for the sailor, in the signal it provides. Lights of different durations, types, and colors tell the experienced sailor direction. Buoys are of various types. Some clang or produce fog signals, others possess a light, and others still mark the channel. "Red, right, returning" — keep the red buoys on the right as you return from sea. "Even red nuns have odd black cans" — even-numbered red nun-type buoys are matched with odd-numbered black can-type buoys. If travelers heed the signs provided, they will have a good chance to navigate successfully where they need or want to be. If signs are ignored, then most assuredly the result will be disaster.

Signs are an important, even integral, aid to the journey of life, setting us on a path that if properly and closely followed will bring us to our desired destination, safely and efficiently. In a very real way signs are a source of liberation; they free us from following erroneous ways and assist us in making wise decisions in the route our life takes. Signs are posted by those who have blazed the path before us, found and negotiated many of the pitfalls and obstacles encountered, and discovered a fruitful and significant prize at the end of the journey. If we are wise we will heed the signs that others provide in order to avoid problems and more directly follow the path home and eventually to God.

Signs of God's presence in the lives of his people have been present from the outset, but they were truly manifest in the famous exodus story. We recall that after 430 years, God raised up from among the Israelites the liberator Moses who, along with his brother Aaron, was given the task of speaking with Pharaoh and leading the Israelites to freedom in the Promised Land. From the outset of their long forty-year journey, God gave the people special signs, both to lead and provide for the community. God gave the community a pillar of cloud by day and a pillar of fire by night to give the people direction in their sojourn (Exodus 13:21-22). The Israelites were also given special signs of God's goodness and beneficent care along the way. When the people complained to Moses that they did not have sufficient food, God rained down manna from the heavens in the morning and provided quail in the evening (Exodus 16:1-36). Immediately thereafter God provided water from the rock when the people again complained that they were famished (Exodus 17:1-7).

In today's First lesson we hear of the greatest sign of God's presence with the people. The Hebrew law, encapsulated in the Decalogue, or what Christians generally call the Ten Commandments, was the road map, the template for how each member of the Israelite community was to conduct his/her life. In a very real way the Decalogue became a source of identity for the community because its uniqueness, compared with the law forms of other contemporary peoples and civilizations, set the Hebrews apart in a few special and significant ways. The Ten Commandments were a distinctive contribution to legal codes of the pre-Christian era. Whereas the Codes of Lipit-Ishtar and Hammurabi were casuistic, that is systems which prescribed certain punishments for specific offenses, the Decalogue is apodictic, defining not punishments but proscribing certain specific actions. For example, rather than providing a punishment if one engages in thievery, the Decalogue emphatically states, "You shall not steal" (Exodus 20:15). Another extremely important and unique element in the Hebrew law was its divisions, clearly defining how one must conduct one's relationship with God and with neighbor. While the last seven commandments describe a person's relationship with others and constitute elements of the natural law, the first three were unique in defining one's relationship with God. This latter idea is most clearly evident in the first commandment, a law which set an absolute priority, namely the oneness of God. Acceptance of monotheism, a belief completely unique to human civilization to this date, became an absolute requirement for any who wished to enter into a relationship with Yahweh. The first commandment thus distinguished Israel from her Near East neighbors in a very significant and fundamental way. In general the Decalogue was a series of special signs, given to the Israelite community by God, which, if followed properly, would bring the people into a right relationship with their Creator and provide the fullness of life today and in the future.

Signs, some of which we readily recognize and others that we might not even consider, govern our world today in many different ways. We have the obvious signs that we daily encounter — the signs that guide the mariner to specific destinations, the road signs that provide information and govern our drive around town, the billboards that advertise the latest products, restaurants, and stores, the signs and symbols that we wear — a cross, wedding or school ring, or special lapel pin that speaks of our membership in some club or organization. These are valuable signs that tell others something about us, but there are many more that we encounter each day and might not recognize.

Like the Ten Commandments for the Israelites, contemporary law, both civil and ecclesiastical, is a special sign that provides direction and allows society to function efficiently and without chaos. The law orders our life. Imagine the roads upon which we travel almost every day without a detailed series of laws to govern our operation upon them. We see every day the destructive results for people and property when drivers violate or ignore the laws which govern our use of the highways. Imagine our nation without laws to regulate financial and banking institutions. Where would people place their hard-earned salaries? What would we do if we needed some extra money to meet the needs of our family? Imagine life today without laws related to commerce and industry. Could we trust that we are getting a safe product at a fair price? The law today might in some circumstances appear to be restrictive, we may perceive that we are being held back by its proscriptions, but the reality is that the law is absolutely necessary for society to function for all peoples. The law is a template, a road map, a series of signs for the daily life of secular human society as assuredly as the Ten Commandments were a special sign of God's love, concern, and favor for the Hebrew people. Without the law and the order it brings, both in civil and church circles, our world would be chaotic, there would be no clear direction, and people would be totally confused on the way they should proceed in order to live a decent and fulfilling life.

Christians might not often think of it, but the church is an important and significant sign of the presence of God in our world. In 1974 Father (now Cardinal) Avery Dulles, S.J., wrote an influential book, *Models of the Church*, in which he described the church

140

as a sacrament, a special sign in a troubled world of the presence of God. Christianity today is an absolutely necessary sign that there is a different approach possible for humankind than that which is generally promoted by secular society. The church is a sign of a different set of values and virtues. Society today says go for the gusto, achieve much, accumulate as much power, wealth, and prestige as possible. A television commercial of a few years back stated it this way, "Who says you can't have it all?" The church must be a counter sign to this prevailing attitude. The contemporary world badly needs the direction which the church as a sign can provide.

Another popular church model uses the Pauline image (1 Corinthians 12:12-31) of "the people of God," necessitating our understanding of the significant responsibility we have of being signs to others of the presence, love, and power of God in our world. Whether we know, want, or accept it, people are not neutral on us. People are either drawn closer to us or pushed further from us by our words and actions. We are a true sign to others; we are in a special way evangelists. An evangelist is a person who not only preaches, but more basically serves as a positive sign that must give proper direction toward God and the Kingdom that we seek. When people think of evangelists, certain images come to mind. We might think of the "Elmer Gantry" image of a street corner preacher who speaks of hellfire and damnation, warning people that if they do not transform their lives soon all will be lost. We might also think of some of our brothers and sisters who choose to evangelize by going door-to-door in our neighborhoods and share with others their understanding of faith. While these stereotypical images are fine, we must not discount the everyday image of evangelization in our daily encounters with others, whether it be with our family, friends, business associates, or a stranger on the street. Each word, each act that issues from our person provides a special opportunity to be a sign to others. We, therefore, must ask ourselves an introspective and possibly difficult question — what do people see and hear from us? Are we evangelizing, being a sign, of Christ's message of love and peace, or are we communicating to others some other missive?

141

As members of the Church we have the obligation, endemic to our common vocation to holiness, to be signs and to witness to the power of Christ in our lives. This is an increasingly difficult task in our world, but it is not an obligation from which we must shy away. Rather, we must see this task as a rare opportunity to share our faith, to be special signs and thereby assist in building the Kingdom of God in our world today.

The church this day is engaged is the special season and discipline of Lent, a time as Isaiah the prophet tells us to set things right (1:18), a time as Joel told us on Ash Wednesday to return to the Lord (2:13b), an opportunity as individuals and community to choose the correct path and begin to walk it toward God and eternal life. This season of grace, itself a sign in the liturgical year, is filled with special symbols that provide direction and purpose to our lives. Ashes speak of our mortality; palms allow us to walk the triumphant road with Jesus into Jerusalem. The disciplines of prayer, fasting, and almsgiving allow us to evaluate our lives and take stock of who we are and where we find ourselves along the road toward God. The Lenten signs, like the law, and the church, provide direction; they assist us to navigate safely toward the paschal mystery — the passion, death, and resurrection of Jesus — and the one and only path that gets us to God. As assuredly as the buoys safely guide mariners and road signs lead us to our destinations, so Lent and its special emblems of God's grace will assist us in our journey in faith toward God.

God sends many signs our way. Some we readily recognize and acknowledge, but for one reason or another we choose another route. Some signs we recognize and reject outwardly; some we don't even recognize. There are, however, many signs which we do recognize, follow, and in the process produce thirty, sixty, a hundred fold (Mark 4:20) for ourselves and others. The Christian path is not easy, but it will be worth the effort. Jesus himself has provided the path and the signs to follow it: "Enter through the narrow gate; for the gate is wide and the road is easy that leads to destruction, and there are many who take it. For the gate is narrow and the road is hard that leads to life, and there are few who find it" (Matthew 7:13-14). May we have the courage to believe the same!

142

Look Inside And Discover Life

Oscar Wilde's short novel, *The Picture of Dorian Gray*, written in the early part of the twentieth century, describes the life of a tortured man who is unable to look honestly at his life. He refuses to look inside and accept who he truly is. Dorian is a physically handsome young man who possesses power, wealth, and prestige, the three great assets and temptations of contemporary life. An artist, Basil Hallward, who is enamored at Dorian's presence, paints a portrait of him, which is indeed a master work. The portrait magically displays the true Dorian who lives inside the physical body — one who is anything but beautiful and handsome. Dorian uses his power to take advantage of others, his wealth to undercut people, and his prestige to place himself in positions of authority where he has the opportunity to do good for others, but always seems to act for his betterment alone. The exterior facade of a handsome and well-groomed man masks the growing ugliness which he carries inside.

One day Dorian observes his portrait and notes how it has changed. The eyes and face are different. They show a man who is sinister and evil. Dorian locks the picture in his attic, but the image will not leave him. In a fit of rage he kills the artist, Basil Hallward, an act which makes the portrait grow even uglier. In the end Dorian Gray cannot live with himself. His outside beauty remains while inside his corruption grows. The portrait shows the true person — the one whom Dorian knows but is unwilling to accept, the one no one else can see.

Dorian Gray died as a tortured soul because he had no capacity to see himself as he really was. He was unable to take the sometimes perilous introspective journey of searching one's soul and honestly looking at one's life in total, especially our relationships with family, friends, associates, and most profoundly God. God sent signs, especially his periodic viewing of the portrait, that were signals he needed to take stock of his life. His refusal to receive and act upon these signs cost him everything.

Scripture is quite clear that the Hebrews were a people "peculiarly God's own"; they were a community special to God. Yet, we know that the relationship was not always harmonious; their actions were repeatedly inconsistent in maintaining a relationship with God. The alliance had many ups and downs, highs and lows. By reviewing the story of the association between Yahweh and the Israelites, it is quite evident that both the community of Israel as a whole and most of its individuals were not able to look inside at their lives, honestly see what was present, and judge what needed to be done to make the relationship what it should be. The result of this inability or refusal to look inside over time brought many trials, problems, and challenges to rulers and common citizens. This failure to evaluate seriously the life of the community eventually led to frustration on God's part and exile for the nation as a whole.

The story of Israel's up and down relationship with God unfolds in a dramatic way during the community's sojourn in the desert. The books of Exodus, Numbers, and Deuteronomy relate many incidents of the people complaining out of frustration with some aspect of their lives, generally over the lack of some item. Typically the people complained against Moses and his brother Aaron. As the human leaders of the nation, it was natural that they were the lightning rod that would attract most of the bitterness of the people. The complaints are often a litany of yearning for their former life in Egypt, protests over the lack of food and water along the journey, and their disgust with manna. Rarely did the people complain against God.

In today's lesson, however, the people complain to Moses and to God. This passage is the last and most severe of the complaint stories that are recorded in the book of Numbers. Again the people

144

are disgusted with the food and want more water, but their protests are of a higher order since now they complain to God as well as Moses. The people seem oblivious to all God has done for them — their rescue from the Egyptians, escape through the Red Sea, provisions of water, quail, and manna, not to mention the physical sign of God's presence in the community at all times with the pillar of cloud by day and column of fire by night. The Israelites are apparently unable to look at their situation, to be thankful for what they have and what has been provided, and to trust that anything else needed will be provided by God. Their vision, like that of Dorian Gray, is limited to themselves and their immediate situation. They are not ready nor apparently willing to look inside and discover their true selves.

The complaint of the people against Moses and God brings a swift, powerful, and deadly response from Yahweh. Serpents are sent by God to punish the people for their incessant complaints, lack of gratitude, and inability to look at their interior lives and judge honestly the relationship that exists in the community at large and in the hearts of individuals with God. The serpent was a symbol of evil power and chaos; the cult of the snake was widely practiced by the people of Canaan at the time. God provided water and manna, but he was also prepared to bring the evil of punishment as might be necessary to teach the Israelites a lesson. As parents must discipline their children to correct their relationship, so Yahweh, the divine Father of the Hebrew nation, was forced to act in order to right the improper thinking of the community as a whole.

The presence of the serpents and their poisonous bite, bringing death to many in the community, brings a rapid plea of confession and spirit of contrition from the people. This is the second time in Numbers that the people have sought confession of their sin after rebellion against Yahweh, the other incident being the famous spy story in Numbers, chapters 13 and 14. While it might appear on a first look that the use of a serpent mounted on a pole to cure those bitten is a case of sympathetic magic, the author, whom scholars believe to be the Yahwist writer of the Pentateuch tradition, takes great care to inform the reader that it was Yahweh who healed the people, not some sorcery provided by a bronze serpent.

145

It is absolutely key to notice, however, that God does not immediately save the people when he is petitioned. The people, realizing their sin, or at least that they could do nothing about the situation themselves, came to Moses and asked that he beseech God to take the snakes away. Yahweh, we must note, does not take the snakes away at all, but rather he tells Moses to make the bronze serpent and to tell the people who have been bitten that they must look upon this image in order to be healed. This seemingly subtle, but actually very profound action by God demonstrates quite clearly that Yahweh expects the people to make an overt gesture in order to be healed. God wishes the people to do something in order to correct the breech in their relationship with the Creator. The people are generally hesitant to act; their stubbornness has estranged them from God. God is willing to act to rescue his people, as he had done so many times in the past, but Yahweh does something more than merely ridding the region of serpents. God brings a restoration of health, to individuals and the community, but only after each individual makes the decision to return. Certainly God could have cured all and rid the land of the snakes with a word, action, or even a thought, but in his wisdom, Yahweh taught the people an important lesson. God wants each Israelite who has complained to take the confession of sin and the need for God's deliverance to heart. Yahweh teaches that confession of sin and forgiveness are both a community and individual responsibility, but this can only happen after one has taken the inward journey, discovered what is inside, and at least initiated the process of getting one's spiritual house in order.

Lent is a special and sacred journey that provides many opportunities for us to look seriously at our lives and make changes and corrections as may be required. We might look great on the outside, like Dorian Gray and the Israelites, but as the scriptures tell us explicitly, "The Lord looks on the heart" (1 Samuel 16:7c). We need to look inside, therefore, where God sees us, and honestly observe and judge what is present. During our journey of introspection we will discover many significant talents and gifts, some of which we have previously discovered and use often and well, and others that may be latent and await their utilization. We will

146

also find some things that we probably don't want to discover and certainly prefer not to admit are present in us. True self awareness and asking the difficult question, "Who am I?" will not allow us to deny what we find on our journey. We must do our best to accept what we find and possibly the new discovery of who we are. The great downfall of the Israelites was that they refused to look inside and, thus, suffered greatly. God, however, rescued them, because they took the opportunity and possessed the common sense to reach out to God. Dorian Gray, on the other hand, never was so fortunate. He died a tortured man without any rescue. If we are not careful, our fate may be similar.

The Christian message of hope proclaimed by Jesus Christ, our Lord and Redeemer, must be for us a bulwark that encourages us to act now to get our spiritual house in order as we traverse the road of our common Lenten journey. Our action must begin with the ofttimes perilous journey to our very core being in order to discover what is truly there, and to commit ourselves to make every effort to transform our lives and make them more consistent with the demands of our contract with God, signed at our baptism.

In order to place our spiritual house in order we must first humble ourselves before self, neighbor, and God through the process and special gift of reconciliation, one of the basic tenets of the Lenten journey. Reconciliation is a special journey that must begin with oneself. We recall in the famous parable of The Prodigal Son that the young man was not able to gain the forgiveness of his father until he had first taken the inward journey, arrived at the conclusion that his actions were wrong, come to a change of heart and mind, and then started his homeward trip, emblematic of his return to God. Dorian Gray never made this first step and, thus, was lost. The Israelites negotiated this first link in the reconciliation chain only after Yahweh sent serpents to punish the people for their actions.

Once we have gained reconciliation with ourselves then we can begin to reach out and seek to forgive and be forgiven by others. All of us have found ourselves in situations where we are at odds with others and many times hard feelings are the result. Many times we don't want to let go of our anger; we would rather stew

147

and fester, creating a tense situation which only exacerbates itself with time. We need to cut the ball and chain of past hurts that hold us back and seek to be reconciled with others. We need to negotiate this second segment of the process of reconciliation in order to reach the last and ultimate goal, reunion with God.

God, as seen in today's lesson and many other passages of scripture, stands willing and ready to receive us upon our return. God's invitation to a resumption of a good relationship is always present, but we must initiate this restoration. God will not beat us over the head nor tie our hands and demand compliance. The gift of free will that makes humankind unique from the rest of God's creation will not be violated by God. We always have the opportunity to say yes or no. After we have found reconciliation with self and others, it is possible and even necessary to complete the full process and go to God, as we recall again from the parable of The Prodigal Son. We can remember here, however, that reconciliation requires not even one word from the son, only his good intent, a condition made possible by his earlier interior journey. God is waiting, but we must respond.

Once we have achieved reconciliation then the task of getting our spiritual house in order can proceed forward. We need now to do our best to accept who we are and the lot and status of life we have been given. Often we hear people complain about what is not present in their lives — insufficient economic resources, a job that is less than satisfying, personal relationships that are not fulfilling, a future that does not seem to be bright. Concentrating on all the negatives and/or incompletenesses of one's life does not accomplish anything that is good; it leads us in the reverse direction that we seek. The Israelites were certainly guilty in this vein; they looked at their lives, wished there was more, and then complained about what they did not have. They and all of us need to place our thoughts on what we have and what is today. Having a more positive outlook on life helps all, not only ourselves but others to whom we communicate by words and actions. Yes, things might be better and we should always strive to improve who we are personally and our lot in life. Let us, however, not constantly complain about who we are or what we lack, but rather, may we concentrate on what we have and the opportunities we possess.

Restoring our spiritual house also necessitates our cooperation in refusing to participate in behavior that is harmful to others. Dorian Gray was perfectly kept on the outside, but his words and actions, through his addictions to power, wealth, and prestige, were highly destructive to others. We must reject the fascination of our world with these three great temptations and willfully choose another road, one that builds up rather than tears down individuals, groups, or even attitudes, opinions, and differing ideas. Having the courage to challenge people we observe engaging in such destructive behavior is also important. This is not an easy road to negotiate and takes some delicacy and discretion, but the strength of our convictions and our certain belief in what is right must be our guide.

Once we have been reconciled, have accepted who we are, and made a commitment not to engage in hurtful behavior to others, we are ready to map out our future course. All people need to set some goals and have some dreams and hopes for the future. Such an attitude keeps us moving forward and never allows us to stagnate, a condition, which if allowed to control us, will draw us into a life of complacency and destroy our ability to make a contribution to society and the church.

Dorian Gray was a despicable man, but no one was able to observe this reality on the outside. He presented himself to others as a handsome, healthy, and seemingly productive individual, a man who "had it all together." Inside, however, he was filled with rapaciousness. He was corrupted by his infection with the desire for power, wealth, and prestige. He could not see his true self; his self awareness was minimal. As our Lenten journey continues let us be filled with the desire to place our spiritual houses in order. Let us begin by looking inward and taking the ofttimes perilous journey of introspection. Let us be honest, sort out problems, and then begin to build our lives anew. We start by being reconciled, move to personal acceptance, refuse to participate in acts that hurt others, and finally set a straight course for the future. Today, may we take the first step on this course, an act that will bring us closer to God today and eternal life tomorrow.

Obedience To God's Plan

In a vast field that stretched as far as the eye could see, a great multitude of people milled about waiting for something to happen. Quite unexpectedly a messenger came into the midst of the people and announced, "You are to walk around this field 25 times carrying a baton." The people were a bit mystified by these words and asked, "What will happen when we finish?" "You will learn the answer when you are done," came the reply. So the crowd ambled off to make its first lap of the field. It took almost a full day at a leisurely pace to walk around the field, but they eventually made the circuit the first time. This feat called for a celebration.

As the crowd celebrated they decided, just for the heck of it, to make the next lap more interesting. They broke into teams to race against each other. The task would not be so boring and winners and losers could be determined. This would transform a mundane task into a fun-filled event. It certainly did not seem that they had to do the task exactly as they were told. So the people separated themselves into five teams, the Reds, Yellows, Blacks, Browns, and Whites. There were some in the great multitude, however, who refused to join the teams. They called themselves "The Others" because they did something different than the teams. Strangely, it was The Others who were given the baton to carry, since the teams argued amongst themselves over which group should have it. The five teams, the Reds, Yellows, Blacks, Browns, and Whites, took their marks and then took off at breakneck speed. The Yellow team won the second lap. The teams decided after the second circuit of the field, just for the heck of it, that they would station various members of each team at select sites around the field. In this way no one would have to run the whole distance but rather each would run an individual segment of the whole. Thus, the relay race was invented. As the five teams raced around the field in relays, The Others simply continued on their way around the field. The teams thought The Others were "out of it."

The competition between the teams became more and more intense. Soon the racing teams realized that slow runners were a liability to their chance to win. They decided, therefore, that only the fast runners would compete. This, however, did not seem to satisfy those who were the best on each team, so it was decided, just for the heck of it, that each team would be represented by one individual and races would be held in measured distances. In one race the representative of the Browns won and in another it was the Black team member who was victorious. Meanwhile, The Others continued to plod their way around the field, lap after lap after lap. When they completed all 25 laps, they held a celebration. When the messenger arrived in the midst of the party, The Others asked, "You told us at the beginning that we would learn our reward when we finished. We have completed the 25 laps of the field, what will be get?" "Your reward," said the messenger, "is that you made it." The Others were stunned. "Is that all there is? We have made this long journey just to say we made it." When The Others thought about their accomplishment, however, they had to agree that this was the reason they were celebrating — because they had made it; they had done what they were asked to do. "But what about the teams?" asked one of The Others, seeing that none of them were present. "The teams," said the messenger, "as you can see they didn't make it. And that's the heck of it!"[1]

The teams thought themselves to be rather important. They were bored and tired of doing what they had been asked to do. Thus, just for the heck of it, they went out on their own, and "did their own thing" as people say today. But in the end they never finished the task; they didn't make it to the finish line. The Others, however, simply did what they were asked to do. Their actions and their methods were not flashy; they did not impress the teams with their accomplishment. They simply did what the messenger asked of them; they demonstrated an obedient attitude toward the instructions they were given, and through such simple obedience they met their goal, crossed the finished line, and completed the race. We must possess a similar attitude of obedience if we are to cross the finish line of eternal life with God.

Today's First lesson from the prophet Jeremiah is one of the most significant in all the prophetic books and possibly in all of the Hebrew Scriptures, what we Christians generally call the Old Testament. Scholars disagree on whether this passage comes directly from the mouth of the prophet or is part of the Deuteronomist tradition, but the message and its significance for the people to whom it was proclaimed and to Christian community is not in dispute. Jeremiah wrote to the pre-exilic nation of Judah in the seventh century B.C.E. The prophet was well aware of the nation's lack of faith in following God's commands. The fall of the Northern Kingdom of Israel was an historic fact; the rebellion of the people during the period of the judges, kings, and prophets was known and acknowledged by all. The Covenant written on stone, the Decalogue, had in many ways been a failure because it had been transgressed so many times by all the people. The people had repeatedly turned away from God. There was a need for some new agreement or covenant, one that would call the Hebrews to a renewed sense of their commitment and responsibility in their relationship with Yahweh.

God, through the prophet, expresses a radically new type of covenant, one that is better for Yahweh and for the people. While God most assuredly was frustrated with the people's lack of faithfulness, the people also may have asked what assurance they had. If the nation of Judah was restored to God and subsequently fell, would a fate similar to Israel befall it? Thus, the need for a new type of commitment and covenant was believed necessary. This new covenant would, as Jeremiah says, be written in the hearts and minds of the people. The prophet seems to indicate that the Spirit of God will move the hearts of the people to be more obedient to the divine law. God is thus challenging the people to obey God's law, not written strictly on stone tablets that are kept in an ark, but etched in a much more personal way on the hearts of each and

153

every member of the community. The most important lesson to learn is that God is telling the people that they must develop an obedient attitude toward the law. One must follow what God asks in a spirit of joy, openness, and confidence that doing things as God bids will prove beneficial for the individual and the nation. It is clear that the "end-runs" and other varied paths chosen by the people over the course of many generations have all proved unsuccessful. These alternate chosen paths have led to the breaking and often disregard for the covenant time and time again. There is an absolute need for the people to be converted to an attitude of openness, allowing God to operate and to direct their lives. With a proper attitude, one guided by obedience to God's law and plan, the prophet predicts a restoration for the people of Judah and a renewal of the nation's relationship with Yahweh.

For many centuries the Christian community has understood that the fulfillment of this passage in Jeremiah is seen in the emergence of the church, those who profess Jesus as Savior and Lord. While this interpretation may bring justification to the church today and its dominance of the Western world in the common era, the more significant aspect of this prophetic utterance is that it provides a vital message for our contemporary society, namely the absolute need to cooperate with and be obedient to God's plan. We remember how the Hebrew people struggled with God's plan. This is the overriding reason why Yahweh gives the prophet Jeremiah in today's lesson a new covenant to share with the people, one that is more personal. God, despite disappointment, always provided a new path, another chance and possibility for renewal.

God has provided an opportunity for all of us, the Christian community, to enjoy the promise and privilege that the covenant gave to the Hebrews, our ancestors in the faith. When the message of salvation brought by Jesus Christ was not well received by the Jews, the privileges and the responsibilities of this special relationship with the Son of God were passed on to us. As beneficiaries of this message and promise, we have many joys and opportunities, but also several significant obligations that at times are burdens.

We have the time now, during the holy season of Lent, to take stock of our lives, and conduct a personal inventory of who we are, where we are going, what we wish to be, and what is our relationship with God. God's plan for our world and our personal lives is a mystery revealed day by day in the events we encounter. Often we struggle greatly with God's plan; we simply do not want to cooperate fully, or if we are honest, at times, even slightly cooperate. We are rebellious; we simply do not want to do what we are asked to do. We refuse to surrender our will and autonomy, for to lose personal control in today's world is viewed as weakness and problematic. We need to be in charge of our lives; we feel the absolute need to call the shots and we are willing to surrender nothing over which we can exercise control!

People today are reticent to accept advice and we generally do not like to be told what to do or how to do it. Like the teams in the story, when we are given a task, we prefer to find a way that excites us, one that provides relief from the mundane and routine duties of our human existence. We want to do things our way! While there is certainly no crime in being innovative, many times our wishes lead us toward goals and conclusions that are inconsistent with the ideas of the one who gave us the task originally. This is true not only with our day-to-day duties at home and work, but consider all the ways we have done everything we can think of to circumvent God's plan. The divine plan for us as a community and individuals is revealed in many varied ways — through events, circumstances, and most profoundly people. In some ways God's plan is all around us. Like the light from a burning candle that emanates out in all directions and is, thus, impossible to avoid, so God's plan is ever present, if we have the eyes and ears to see and hear its manifestations. Sometimes, however, we run away from the light; we hide because we don't want to deal with what God has planned for us. At other times we recognize the light, but choose not to participate; we simply do nothing and try to ignore the plan. There are times, as well, when we intentionally frustrate the plan and do just the opposite of what we are asked.

God's plan is generally mysterious and, thus, often we cannot "see" or possibly understand what God asks of us. We diligently search through prayer but can find few answers. We call out to the Father, but we receive no clear response. In our frustration and impatience we often find ourselves "doing our own thing," for we have not received the message we so earnestly wish to receive concerning the proper road to follow.

Lent is a sacred time when we journey toward the celebration of the Paschal mystery, the passion, death, and resurrection of Jesus Christ. Our Lord spent long periods in prayer with his Father so he could be faithful to God's will, the message he was to proclaim, and the mission and kingdom that he was asked to inaugurate. We know and believe that Jesus was divine, the Son of God, but he was human as well and, thus, most assuredly had doubts and was at times uncertain. But he was obedient to the end to God's plan in his life. Jesus did not take the fancy, exciting, or fun-filled route to the completion of his work. He knew that ultimately there was one and only one way to do what the Father had asked of him and that was by following God's plan. As our Lenten journey continues let us seek strength from God to stay on the correct path and to avoid obstacles and pitfalls which tempt us to another route. May we have the courage to follow God's plan faithfully, as did Jesus. May we have the courage to follow the narrow road and the one less traveled — the only path that leads to death, resurrection, and in the end, eternal life.

----

1. Paraphrased from "The Game," in John R. Aurelio. *Colors! Stories of the Kingdom* (New York: Crossroad, 1993), pp. 81-84.

The Paradox Of Death

The motion picture *Patton*, produced in 1970, won eight academy awards, including one for George C. Scott as best actor, in his portrayal of the famous American World War II army general. The film opens in a rather odd manner. Patton, in full military regalia, stands atop a platform; he is addressing his troops before they enter battle. In the course of his comments he states, "Some people say it is glorious to die for your country. But I say that the objective of war is to make the other guy die for his country." That simple statement says something very profound about what we as a society think of death. We see it as something that is to be shunned and avoided; it is dishonorable to die. Certainly anyone in a normal situation wants to live and desires that all friends and loved ones remain healthy and active. Still, for the Christian, one's attitude toward death must be different. We have been given life by God for the ultimate purpose to return to our Creator. We are on a journey which leads to God, but one can only arrive at the final destination through death.

Lent is a journey which in many ways simulates our whole life path, from birth to death. We began this season on Ash Wednesday when we received the sign of ashes, which not only spoke of our mortality but also of the journey that we entered. During this season we have gone to the desert with Jesus to be tested by Satan with the great temptations which have haunted humans for ages — power, wealth, and prestige. We next went to a high mountain, with Jesus, Peter, James, and John, and we saw the Lord transfigured. It was a momentary external transformation, but what did that miraculous event in Jesus' life do to transform us on the inside? We have walked beside Jesus in the heat of the day and the cool of the evening, experiencing along the way his triumphs and his difficulties. Now we enter the final part of the journey, a road that leads to death, but also to resurrection and eternal life.

We cannot experience the joy of Easter without first passing through the suffering of Good Friday. Today's first lesson from the prophet Isaiah, one of the famous "suffering servant" passages, demonstrates clearly the need to pass through death in order to find life. The servant does not try to avoid the humiliation and indignation which is his lot in life. The servant refuses to be rebellious, but rather willingly allows others to strike and spit upon him, all the while listening to insults. In the end God will vindicate him; God will bring him to victory.

It is only through such an attitude that finds promise, possibility, and even victory in the midst of pain, suffering, and humiliation that we can find any way to negotiate our world with all its vicissitudes, hurdles, and obstacles. Still, we might rightly ask why the world suffers. Why do pain, problems, and suffering exist in such abundance? We all believe that God is all good, all love, full of compassion, and all powerful. This is how we define God; we know this is true. Thus, the question bears repeating: Why does our world suffer? Why do wars exist and people die in innocence? Why do people in positions of public trust commit acts that cause others not only to lose faith in the individual, but in the system as well? Why do people fight one another when the only question between them is the color of their skin, their political preference, or religious belief?

One answer to these challenging questions is personal choice, our free will to say yes or no to God at any time in any way. Soren Kierkegaard, the famous nineteenth century existentialist philosopher and theologian, once wrote, "Faith is a matter of choice, our personal decision in finding God." This personal decision, our free will, is why the world suffers. It is free will that allows the drunk to drive and kill others. It is free will that allows people in public service to break the law and thus lower the integrity of the system. It is free will that places certain members and groups in society on the fringe and does not allow them to participate. Free will moves us closer to or further from God. As Kierkegaard wrote, it is our decision; faith is our choice.

It is free choice that allows the suffering servant to lay down his dignity and ultimately his life for others. The Lord was able to find promise where no hope was present and to snatch victory from the jaws of defeat. His attitude toward death was anything but shameful. On the human level Jesus most assuredly was fearful of his death, but his faith and confidence in his Father were so great that he could go forward with complete assurance that his fear would be conquered, pain would be transformed to joy, and death would lead to eternal life. Thus, to die was the ultimate good, for it produced so much for so many. Jesus, the suffering servant, today enters Jerusalem in triumph. He is the one who will eat dinner with his disciples and then willingly choose death for the freedom and salvation of sinful humanity. He was an innocent victim of the hatred of human beings. But through the transformation of hatred, Jesus will rise and bring all people for all time the possibility of salvation.

Jesus' journey to death and resurrection must give us hope. It is a hope, born in difficulty, which says, despite the paradox, that life can only come from death. If we are willing to continue the Lenten journey with Jesus to the end; if we will walk with him — then we too will find good through evil, triumph through defeat, and life through death. Let us, therefore, continue our walk with Jesus; let us stay close to him and in the process find life without end!

Death Leads To Life

Long ago on a high mountaintop three trees were speaking about their future dreams. The first tree said, "I would really like to be made into a cradle so that a newborn baby might rest comfortably and I could support that new life." The second tree looked down at a small stream that was flowing into a big river and said, "I want to be made into a great ship so I can carry useful cargo to all corners of the world." The third tree viewed the valley from its mountaintop and said, "I don't want to be made into anything. I just want to remain here and grow tall so I can remind people to raise their eyes and think of God in heaven who loves them so much."

Years passed and the trees grew tall and mighty. Then one day three woodcutters climbed the mountain in order to harvest some trees. As they cut down the first tree one of the men said, "We will make this one into a manger." The tree shook its branches in protest; it did not want to become a feed box for animals. It had grander ideas for its beauty. But the woodcutters made it into a manger and sold it to an innkeeper in a small town called Bethlehem. And when the Lord Jesus was born, he was placed in that manger. Suddenly the first tree realized it was cradling the greatest treasure the world had ever seen. As the woodcutters cut down the second tree, they said, "We will make this into a fishing boat." The woodcutters did as they planned and a man named Simon Peter bought it. And when the Lord Jesus needed a place from which to address the crowds that were pressing upon him, he got into the little fishing boat and proclaimed the Good News. And the second tree suddenly realized it was carrying a most precious cargo, the King of heaven and earth. The woodcutters then came to the third tree and said, "The Romans are paying good money these days for wooden beams for their crosses. We will cut this tree into beams for a cross." The tree protested so hard that its leaves began to shake and then fall onto the ground, but it was cut down, nonetheless, and made into beams.

One Friday morning the third tree was startled when its beams were taken from a woodpile and shoved onto the shoulders of a man. The tree flinched when soldiers nailed the man's hands to the wood; the tree felt shamed and humiliated. But early on Sunday morning, as the dawn appeared, the earth trembled with joy beneath the tree. The tree knew that the Lord of all the earth had been crucified on its cross, but now God's love had changed everything. And the cross from that third tree stands tall to remind people to raise their eyes and think of the God in heaven who loves them. And did you notice, how, in each case, being cut down was the price that was paid for entering into God's glory?

The three trees all had ideas of what they wanted; they had dreams for their futures. But what they wanted and how it came about did not happen in the way they expected. They did not realize that being cut down was the price for entry into God's glory. They did not understand it, but they needed to be molded and transformed, a process which took a sense of dying to their own wants and desires. On Good Friday we commemorate Jesus' death, his complete sacrifice. Saint Paul summarizes Jesus' action well: "And being found in human form he humbled himself and became obedient to the point of death — even death on a cross" (Philippians 2:8). But Jesus' death was salvific for us. The Lord's supreme, total, and uncompromising sacrifice brought life. We who wish to follow in his footsteps must be willing to sacrifice, to die to self, in order to bring life to ourselves and others in the world.

Today's familiar lesson is the fourth of the famous Suffering Servant passages presented in Deutero-Isaiah, written during the period of Israel's Babylonian captivity. The Servant dramatically challenges the worldly understanding of power by accomplishing God's purpose not through force, but by gentleness (Isaiah 42:1-4). The Servant is acquainted with suffering and abuse (Isaiah 5:4-7).

In fact, it is through the Servant's humiliation and suffering that God accomplishes the redemption of God's people from the bondage of sin. Scholars over the centuries have debated whether the Servant is a prophetic reference to Jesus (as the New Testament writers seem to indicate) or to the voice of the Hebrew nation. Regardless of the interpretation, the message of the passage is clear.

Today's lesson is a classic example of a paradox. We recall that a paradox is a statement or idea that when first examined appears to be false, but on closer scrutiny is proven to be true. "Meno," a famous dialogue of the great philosopher Plato, presents a classic example of a paradox. In the dialogue Socrates, Plato's protagonist, engages his friend Meno in a conversation and asks, "Is it possible to know that which is not learned?" Meno immediately answers, "No, there is nothing that one knows that is not learned." Socrates, after some reflection, responds that there are many things that people know without learning them, such as how to breathe, the emotions of love and sadness, and the natural instinct to live. Thus, there are things known that are not learned; Socrates' question is a paradox.

In this Suffering Servant passage we are told that the Servant will prosper but the path to this exaltation is the path of suffering. The Servant will not lose life so much as redefine it along lines that demonstrate light breaking through darkness, forgiveness destroying the bondage of sin, and knowledge that leads to righteousness. The Servant tells us that the highest expression of human dignity is found in the demonstration of solidarity with fellow human beings through a love that acknowledges no bounds because its source is God. We hear today, "See, my servant shall prosper; he shall be exalted and lifted up, and shall be very high ... But he was wounded for our transgressions, crushed for our iniquities; upon him was the punishment that made us whole, and by his bruises we are healed" (Isaiah 52:13, 53:5). Such a path to life and harmony with others makes no sense on the surface, especially in today's world. Thus, the Servant's message is a great paradox. The actions of the Servant appear to be all loss, but by such deeds the powerful in the world are startled and astonished. Those who follow the way of the Servant will transform the vision of many and place them on the correct path leading to righteousness.

The surrender of the Servant to the will of God is complete in all ways. We hear today, "He was oppressed, and he was afflicted, yet he did not open his mouth; like a lamb that is led to slaughter, and like a sheep that before its shearers is silent, so he did not open his mouth" (Isaiah 53:7). He knows that he must be molded and transformed by God, to go places and do things that he would rather not do, but he is willing to forego his personal needs for the needs of others, even to the point of taking on the sins of the community, though he is innocent. The Servant is totally unselfish; he has no fear for himself, but rather has developed a relationship with God of complete trust. He has absolute certainty that God's will for him will be profitable for the world and thus he is willing to endure whatever God asks of him.

The paradoxical nature of today's famous passage from the Prophet Isaiah can be directly applied to our Good Friday commemoration. On the surface Jesus' ignominious death on the cross seems to make no sense. We remember, however, what Saint Paul (1 Corinthians 1:18) said about this apparent contradiction in our faith, "For the message about the cross is foolishness to those who are perishing, but to us who have been saved it is the power of God."

The cross and its guarantee of pain are the greatest of all paradoxes. Jesus expresses this clearly in the Gospels. "Very truly, I tell you, unless a grain of wheat falls into the earth and dies, it remains just a single grain; but if it dies, it bears much fruit" (John 12:24). Again Jesus tells us, "For those who want to save their life will lose it, and those who lose their life for my sake, will save it" (Luke 9:24). The cross is not an option for those who wish to be disciples. The Lord makes this expressly clear as well, "If any want to become my followers, let them deny themselves and take up their cross and follow me" (Matthew 16:24). Thus, we know from scripture that there is one and only one way to enter into the eternal life promised us by God and that is by dying to self, as did Jesus, so as to rise renewed in Christ. Our sights must be set on the goal as Paul presents it, "What no eye has seen, nor ear heard, nor the human heart conceived, what God has prepared for those who love him" (1 Corinthians 1:9).

Contemporary society stands in complete rebellion against any idea that one must surrender oneself in any way. Years back there was a television commercial which proudly boasted, "Who says you can't have it all!" That attitude remains pervasive in our world, especially the prosperous American society in which we live. Society celebrates achievement and winners; losers and non-achievers are cast aside as unproductive, unimportant, and certainly not worthy of our time or attention. It makes no sense at all to people today to suffer intentionally, especially when for most there is absolutely no need. Besides we know that the world of hard knocks will come our way; why would we want to invite it to arrive early?

In every human way Jesus' life and mission appeared to be a failure. His master plan seemed to all to end on Good Friday when he was nailed to the cross and all but a select few of his faithful followers abandoned him. Yet, as we recall from Saint John's passion narrative, Jesus' death was his greatest victory. The thorns he wore were his crown and the cross upon which he died was his throne. Jesus' sacrifice on the cross, like all the actions of his life, contradicted the prevailing culture and societal norms. He challenged rules of all sorts. He freely associated with women, even some like Mary Magdalen who were considered indecent; he reached out to the ritually unclean such as lepers; he broke the sabbath laws, choosing in the process to establish a higher order of behavior. Jesus never feared people in positions of power and authority, such as the Pharisees, scribes, and elders, but rather challenged them to see another perspective on life. He never cowed to their threats, but rather steadfastly and courageously practiced his ministry to all who were willing to walk with or listen to him. Jesus proceeded forward unconcerned about what others thought; he knew his Father's will and did what was necessary at the appropriate times to carry it out.

Discipleship necessitates that we follow Jesus in every aspect of our lives. We know that this common call of the baptized manifests itself in service to God through our assistance of our brothers and sisters in need. It also means that we must preach and proclaim God's word to others. This need not be done on a street corner or in the door-to-door sale of religion, but it must be, and probably is most profoundly accomplished, through the everyday lives we lead. Every word and every action is an opportunity to tell others about our faith and what we proclaim about Jesus of Nazareth.

Discipleship also means, however, that we must follow Jesus to the cross; we must die to ourselves so others may live. In many ways this might be the greatest challenge to contemporary discipleship. People today are rather comfortable participating in some sort of service to others. It has become in vogue and is even popular in many circles individually or in groups, to assist at soup kitchens, visit the sick and elderly in nursing homes, or collect food, clothing, and other daily necessities and distribute them to the poor. Preaching by our actions is another thing we have been trained to do in contemporary life and our level of comfort with this Christian calling is fairly high. But to die to oneself, to deny what we have and even at times who we are is beyond the comprehension of most today. The denial of our self-autonomy, to sacrifice totally for others, something that loving parents are often called to do, is very difficult for most people. Lowering and humbling ourselves in order to raise up others does not make sense. It is a paradox as assuredly as Jesus' self-sacrifice on the cross was paradoxical for the salvation of the world. If we trust God, however, then we will be able to die to self and in the process raise up not only others but ourselves as well. Such ideas are difficult, but the difficult in life is many times the best option. This is the narrow road of which Jesus spoke when he addressed his disciples in the Sermon on the Mount (Matthew 7:13-14). It is the road less traveled, but the only path that leads to life eternal.

The cross is a paradox and thus it doesn't make sense, but it truly is the only hope for Christian salvation. We need not suffer and die in a physical way as did Jesus, as we recall the great events of Good Friday, but our spiritual martyrdom, like that suffered by Mary of Nazareth, to a lesser or greater degree, is required. Mary, the Sorrowful Mother, who kept vigil beneath the cross of her Son, can be a great model for us. She unhesitatingly said yes when invited by God, through the words of the Angel Gabriel, to become the mother of Jesus. Her great *fiat* would over the course of Jesus' life bring her much pain and suffering and many situations that she probably never fully understood. Yet, she was willing to endure the pain and walk the road with Jesus. We too must walk the *Via Dolorosa* and be willing to be the Suffering Servant who lays down his life for others.

Life throws all sorts of possibilities, people, events, circumstances, joys, and sorrows our way. Like all of us, the trees on the mountaintop had plans for their future; they, again like all of us, at the outset, were unwilling to allow their hopes to proceed in any way other than what they had planned. Yet in the end, they learned the lesson that if they were willing to die to self in their needs and wants, God through his master plan would bring to fruition their needs and would most importantly bring them home. We must learn the same lesson. The crosses of life will not be pleasant; we will suffer. But, as paradoxical as it seems and is in reality, the cross must be our only hope. Let us today fully enter into Christ's suffering. Let us humble ourselves and die to self, at least to some extent, so that others might benefit. It is the Lord we follow; it is Christ we seek to emulate; it is Jesus who brings us today through death to everlasting life.

Jesus Brings Us To New Life

Pastor David Johnson was all prepared, he thought, for his Easter sermon. Having only graduated from the seminary three months prior to taking his present position at the Maple Street Community Church, he possessed all the latest and most interesting theology. He made the final touches to his sermon on Holy Saturday morning and outlined its content to his wife. He told her that his sermon was based on theology of Paul Tillich, who spoke of the resurrection as a symbol that the estrangement from our authentic self was over. God has made possible the New Being, and if people would accept this truth, their unauthentic existence would end and new life would begin. His wife shook her head, but David didn't seem to notice.

Early that evening David drove to the church for the rehearsal of the sunrise service the next morning. When the practice ended, a youth, lovingly called "Tiny" because of his 6-foot 5-inch frame, asked, "Pastor, can you give me a ride home?" David said he would be glad to do so but that the young man would have to give him directions. With Tiny pointing the way, David delivered the youth home without incident. When he left, however, he could not remember if he was to turn right at the end of the cement and left at the crossroads or the other way around. It had only taken ten minutes to reach Tiny's home, but now after twenty minutes of driving he found himself on a deserted dirt road, totally lost. When the car sputtered, he realized he was out of gas.

David was overcome with anxiety. It was 10 p.m. on Holy Saturday evening. He was lost and out of gas, and he needed to be at

169

the church by 6 a.m. to set up for the sunrise service. He got out of the car and began to walk. Ten minutes later he saw some bright lights up ahead on the right. As he drew closer he could see that the lights came from a bar, the neon sign reading "The Boondocks." Everyone, including those new to the community like David, knew that this was one of the seediest taverns in town. As he walked to the front door, he saw a group of parked motorcycles which made him nervous. Upon entering the bar he smelled rancid beer and the stench of tobacco. He did not see anyone he recognized, a fact that was both good and bad. He wondered what church members might think if they knew their pastor was at "The Boondocks" on Holy Saturday night.

David approached the bar intending to ask for a ride to town but found himself ordering a Coke and, noticing a billiards table behind him, soon engaged in a game. David had played pool since he was six and was very good. This night, however, he was fantastic; he twice ran the table after the break. This action was noticed by Turk, a short but powerful "biker" who, taking off his leather jacket, challenged David to a game. Turk was good, but that evening David was better. After three consecutive wins Turk conceded defeat. He bought David another Coke and announced that henceforth David would be called "Shark." He then asked the inevitable question, "What do you do?" David was uncertain whether to tell the truth or lie, but he summoned his courage and said, "I'm a minister in town at the Maple Street Community Church." The crowd was shocked and began to mumble, but from the background Turk bellowed, "Quiet!"

Immediately the mood in the bar changed and the patrons, one-by-one began to tell their stories. When Turk's turn came he began, "I've never been to church. My mother was never married so people told her she was not good enough for any church. I've never been to Sunday school either. What I know about the Bible comes from television. I don't even know what we celebrate at Easter." The eyes of all the patrons trained on David, who realized that Turk had given him an invitation and he needed to respond. Thus, David began to tell all assembled about Jesus. He told about his birth and how when he was old enough he began a public ministry.

170

He told them that those who were rich and powerful had little time or energy for Jesus, who reached out in a special way to those who were despised by society at large. He did many wonderful things, cured many of diseases, forgave sins, and demonstrated love in every word and action of his life.

After three years of active work, Jesus, who mostly stayed in the northern section of his nation, ventured south to the capital city of Jerusalem. There he entered the city one Sunday morning in great triumph as people shouted, "Hosanna!" and laid palm branches on the ground for him. But later that same week those who were his enemies plotted against him. On Thursday evening he was arrested and tried in an unjust kangaroo court. The next day he was led to crucifixion, wearing a crown of thorns. All his best friends abandoned him, save a couple who watched all these horrible events. People mocked him saying, "All hail, King of the Jews!" Because he was tortured so severely, Jesus died on the cross after about three hours. His loyal friends took him down and laid him in a tomb. Upon hearing the story several of those in the bar began to cry openly.

David then told the men that on Sunday morning Jesus' friends went to the tomb to visit, but they met two angels who told them that Jesus was no longer there; he had risen and was alive. Later that day Jesus appeared to his friends, the same ones who had abandoned him just a few days before.

Turk and the others were impressed but they said, "That is a crazy story." David responded, "It's a crazy world. But our God can turn losers into winners; he has shown many times that what most believe is weakness in a person is truly strength. He demonstrated that those despised by society might be your best friends. By raising his Son from death, God has destroyed death forever."

When all was said, David then told Turk about his car problem. Quickly the rugged "biker" siphoned some gas from another vehicle, gave David directions, and sent him on his way. When he arrived home, his wife, who was obviously concerned about her husband's late return, told him that he needed to get to bed and rest, but he responded, "I need to rewrite my sermon." The next day David did not talk about New Being or estrangement from

171

authentic selfhood; he simply told the story of how God raised Jesus from the dead and in the process gave him and all people new life and hope. People in the congregation thought the sermon was good but what really got them talking was the strange group of visitors who parked their shiny motorcycles in front of the church and sat in one of the front pews. When one of the ushers inquired about the visitors, one burly man, obviously uncomfortable in a suit and tie, growled, "We are friends of Shark."

Pastor Johnson's encounter with Turk and his friends at "The Boondocks" is a story of transformation and conversion, the movement from death to life. A chance and unintended meeting between a young and inexperienced minister and a hard-bitten "biker" allowed both to cast off blindness, the veil that kept them in darkness, and to discover new vistas never before explored.

On this festival day of Easter Sunday, when Jesus Christ rose from the dead, thereby proving his divinity and conquering the death of sin forever, we are challenged to see our need for transformation, our opportunity to cast off whatever in life is the veil that obscures God's love and presence. Easter is a celebration of Jesus' complete reversal of fate, moving from what appeared to be the defeat of death to the victory of life. With faith we can do the same!

From the dawn of God's plan for human salvation he has provided all that was necessary not only to survive but to do well and be successful. The Hebrews experienced God's providence in their lives. God was present every step of the way, even when the people strayed off the correct path that was shown them, or even in some cases completely reversed direction. God was with the Israelites every moment during their forty-year sojourn in the desert following their exodus from Egypt. When the people sinned and were, as a consequence, subjected to the rule of other peoples, such as the Philistines, God raised up judges who rallied the people and brought victory to Israel. God was the one who provided a king for the Hebrew people, so they could be like all the other nations in their region, even though the prophets warned against such a move. Thus, Saul, David, and Solomon reigned over the united Kingdom of Israel and Judah before the loss of the Northern Kingdom to the

172

Assyrians. God also sent prophets to guide, cajole, and prophesy to the people in an effort to get them back onto the path of life.

Isaiah, one of the greatest of prophets, wrote the first third of this great book of scripture, to the people of Judah after the fall of the Northern Kingdom. The people may well have been uncertain about their future and what God might do with their nation. In response to this possible consternation, Isaiah writes, as we hear in today's First Lesson, in beautiful imagery of how God will remain faithful to the people every step of their journey. God will provide in his house a banquet of the richest foods and choicest wines. God will take away the veil that has shrouded the people of all nations and kept them from knowing and loving God fully. The destructive force of death, brought about by sin, the lot of all people in the past, will be destroyed forever. God will herald a new day for the people of Judah. On this day God, acting like a loving mother caring for her child, will wipe away the tears of the nation; the disgrace of the people will be removed.

Isaiah in this powerful and poetic passage is describing how God will completely reverse the fortunes of the Hebrew people. In the past God's activity had led to the annihilation of nations, Israel being prominent in the minds of the people of Judah, but in the age to come God will transform the people's hearts and minds. Sorrow will be replaced with joy, death with life, and this will happen in unimaginable proportions. The prophet proclaims that on this festival day, when God reverses the fortunes of the people, all will be glad and rejoice, for the day of salvation is at hand. Clearly Isaiah is painting a beautiful canvas, using vivid imagery, of the pardon and victory that God will win for us.

Easter is a celebration of God's great victory, not only for Jesus in his resurrection, but equally importantly for the transformation that is possible for us. God's ability to reverse the irreversible, to bring life from death, must be our great source of hope. All of us in some ways need to reverse the patterns in our life that often run counter to the Christian life to which we have all been called through baptism. Some of us fight the demons of persistent habits that seem to plague us as certain as disease can ravage our bodies. Some of us are plagued with habits of vice that take us down the wrong road. Others exhibit behavior or possess addictions that are destructive to us and which present to those we encounter a picture we do not want them to see. Many times we can seemingly find no way to break the cycle or to reverse the trend, but the power of Christ's resurrection, his destruction of eternal death, can put us back on the proper road, right the ship of our personal behavior, and steer us in the direction toward God and life.

The reversals in life can appear in other venues. Some people suffer misfortunes in their day-to-day work environment. Many find no joy, often because of boredom or routine, in their daily tasks at the office or at home. Under these conditions we need a change, a reversal of our path. The Easter mystery can reverse this pattern of routine in our lives as well. There are many people who are caught in a rut with their personal relationships. At times we cannot get to first base in trying to make friends with certain individuals; we find it impossible to break the ice with some people. With other people we can speak but there is no connection; we are on different wavelengths and cannot seem to communicate adequately. Still other people we ignore, possibly intentionally, because we "know" we cannot get along and be cordial. The power of Jesus' resurrection can transform our hardened hearts and open the hearts of others, allowing wonderful things to happen.

Most of us, if we are honest, need to do some work to place our relationship with God on a firmer foundation. Sometimes we know we are heading in the wrong direction; we have intentionally ignored the warning signs that have been placed along our path and willingly taken another route. Other times our direction is only slightly off, but we need an extra boost of encouragement to strengthen us to walk ever more closely with Christ. The power of the Easter message allowed Turk and his "biker" friends to get back onto the correct path in their lives; they again entered into a relationship with the Lord. Even Pastor Johnson, who knew all the intricacies of theology, experienced how the fundamental message of Jesus' triumph can reverse trends that keep us blind to many situations, circumstances, and individuals. The same can be true for us. Christ's resurrection must be meaningful for us today; it cannot simply be an event of history 2,000 years ago. The miracle can and must continue today.

As we, the Christian community, celebrate the most significant event in human history, the pinnacle moment of salvation history in Jesus' resurrection, let us possess the conviction that this festival milestone has meaning for us today. Let us be transformed by the power of the resurrection story. Jesus rose from the dead; the apostles rose from their fear and lethargy; Turk and Pastor Johnson gained new vistas on life. May we too be transformed by the power of Jesus, who suffered and died, but today rises and brings us the possibility of eternal life.

Teammates In The
Cause Of The Lord

"Outlined against a blue-gray October sky, the Four Horse-men rode again. In dramatic lore they are known as Famine, Pesti-lence, Destruction, and Death. These are only aliases. Their real names are Stuldreher, Miller, Crowley, and Layden. They formed the crest of the South Bend cyclone before which another fighting Army football team was swept over the precipice at the Polo Grounds yesterday afternoon as 55,000 spectators peered down on the bewildering panorama spread on the green plain below." Grantland Rice, a well-known sports columnist in the first half of the twentieth century, wrote those memorable words on Saturday afternoon, October 19, 1924. With these words a legend was started, for Notre Dame football, for the team's immortal coach Knute Rockne and, that day especially, for the Four Horsemen of Notre Dame.

Who were the Four Horsemen? Elmer Layden, Harry Stul-dreher, Jim Crowley, and Don Miller were the talented offensive backfield for the Notre Dame football team in the late 1920s. There is no doubt that they were great players. Football fans then and now remember their names and their exploits on the gridiron. All four have been enshrined in the College Football Hall of Fame.

Most people know, however, that there are eleven players on a football team. What about the other seven? Who were they; what did they do? History knows them as the "Seven Mules." Few if anyone remember their names; only one of them, "Rip" Miller, is a member of the College Football Hall of Fame. Still, I am certain

177

that the Four Horsemen knew them. In fact, the same Grantland Rice who immortalized the Horsemen said that this talented backfield attributed all their success to the Mules. They were the ones who stood in front, did the blocking, ran interference, and paved the way for the two halfbacks, the fullback, and quarterback to run the plays, score touchdowns, and bring victory to Notre Dame.

The Four Horsemen and the Seven Mules were a team. They knew that they needed each other. Without the Mules the Horsemen probably would have been an ordinary college football backfield. But the combination of the Mules and the Horsemen brought greatness, fame, and legend to Miller, Layden, Crowley, and Stuldreher, and to Notre Dame football as well.

The fabled Four Horseman and the unheralded Seven Mules were a team that worked together and in the process brought fame and legend to college football. While the sports world may remember certain members of this fabled team, and seemingly forgotten others, the players themselves knew their need for each other. Their mutual assistance was a microcosm of how people can work together toward a common goal and a good illustration of the call of the Christian community to be teammates, working together in the cause of the Lord.

Luke, in the Acts of the Apostles, his second great book of scripture, describes the lives of the first devoted followers of Jesus Christ, namely the Christian community. We hear about how they chose their leaders, especially after Judas' defection and betrayal of Jesus. Luke also describes the prayer life of this fledgling community. In today's lesson we are provided with important insight into the common life that these men and women lived. This communal lifestyle was the foundation from which their mission of the promulgation of Jesus' message would be generated. Besides their rock faith, the communal life was the great source of strength. It helped the community to live a common ethic and vision; it provided a base from which the works of the Lord could be generated. It was a way of life that marked who they were and thus became a source of the witness that was necessary for the community to recruit new members and to be visible in the midst of a non-believing society.

The community life which the apostles and other disciples of Jesus led was marked by four basic elements. First, Luke tells us that the members were in unity of mind and heart. This element was most basic; it was the ideal from which all the others flowed. Next, the community members shared all their possessions. This does not mean that people did not have personal property, but rather that members of the new way shared the things they had with others. Third, the fledgling community was marked by its powerful witness of the gospel. This was the group's common ministry; it was the way people demonstrated their belief and proclaimed the message of Christ to the world. Lastly, the community was special in that the grace of God rested upon its members. God was with this group of men and women in a special way. It was to this group that the Holy Spirit was originally sent. The community life of these first followers of Jesus was not imposed upon them, but rather, was voluntarily accepted. This was the way these men and women chose to live their lives of discipleship.

The ideas that Luke expresses as part of the communal life of the first Christians have their genesis in two basic arenas. Some of these concepts have their roots in Greek ideals and practice. Greeks of the period shared a common myth that people in primitive times lived in an ideal state in which there was no personal ownership; everything was held in common. For the Greeks as well friendship meant that people held everything in common. This idea was expressed best by Aristotle who called a friendship "one soul dwelling in two bodies." The Old Testament is also an important source for the community ideals of the first Christians. In Deuteronomy (15:4ff) we are told that God established the ideal in Israel that there would be no needy members in the community, but rather, all would share. The ideas of the Jews and Greeks was brought together by Jesus himself. When Luke reports that things would be sold and the proceeds laid at the feet of the apostles, he is referring to the Christian community's common effort to serve Jesus and the mission. All was to be laid at the feet of the apostles, who represented Jesus.

The Christian ideal articulated in today's lesson from Acts appears to be in direct conflict with our contemporary world. We are accustomed to leaders and followers, to those with great power and those with little, to those with many resources and to those with few, to those with much influence and to those with barely any, to those with privilege and to those without. We are also accustomed to people "doing their own thing," to entrepreneurs who make it big, to those who make the headlines of the daily newspapers because of their personal exploits and accomplishments. Contemporary life almost programs us to seek the highest and most lucrative position, the best salary, and the most influential friends. This is the era of the individual. The ideal of teamwork is not in vogue; its importance seems to have been lost on contemporary society. The common good and goal are not viewed with the importance they once held in our world. These ideals have become subservient to the individual.

An image from the ancient Greek drama *Oedipus Rex* accurately describes the situation of people today. In the play the protagonist is asked what has become known as the Riddle of the Sphinx: "What has four legs in the morning, two in the afternoon, and three in the evening?" The answer is a human being. In the early days of our life we crawl and, thus, use four "legs" to get around. We are totally dependent upon others for everything at this stage in our life. We are willing to be fed, changed, carried, put to bed. Our independence is minimal. In the great afternoon or middle of life, we walk upright on two feet. Gradually as we mature we become more and more independent and, thus, less and less dependent on others. There is no need to be a team player at this stage in life since we can do all that we need done by ourselves. In the latter stages of life, for many there is again the need for a third leg, a cane, walker, or a helping hand. We revert to the need of our childhood; we are more open to people helping us as we simply cannot do these things alone. We are once again team players. The Riddle of the Sphinx demonstrates that the majority of our life is spent in a mode of autonomy and self help; we feel we are a burden if we seek assistance or play as a team. We will do all that we can ourselves for as long as it is possible. This is our world today, but it need not be that way.

We need to be converted to the reality that we need each other. Simply because autonomy and independence rule today should not mean that these concepts are the ideal. Maybe we can learn something about teamwork from the Four Horsemen and Seven Mules, the understanding of the ancient Greeks, and especially those first followers of Jesus. The common good of all believers must be the ideal we strive to reach in our lives.

How can we be true teammates in the mission that is the cause of the Lord? First, we must possess an attitude of equality that does not allow us to place ourselves above others. Inequality among peoples can be seen in societal structures, companies and businesses, and even the church where people in positions of power and authority use these devices in ways that are self-aggrandizing or harmful to others. Another attitude is necessary, one that demonstrates solidarity with those we lead and appreciation for the gifts and talents others possess. There is no need to compromise one's ability to lead and supervise, but the methods we use in these positions of authority are critical.

We must lead by example. If we are to be true teammates with the Christian community, we cannot separate ourselves from the whole. We must be willing to do what everyone else does, to proverbially get our hands dirty in our daily tasks, whatever they may be. Those on a team should not feel that others are too important to "lower themselves" to do tasks assigned to others. Should we not be willing to do anything that we ask another person to do?

True teammates give encouragement to others. We are at our best when we help others, through our words and actions, to give their best effort. We demonstrate good teamwork when we take the time to congratulate others on what they have accomplished; we need to say, "Thank you," and truly mean it when someone does something for us, even if it be some routine and generally accepted act of kindness. We must never be demeaning to others in our words, exalting our self-importance, especially to the detriment of others.

The need and ability to share is also critical to good teamwork. Can we be true teammates in the cause of the Lord when one person has an abundance and others live in want? How can a true community of the faithful be formed when we separate ourselves

181

from others because of the advantages and opportunities that have come our way? Do we, as individual Christians, as a church community, as a state or nation, owe anything to those who through no fault of their own or lack of initiative, but mostly through unfortunate circumstance, have not been productive, made the grade, or achieved what others expected of them?

Teamwork does not happen overnight; it will take time, but we must begin today. Excuses will always be present, but we cannot allow these to cloud our vision. Our mission and cause, the work of Jesus Christ, is far too valuable to allow personal pride, arrogance, or need for self-gratification to get in the way. We need to be teammates in our common goal of building the Kingdom of God in our world.

Our work is the work of Christ for we are his body, as Saint Paul reminds us (1 Corinthians 12). We act most strongly as teammates when we become the Christ to others. Saint Teresa of Avila, the sixteenth century mystic and church reformer, expressed this idea powerfully in a famous prayer: "Christ has no hands but yours, no hands no feet but yours. Yours are the eyes with which Christ looks with compassion on the world. Christ has no hands but yours." My friends, may we believe, act, and profess the same!

Negotiating The Trials Of Life

"In the seventh year of his reign, two days before his sixty-fifth birthday, in the presence of a full consistory of cardinals, Jean Marie Barette, Pope Gregory XVII, signed an instrument of abdication, took off the Fisherman's ring, handed his seal to the Cardinal Camerlengo and made a curt speech of farewell." So begins the power novel *The Clowns of God*, the second volume of a trilogy of tales about popes and faith written by Morris West, the Australian-born author. In the story the Pope has seen a vision of the Second Coming. He feels that the message of Christ's return must be promulgated throughout the world. Therefore, he gathers his closest advisors, the curia and college of cardinals, and asks their advice. They tell him that such a message cannot be published. "It will throw the world into a panic," they claim. The Pope is confused but feels that he has only one alternative; he must be true to himself. Thus, he decides to abdicate his position. This he does, placing himself under the obedience of an abbot in a monastery outside of Rome.

After one week at the monastery, Jean Marie receives his first visitor. His name is Carl Mendelius, a long-time friend and former Jesuit priest, who now as a married man is teaching theology in a prestigious German university. The two friends speak and begin to map out a strategy for the promulgation of Jean Marie's vision to the world.

The plan is foiled, however, before it can be enacted. Mendelius, working in Germany, is felled by a letter bomb sent by a would-be assassin just as he made ready to present the text of the message to a group of the world's scholars. Meanwhile, Jean Marie, in England to give a speech that will reveal the message, suffers a severe heart attack. As he clings to life in a London hospital, the former pope receives a strange visitor. The man is young, about thirty years old. He is tall, strong, and speaks with a Middle Eastern accent, although his origin seems a mystery. He wears a beautiful and ancient ring which has inscribed on it the Christian symbol of a fish. This man calls himself Mr. Atha. The stranger tells Jean Marie that he must persevere but that the message which he feels must be told is already present if people will only recognize it.

Several weeks later Jean Marie returns to his native France to recuperate fully. One day he goes for a walk in Parisian park. He sits down and observes the scene. There is a group of children playing nearby. They are a special group; they are mentally handicapped. He sees that these children each day live a great trial of faith, and they don't even realize it. These children live for the moment and endure their handicap with no fear and apparent concern. In this experience Jean Marie begins to realize that the essential message of his vision is to accept God's plan and to endure the trials of faith. He can see this in the unpretentious lives of these children whom he calls the "Clowns of God."

Months later Jean Marie is present with his new-found friends, the Clowns of God. They have gone to a remote mountain villa to celebrate the Christmas feast. To this isolated place Mr. Atha comes quite unexpectedly. Jesus, the Christ, has returned as was predicted to claim his own. Jean Marie has endured the great trial of faith and discovered God in the process.

Morris West's epic tale illustrates an important lesson in every human life, namely the need to persevere, to maneuver through the maze of life, a journey which only seems to become more complex with time. Summoning the courage and strength to navigate the ofttimes troublesome waters of daily life is not easy, but in securing assistance we can generally count on our brothers and sisters, the Christian community, and we can always count on God. When the path we need to trod is strewn with obstacles and hurdles we may despair, but we need not knowing others will help. We need to negotiate these trials of faith with others at our side.

184

It is hard to imagine the difficulty of the life of the first followers of Jesus. The apostles and the other disciples of Jesus, like their
ancestors during the period of the patriarchs, Abraham and Moses,
lived in a very hostile environment that was not open to their presence or the message given them by God to promulgate. Some of
the trials most assuredly came from the community's lack of ac-
ceptability by the ruling forces or possibly its forced ostracization
from the elite. Because the forces around them were numerous and
powerful, the people banded together to gain strength from their
numbers. The Acts of the Apostles tells us that the fledgling Christian community was united in mind and heart. The unity of the
community helped its members endure the great trials that came
their way. The people needed each other and they were happy to
express that necessity in their lives.

Peter, who we hear in today's lesson giving a speech to Jewish
leaders, was converted to the knowledge of a higher reality in his
life and gained a greater depth of faith through the miracle of the
resurrection. Peter had endured several trials of faith as reported in
the Gospels. He could not understand Jesus' need to suffer and die
and he abandoned the Lord when he needed him most through his
infamous three denials. Now, after the resurrection, Peter is a new
man. He speaks out fearlessly in his speech, which is similar in
several ways to the one delivered on the day of Pentecost. Peter
begins by correcting the false impression that he was responsible
for the renewed health of the crippled beggar. He then says that
God glorified Jesus, but the Jerusalem Jews nonetheless handed
him over to Pilate. Lastly, Peter invites the Jewish leaders who
were responsible for Jesus' death to repent and return to God. Peter's
new resurrected faith gives him the strength and courage to carry
out his mission as a fully committed follower of Jesus Christ.

The speech which Peter makes in Solomon's Portico has one
additional dimension that is critical — an emphasis on faith. Peter's
newly-found resurrected faith was necessary for him to negotiate
the trials of life that would come his way. He was successful in his
mission because he could count on the help of his fellow disciples
and most especially Jesus. He was able to do miraculous things,
such as the cure of the crippled beggar, because, as we are told by

Saint Luke, the name of Jesus has great power. Jesus' glorification and resurrection brought great power to the name. It was Peter's great faith in the name of Jesus, in turn, that brought healing to the beggar.

The Jews whom Peter addresses serve as a contrast to the great faith of the apostle. These religious leaders rejected Jesus, even when the Procurator Pilate was ready to release him. In a great twist of irony, the Jews ask for the life of an insurrectionist and murderer, Barrabas, to be spared, while they, in turn, are responsible for the execution murder of Jesus. Thus, Peter calls for repentance as the first step for the Jews to get their lives back on track, so they can safely navigate through the maze of trials that life will bring. The Jewish leaders will need faith in the resurrection as well.

Easter is a season that provides the opportunity to ponder the resurrection and to discover how this greatest event in all salvation history can be transformative in the renewal of our faith. All of us, to a lesser or greater extent, need to have our faith deepened; it needs to be made more full and complete. This can happen when we allow the resurrection to make a difference in our lives, to be more than an event, but a way of living our life. There is no question that Peter and the other disciples of Jesus possessed faith before the resurrection. Without faith it would have been impossible for any of them to have answered the call to be followers of the Lord. We recall that the Gospel evangelists tell us that the apostles "immediately left everything" to become his disciples. This could not have happened without faith. Yet, there is no question that the resurrection transformed them; the disciples became new creations in their resurrected faith. They were given a renewed faith that would be necessary to negotiate through the vicissitudes, hurdles, and obstacles of the Christian life.

We have many trials of faith that come our way. God throws many curve balls in our direction. People, circumstances, and situations enter out lives and become great trials of faith. In baseball when a pitcher throws a curve, batters tend to bail out of the batter's box, fearful that they may be hit by the pitch, but we must stand our ground when God throws the curve that might throw us off course or off stride. We need to make solid contact with the pitch

186

and we can only do so by meeting the curve head on and refusing to bail out of the batter's box.

What are the trials of faith that have come your way? For some the great trial might be one's day-to-day nine to five job. We work very hard each day and believe that our efforts are not appreciated, possibly not even noticed. Sometimes a person or situation at work is troublesome and makes our time on the job a real cross. There are times as well when we might not receive the raise we know we deserve or, as unfortunately happens sometimes, we lose our job. Many people have the trial of a sick family member, friend, or associate that takes its toll on them. We must make extra time that we simply do not have to be with someone at the hour of need. Sometimes trials of ill-health end in death. At these times we are not sure what to do or where to turn. The trial and the pain it brings seems insurmountable. For some people the great trial may be a personal failure, either in a task, a relationship, or a commitment. If we fail to meet our own personal goals, we often become disheartened and get down on ourselves. If we are not careful, this can lead to self-doubt or, worse still, a poor self-image. When we realize that we have let down someone and our failure cost others in some way, we feel poorly and seek a way to right ourselves. There are those times as well when the great trial is our relationship with God. We wonder why God does not listen, act on our behalf, or grant our requests in the manner and time we know is correct. We become frustrated, even angry with God, creating a rift that leads us, for a time, to choose not to communicate with the source of all love and goodness.

Trials of faith will come our way, in different ways, varied forms, and multiple occasions. How will we respond? Jean Marie Barette was able to endure his great trial of faith through the example of the Clowns of God, whose unpretentious nature and ability to live for the moment taught him some important lessons for life. In a similar way, after the resurrection, Peter had need for greater faith, for the tasks he was assigned were monumental. He realized he could rely on the fledgling Christian community and most especially upon Jesus. There are people who help us, as well, to find our way through the maze of faith's trials. We, like the first disciples, need to build community; we need to help one another. We need to return to the Lord and seek our strength and solace in him. If we have even the slightest doubt of God's abiding presence, love, and care for us, picture this image. It is a hot summer day and a little girl stands on the edge of a big swimming pool. She looks down at the shimmering water and is filled with fear because she knows the water is deep and she cannot swim. She begins to cry. Then she lifts her eyes slightly and she sees her mother with arms outstretched. Mom says, "Go ahead; jump in. There is nothing to fear. I will save you and hold you up." In a similar way, Jesus has his arms outstretched on the cross, and he says to all of us, "Go ahead; take a chance with me. Jump in; I will save you. I will bring you to eternal life."

Resurrection Faith:
Our Source For Accomplishment

Joshua and the Children, by Joseph Girzone, the second in a multi-volume series that describes the life and ministry of a messianic figure named Joshua, tells a tale of the creation of peace in the midst of a sea of hatred and long-standing rivalry. Joshua appeared unceremoniously one day in a small town, typical for the area. The town was host to four different churches, Presbyterian, Roman Catholic, Anglican, and Wesleyan, but these Christian communions were divided, with the Protestants and the Catholics not seeing eye-to-eye with each other, a condition which had been the lived experience of the people for many generations. Joshua had a plan to break the cycle of hatred and the violence which often accompanied it, he began to work with children and show them that peace and harmony between peoples was possible.

Each day Joshua, whose origin was uncertain and whose carefree attitude toward life, organized religion, and politics was quite unique, met with the children in the town square. He played games with the children, showed them some wonderful magic, and even played music (although rather poorly) with them. But most importantly, Joshua taught the children that division between peoples because of religion need not be the reality; there was no reason why Catholics and Protestants could not work together, be friends, and live in peace. Joshua had great faith; he spoke to his Father frequently and gained strength for his mission from these numerous conversations. This was a strange concept, even to the children, who from the day of their birth had been taught to be wary of and even hate those who were not like them. Joshua organized the children in a march to the neighboring city, a march for peace and unity. He organized a soccer game, not between the two groups, but between two teams whose members belonged to both groups. The parents were impressed, but they began to wonder who this person was and to question his motive. For the adults, what Joshua had accomplished was too good to be true and, thus, they continued to be wary.

Joshua's unusual personality and what he was doing attracted lots of attention. Everyone in town knew him. He was a frequent guest to the houses of many, and he appreciated the invitations because he had no house of his own. Joshua worshiped at all four churches at different times. He often told people who questioned his movement between congregations that his Father was present with all people. No one group had a monopoly on the favor of God. Joshua also attracted lots of attention in other places. The Catholic and the Anglican bishops came to meet him and were so impressed that they issued a joint statement endorsing his good work with the children with the hope that it would be fostered and continued. A local paper came and interviewed him and his children disciples, making him a celebrity.

The forces of evil, those who did not want the status quo of hatred and violence to be disturbed, raised their ugly head. A plot was hatched against Joshua by people from both sides. They could not stand the fact that one man's faith and initiative had accomplished so much in a relatively short amount of time. They came to the village square where Joshua was instructing the children as he did most every day. Shots rang out. Joshua was hit, so too was a little girl, to the horror of the marksman who through his scope saw he had shot his own daughter. But with his last ounces of strength Joshua reached out and touched the girl, and she was instantly made whole once again. Joshua died that day, but the next day when people looked into the coffin prepared for his burial they found nothing. What had happened to this man of peace who taught the people what was possible with faith? No one would ever know for sure.

Joshua was a man who possessed total faith amidst a sea of people, in the town and nation, who purposely chose to have none.

190

He was able to accomplish the impossible, to bring peace to the hearts and minds of people through his work with children while others continued to spread hatred and violence. Joshua, the man of faith, the Christ who came to that small town, won the day, challenging others to follow his lead.

Saint Peter, as he is depicted in the Acts of the Apostles, possessed great faith in the Lord, but as we can recall, he did not begin that way. In the Gospel, Peter is portrayed as one who does not understand Jesus' plan. As soon as the Lord tells Peter he is the rock, he then reveals that suffering and death are in the future. This is something Peter cannot imagine: "God forbid it, Lord! This must never happen to you." Jesus must reprimand one of his chosen twelve, "Get behind me, Satan! You are a stumbling block to me; for you are setting your mind not on divine things but on human things" (Matthew 16:22-23). Peter, as we also recall, was the one, who, when Jesus needed him the most, denied the Lord three times.

The resurrection obviously made a great difference in Peter's life. Somehow he was transformed into a new person, one filled with hope. As today's lesson tells us, he is filled with the Holy Spirit. Now Peter can speak out boldly and courageously; he can act with total confidence in the name of Jesus. The resurrection has filled him with so much faith that he is able to do what is humanly impossible. Peter acts in the place of Christ; he does good deeds and heals because his newfound faith, generated by the resurrection, is centered in the one who can do all things for all people at all times.

The ruling Jewish religious officials were concerned about the source of the disciples' teaching. They were worried that emphasis on the resurrection could lead to a major insurrection that might bring serious political repercussions. But Peter was not concerned about what his actions would cost the Jewish leaders. He needed to demonstrate that his renewed faith in Jesus was the source of the good he had accomplished. Peter wanted others to know that his example was not unique; others who possessed great faith in the resurrection of Jesus could do incredible things as well. Peter's actions imply that since salvation comes through only one name, that all must make a commitment to that name — Jesus of Nazareth.

Faith must be the true source of all that we do, but, unfortunately, there are people who feel that the source of their accomplishment is their own initiative and work. No right-thinking person would deny that hard work is absolutely necessary for the accomplishment of tasks and the achievement of goals. Personal initiative is equally important. If we cannot find the strength, motivation, and initiative daily to do what God asks of us, nothing will ever be accomplished. God gives us much talent, many opportunities, plus the purpose and initiative for our endeavors; we have all the tools necessary. Thus, we must acknowledge and fully own the reality that God is the ultimate source of what we do. If we think that we have done it alone, that God was not involved from the very outset, then our thinking is skewed, limited, and even foolish. Unfortunately, too many people in our world think this way, and their limited vision and scope directly curtail and possibly produce adverse effects on what they do and how much they accomplish.

Some people do not possess the requisite faith and thus limit their effectiveness and ability to accomplish things that seem beyond their reason, time, or talent. Many Americans these days have lost faith in the government process. They see partisan politics and gridlock rampant in the national Congress, as well as state and local governments. This lack of faith is manifest most noticeably through the great apathy that people today take toward voting, their general lack of interest in the electoral process, and their disinterest in what happens in our state and national capitals. Many people have lost faith in institutions. When the school, company, or fraternal organization does not do things "our way," following a method or path which *we* know is clearly wrong, we become upset and lose faith.

People today have lost faith in systems and policies as well. We have difficulty understanding and, thus, accepting why "the system" or the policy of some group necessitates so much "red tape." We become frustrated, grow impatient, and at times even angry. Our feelings oftentimes translate into a lack of faith in the system and policies that are used. We refuse to participate; we opt out. People today often lose faith in the judicial system. The system of *juris prudence* used in the United States is probably the best available, but it is highly imperfect. How many times have we seen people who are clearly (at least in our minds) guilty set free on some legal technicality or superficial error by the police or an attorney? How many times have well-trained lawyers been able to manipulate the system toward a verdict that in the minds of many is clearly in error? There are times as well when innocent people are unjustly convicted and serve long sentences before the error is discovered and rectified.

Possibly our most notable loss of faith is when we can no longer trust people. How many times have family members, trusted friends, or associates let us down or disappointed us? Sometimes people don't come through; they fail to meet their commitments. When we need people the most, they fail to be present. Such occurrences create a loss of faith in us.

Unquestionably the ultimate source of faith we need is in Christ and the power of his resurrection. Jesus tells us in the Gospels, "If you had faith the size of a mustard seed, you could say to the mulberry tree, 'Be uprooted and planted in the sea,' and it would obey you" (Luke 17:6). On one level this seems like a small amount of faith, only a mustard seed of faith is necessary for such a monumental, superhuman task, but Jesus is referring to true, unquestioning, and unconditional faith in him and the message his Father gave to the world. The apostles, after the resurrection, possessed this true and uncompromising faith, allowing them to go forward — to preach, to heal, and to witness so powerfully in the midst of a hostile world, one that was not open to their new way nor the message their Master, Jesus Christ, had given to the world. To most, as today's lesson tells us, Jesus was the stone rejected by the builders, but to those who believe, those who were transformed by the resurrection, he became the cornerstone of their lives. Without Jesus we can accomplish some things. We can operate and complete the limited and finite tasks of our world, but with Jesus and, most importantly, true, unconditional faith in his resurrection, we can do what seems to be impossible. We can say to the mulberry tree, "Be uprooted and planted in the sea," and it will happen.

Today's active, busy, and increasingly complex world throws us many "curve balls," people, events, circumstances, and situations that we might label as trials of faith. We are asked to negotiate these obstacles and hurdles, but the accomplishment of these endeavors, the ability to get to the other side of our trials of faith and accomplish the many tasks that come our way, can only happen when we possess absolute faith in the resurrected Christ. The Easter event must, therefore, be transformative in our lives as it was in the lives of those first followers of Jesus. The reason to celebrate the Easter season is to demonstrate its efficacy in our lives. Jesus' rising from the dead 2,000 years ago must be the source of ultimate hope for our world. If we truly believe that the Lord conquered the grave and destroyed the death of sin forever, then our attitude and our faith can be translated into actions of great accomplishment. Without our faith in the power of the resurrection, however, what we accomplish will be limited, for it will be only what is humanly possible.

Great faith in the resurrection is the solution to the loss of faith which our world so deeply experiences today. Faith in Jesus' ability to conquer death will allow us to negotiate through the trials of life — sickness and death, unemployment, disappointments, loss, and failure. Our uncompromising belief in the resurrection will bring new hope so we can regain confidence in government, institutions, systems and policies, the judicial system, and, most importantly, people. With faith we can accomplish the different tasks that today seem impossible, at least at the outset. If we trust sufficiently in the power of the resurrection to transform our lives, as it did Peter and the other apostles, then we truly will accomplish great things.

In Joseph Girzone's book *Joshua and the Children*, a messianic figure with absolute and uncompromising faith in his Father organizes a grass roots program to bring people together in order to end years of violence and hatred. People felt the situation was hopeless and, thus, they had given up. Even good church-going folks believed the situation was beyond change. But Joshua showed what could be accomplished through great faith. In a similar way Peter, transformed by the power of the resurrection into a man of unconditional faith in Christ, was able to accomplish wonderful things. We can do the same!

As we celebrate the Easter season, let us seek the faith that Jesus possessed in his Father. Let us be transformed by the power of the resurrection. May we accomplish great things through faith, moving day-by-day closer to Jesus, salvation, and eternal life with God.

Transforming Our Mind To Christ

Sir Launfal, a knight errant, methodically checked his list for the third time. He readied everything for his great adventure that would begin tomorrow. His sword was sharp, his shield was polished, and his horse was rested and fed. Finally he knelt down and prayed, "Dear Lord, tomorrow I begin my great quest in your name. Guide me in my search for your Holy Grail, the cup you used when you ate your last meal with your apostles. Make me pure, for only if I am pure will I find your cup."

He fell into a deep sleep and began to dream. In his dream it was the next day and he began his quest. He bid farewell to all at the castle and rode out the gates on his beautiful horse. Just on the other side of the gate, however, a beggar stopped him. "How annoying," thought Sir Launfal. At this high moment he did not want to be bothered by a beggar. Who needed such an interruption in the great quest for the Holy Grail? Disdainfully, the knight flung a penny at the beggar and rode on.

Time, in fact many years, passed in his dream. He looked everywhere for the Holy Grail. He fought many battles but in the process he did not even obtain a glimmer of hope to find the Grail. Sir Launfal was discouraged. He had become an old man and had failed in his quest. He decided to return home. As he arrived at the castle gate, the guard did not recognize him. "No beggars allowed here!" the guard shouted. "Who needs such people anyhow?" The guard then forcefully drove Sir Launfal away. He was dejected; he felt alone. He had been rejected, even by those in his own home.

Finally the knight sat down and pulled the last crust of bread from his pocket. As he began to eat, he noticed a beggar near him. It was the same beggar who had been at the gate so many years ago when he began his quest. Sir Launfal broke the bread in two and gave the beggar half. Then he went to the brook and drew water for them to drink. As they ate and drank from his wooden bowl, Sir Launfal realized that the stale bread tasted as if it was fresh and the water was like fine wine. He turned toward the beggar, but he was gone. In his place was the shining presence of Christ. He heard Jesus say:

> Not what we give, but what we share
> For the gift without the giver is bare.
> Who gives himself with alms feeds three
> Himself, his hungry neighbor, and me.

The knight looked down at his wooden bowl. It was no longer there. Instead he held in his hand the Holy Grail. His search was now over.

At that moment Sir Launfal awoke from his dream. It was the next morning and he now knew what to do. There was no need to search for the Holy Grail; it was right in his midst. He only needed to open his eyes and be converted to the mind of Christ and he would find it.

Sir Launfal took a journey to find the Holy Grail, but he had no time for the peasant who seemed to impede his progress toward this great quest. Only when he was personally rejected by one of his own servants and discovered the presence of Christ in one whom he had rejected did he come to realize how he had acted and then begin to change.

The Easter season is all about transformation and conversion, and our personal need to broaden our horizons and to see where God may lead us. Today in our first lesson we hear of a famous conversion, an outsider from the ranks of Israel who learns of the ways of the Lord. His story and the Easter mystery must energize us to seek transformation in our lives, conforming ourselves more closely to the life and mind of Christ.

Philip, one of the select twelve in Jesus' company, having just completed his preaching to the people of Samaria, is now asked to take on another mission, one of conversion and transformation. He is sent by an angel toward the south to meet and then engage in conversation a stranger, one who does not know God. I am sure that Philip was confused and wondered what God intended in sending him to an outsider, an Ethiopian. For a Jew or Jewish-Christian to reach out to an Ethiopian would have been of great interest, even fascination, for Luke's audience. Such a man would not have been a despised and despicable person, but rather, a well-placed and significant person in society, one who was open and receptive to the truth when it was articulated. Thus, Philip's task was to instruct an accepted person in society in the new way; he was to transform this man to the mind of Christ.

The Ethiopian's conversion was one of true acceptance. There is every indication that this man was completely open to receiving God's word when it was explained by the apostle. It was the Ethiopian who invited Philip into his carriage so the Scriptures could be explained to him.. Thus, he was open to learning, and more importantly, to conversion. Moreover, as soon as he achieved an interior conversion, he wished to testify publicly to his newfound faith by his baptism. The Ethiopian eunuch was pro-active; he did not rest on his laurels, but energetically sought God. He was given a special opportunity and he took it. We must do the same!

The Easter season is a time when we celebrate conversion, transformation, and reversals of fortune. As Jesus' resurrection transformed death to life, negotiating a complete reversal of fortunes, so we are called to seek conversion in our own lives. We must transform and conform our lives, minds, and hearts more to the person of Christ. We are all aware of this need and the call to be more Christ-like in our words and actions. We strive daily to be good witnesses to others of the importance of Christ in our lives. We make plenty of errors, we falter and fall, but we hope our direction is clear and we make a concerted effort to follow the Lord's lead, by patterning our lives, in every aspect, after Christ.

All of us in some way need to transform our attitude and mindset to that of Jesus Christ. We need to ask — what is God calling me to do? Sir Launfal was called to search for the Holy Grail, but he came to realize that his quest could only be realized when he was converted to an appreciation for others, thereby following Jesus' lead. Philip was called to go where he might not have wanted to go, to speak with someone he might not have wished to engage in conversation. The eunuch seems to have been open to God's call, but it is probable in his life, also, that at times he was reticent to be transformed.

The story of Sir Launfal and what we learn from today's lesson from the Acts of the Apostles challenge us to ask some serious questions. When God calls us, are we listening? Do we have the courage to answer when God calls, especially when the call is to do something or go somewhere we would rather not? What are we doing to conform our lives to the mind of Christ?

The reasons we give for our inability or unwillingness to listen and to conform ourselves to the mind of Christ are many, but they seem to center about self-autonomy — we do not want to be told what to do. We do not wish to be disturbed, to move beyond our zone of comfortableness. We do not want to think about the sacrifice that might be asked of us in answering God's call. We are content to do what we want to do; we simply do not want to be disturbed. The call might come for us to walk the road of ill-health with a family member, good friend, or colleague at work. As an excuse, we say that such an effort will drag us down and, thus, we would rather not participate. We make all sorts of excuses to satisfy ourselves that we are doing what God asks of us — but are we truly listening and answering the call? We may have to exercise "tough love" in a confrontation with another who exhibits addictive behavior. We say it is too hard and too much trouble to take the right path in dealing with hard issues, and thus we "opt out." It is so much easier to let things slide. We can easily say, and thus rationalize, that the person's inappropriate behavior is not hurting us. We take the easy road and leave the "problem" for someone else.

We all know that God is calling us to change, to be converted, to transform our minds to that of Christ. This is clear because we hear God's voice, in the multiple ways the Lord speaks, telling us to change our habits, to seek reconciliation with another, and to drop past hurts and failures that chain us to the past and impede us from moving toward God. We often prefer, however, to keep up our front; we will not drop our guard for one moment, fearful that God just might give us a punch that could knock some sense into us. God might be calling us to a deeper and renewed relationship, but again we rationalize and say that we don't have sufficient time for what God asks of us. We say our prayers — what more could God possibly want from us? We feel we are giving all we can give.

When God calls, when challenges come our way, we must respond with openness to the possibility so we can be transformed to the mind of Christ. Sir Launfal needed some prodding and the experience of personal rejection to get him to see his need for transformation. What will it be for us? The apostles knew Jesus personally and thus their ability to be transformed might be greater and its exercise easier, but we cannot make excuses for ourselves. Let us listen well to the voice of God, as it is manifest to us in its multiple and varied ways. Let God's word penetrate deeply so we can be transformed. The spirit and power of the resurrection call us to conversion to Christ. May we have the courage to respond, and answer the call of the Lord!

Conversion To Impartiality

Once upon a time a great and powerful king ruled over a vast territory. There was something very strange about this kingdom, however — everything was the same. The people ate the same food, drank the same drink, wore the same clothes, and lived in the same type of homes. The people even did all the same work. There was another oddity about this place. Everything was gray — the food, the drink, the clothes, the houses; there were no other colors.

One day a majestic and very beautiful bird flew from the west into a small village a great distance from the capital city. The bird deposited a yellow egg and flew off. The people were fascinated with their new possession since they had never seen anything but gray. They played with the egg and poked it. In the process the egg broke. Inside was a yellow powder. Anything that came in contact with the powder instantly turned yellow. At the outset a few people's clothes and some other objects turned yellow, but the people were soon so struck with their new discovery that the whole village was "painted" yellow. The next day the same bird flew from the west and deposited a blue egg in another small village. It did not take long before everything in this village was blue. This same scenario repeated itself on seven consecutive days as the majestic bird deposited seven different colored eggs in seven villages.

The king in the capital city, where all was still gray, heard about these strange events and wondered what the sign might mean. He called in his royal councilors and advisors and asked them if anything like this had happened in the past. They checked the ancient manuscripts and discovered that many generations ago the kingdom was ruled by a philosopher king. At the time there was much dissension, strife, and conflict in the kingdom. It was further discovered that the source of this dissension came about from the differences that existed among the people. The king, who wanted peace, believed that the only way to restore harmony was to eliminate all differences among the people. This is why all the people did the same things and all was gray.

The present king was worried that the various colors in the villages would again lead to dissension and strife. Thus, he ordered the royal archers to locate the majestic bird and slay it. The archers found the bird and their arrows were sent straight and true, but they had no effect on the bird, which simply flew away. If the bird could not be stopped, then the people must be, thought the king. Thus, he ordered the people to remove all the colors and return to gray. But the people, who were enamored with the new colors in their lives, refused to obey the king's order. Dissension, strife, and conflict ensued — the very things the king was trying to prevent.

The king was unsure as to what to do until one day the beautiful majestic bird flew into the royal palace and deposited seven different colored eggs. The king was frustrated and angry and in a fit of rage he hurled the eggs in all different directions. They burst into an array of color. The beauty was so magnificent that the king, in a moment of inspiration, knew precisely what he needed to do. He now realized that the bird was a sign that he had been too exclusive in his way of thinking and change was needed, but he had ignored the sign. Thus, the king ordered that all the people must have all the colors. Again there were no differences and, thus, dissension, strife, and conflict ceased and all of the people lived happily ever after.[1]

The king held tight control on the lives of his subjects. In controlling the colors he controlled how the people thought and in general how they lived. He had one and only one way of thinking, one way of acting and responding to situations and, thus, he believed his way was the only way for all. But his perspective was quite limited; he understood life in his own way and lived it on his own terms. But through the intercession of the majestic bird he learned that he needed to be more open; he needed to be converted to a more inclusive understanding of life. He became converted to the absolute need to be impartial.

Scripture scholars say that Acts 10:1—11:18 is one of the most important passages in the whole Acts of the Apostles. This pericope speaks of the conversion of Cornelius, a Roman officer, to the "new way." The story is told is seven separate scenarios with today's first lesson being the climax. It is clear that Luke the evangelist wants his readers to understand the significance he is giving to the story. The use of repetition in the passage, telling the story of Cornelius' vision four times and Peter's dream twice indicates how strongly Luke wants us to grasp the narrative's importance for the fledgling Christian community. Luke tells us that Cornelius was a devout man who feared God and, although as a Gentile he was an outsider to the new community, he was willing to be converted.

The significance of this passage can be seen in several fundamental ways. First, it is clear from the narrative that we are being told that the young Christian community is beginning to reach out to people beyond its immediate purview; leaders of the new way are now ready to seek outsiders, Gentiles, who can be added to the Judeo-Christians who comprise the first followers of Jesus. Secondly, this passage demonstrates how the Christian community began to exercise Jesus' ministry of inclusivity in its application to converts. In his earthly life Jesus reached out in a preferential way to the many "outcasts" of his day — to lepers, the poor, tax collectors, prostitutes, even women. Thus, we can see that the message of the gospel is now directly applied by the first Christians in how they will deal with the varied peoples they will encounter in their efforts to evangelize and spread Christ's message to the world. In this passage Luke creates a scene in which old divisions are broken down. Those who had been at odds with each other, namely Jews and Gentiles, are now brought together in one common community of faith. Peter aptly expresses this idea in 10:34, stating, "I truly understand that God shows no partiality, but in every nation anyone who fears him and does what is right is acceptable to him." In other words, God plays no favorites. God is not exclusive in responding to the needs of his people. On the contrary, God is fully inclusive in his relationship with all.

Today's First lesson is the climax of Cornelius' conversion story. Armed with the knowledge that God shows no partiality, it follows directly that the presence of God in the world, the Holy Spirit, should be bestowed upon this Roman officer and his family. This pericope is often referred to as the "Gentile Pentecost," an appropriate appellation since Cornelius is symbolic of all Gentiles to whom the Holy Spirit goes. The irruption of the Spirit descending upon Cornelius and his family confirms Peter's claim that God shows no partiality. Any potential dilemma concerning the baptism of Cornelius is hereby settled. If God has chosen this man and his family, and by extension all Gentiles, then the new way can do nothing but follow.

The scenario depicted in today's First lesson is an example of the theme of conversion that is predominate in Luke-Acts. The evangelist constantly seeks opportunities for people to find their home in the new way that Jesus has inaugurated. Individuals, like Cornelius, who are converted are emblematic of groups to whom the new Christian community must reach out in a special way. Jesus played no favorites and sought followers among all constituencies; God shows no partiality.

Human history is replete with significant examples of systemic injustice. One example of injustice is how governments, partial to some citizens to the detriment of others, were smashed because people were eventually converted to the need for inclusivity in all human relationships. We need look no further than our land to find one significant example of this reality. Even before the official foundation of the United States in 1776 this land existed half slave and half free, a manner of life that was totally inconsistent with the basic Christian principles upon which the foundational documents of this country, the Declaration of Independence, Constitution, and Bill of Rights, are based. The understanding that all people must enjoy "life, liberty, and the pursuit of happiness" was not being followed for some. Abraham Lincoln's "Emancipation Proclamation" of January 1, 1863, looked good on paper, but the reality was that many African Americans did not enjoy the rights and benefits of other United States' citizens. Martin Luther King, Jr., expressed the situation accurately during his famous "I Have a Dream" speech, proclaimed on the footsteps of the Lincoln Memorial in August 1963 during the historic "March on Washington." He told his audience that Lincoln's proclamation was like a promissory note given to slaves that had been repeatedly returned and marked "insufficient funds." Not until Dr. King and his faithful and courageous associates were able to break through the barriers of racism and discrimination during the Civil Rights Movement of the 1960s was a more inclusive attitude toward people of color in this land appreciated.

More recently in history we can see a repeat performance of the smashing of discrimination in the elimination of the apartheid system in the nation of South Africa. Two brave men, a white politician, F. W. DeKlerk, and a black freedom fighter, Nelson Mandela, formed an unlikely alliance in bringing a new day to a nation in the midst of its darkest hour. In a rather short number of years these two courageous men were able to undo a system that had "enslaved" the majority population of a land for almost fifty years. South Africa, like the United States, Peter, and the king in the story, was converted to the need for an inclusive way of thinking. All people were to be equally valued and treated as full participants in the land.

The need for conversion to a more inclusive way of thinking is necessary for all of us in lesser or greater ways. This new or renewed way of thinking must begin with ourselves. Too often today people go about their daily activities with a poor self image. Many people in our contemporary world feel inadequate, believing that others can do things and they cannot. We often believe ourselves to be inadequate or insufficient in many things — our intelligence, physical appearance, personality, athletic prowess, or worldly power or acceptance. We lower ourselves and raise others. When we think like this we, in a very real sense, have excluded ourselves from the equation of life. We, for many varied reasons, consider ourselves inadequate for the task or the possibility before us. We at times need to be converted to the reality that while we might not be the best in any one thing (although we just might be) it is wrong to denigrate, and thereby, exclude ourselves. Such an attitude subjugates part of God's creation. We are just as important and just as capable as the other person. Our need to be inclusive must obviously start at home.

Once we have come to grips with and have accepted our own person as valued, worthy, and important, then we can begin to be converted to a more inclusive understanding of others. This process is initiated by exercising an inclusive attitude toward others. Many times we possess attitudes which are completely contrary to the impartiality God showed in reaching out to the Roman Gentile, Cornelius. We hold and at times share with others exclusive attitudes that separate us from others. We place ourselves, our group, our institution, or our profession above others in an exclusive manner. Such an attitude leads us to believe that we have all the answers and that others have little if anything significant to contribute. We discriminate in our hearts and remove ourselves from others because of differences in race, ethnic origin, religion, political preference, sexual orientation, and even economic livelihood. Such an attitude of self-righteousness is ultimately detrimental to all concerned. It lowers the inherent human dignity of some and falsely exalts the importance and ideas of others. We need to transform our attitudes, as the king and Peter learned, to an understanding of life that appreciates all ideas, people, and ways of being. We might not agree nor participate in many of the varied ways people think today, but we are asked to appreciate the need to be more inclusive.

Once we have righted our self-understanding and attitudes to a more inclusive perspective, then we must demonstrate this renewed self in our actions and words. We are all aware that attitudes translate into action and words and, thus, the need for transformation is clear. At times, possibly without thinking or realizing it, we discriminate against others by associating with some people and refusing to be with others, by being pleasant to one group but totally ignoring another. Sometimes our actions and words are inconsistent with our Christian call, as articulated in the "Golden Rule," to love others as we wish others to love us. Since all people are created, as the book of Genesis tells us, in the image and likeness of

God, actions and words that denigrate others or demonstrate a preference for one at the disdain of another are incompatible with our vocation as followers of Jesus Christ. He followed what the Father asked of him. We, in turn, must follow Christ's lead in being fully inclusive in all that we do and say. Our actions need not be overt. We can communicate a very anti-Christian philosophy of life in all sorts of subtle ways. We must, therefore, be ever conscious of what we say and do so that our lives communicate a Christ-like attitude and manner of life.

The king in the story refused to give his subjects the colors because he wanted to control their lives, but he learned the error of his way. Both the United States and South Africa practiced segregationist and racist policies of social discrimination that were only smashed when the futility of such approaches was revealed. Today, as the Easter season continues, we are challenged to discover and apply to our lives a more equitable, open, and inclusive understanding of life. God chose the Hebrews, but through the life of Jesus Christ all people for all time can enjoy God's benefits and the promise of eternal life. Jesus showed no partiality. Let us, therefore, reach out to others and demonstrate the boldness and inclusivity of God's love. This is the only route to holiness, the common vocation for all God's people. May we in word and action show the face of Christ to all we meet today and each day of our lives.

---

1. "Colors," paraphrased from John R. Aurelio, *Colors! Stories of the Kingdom* (New York: Crossroad, 1993), pp. 134-136.

Ascension Of Our Lord
Acts 1:1-11

Witnesses To The Whole World

A woman involved in a weekly Bible study made a significant discovery quite accidentally in her basement. One day she noticed that some potatoes had sprouted in the darkest corner of the room. At first she could not figure out how they had received any light to grow. Then she noticed that she had hung a copper kettle from a rafter near the cellar window. She kept the kettle so brightly polished that it reflected the rays of the sun onto the potatoes. She exclaimed privately, "When I saw that reflection, I thought, I may not be a preacher or a teacher with the ability to expound upon the scriptures, but at least I can be a copper kettle Christian. I can catch the rays of the Son of God and reflect his light to someone in a dark corner of life."

One day a young missionary spotted a woodcutter hard at work in the forest. "What a perfect opportunity," thought the missionary, when he learned that the woodcutter had never heard of the Lord, "for me to make a convert for Jesus." All day the man chopped wood, carried it to his wagon, and then walked back to chop another load. After a good long time, the missionary, who had been telling the woodcutter about the life and message of Jesus said, "Well, are you ready now to accept and believe in Jesus Christ?" "I don't know," replied the woodcutter. "All day long you spoke to me of this man Jesus who helps us with our burdens and assists us with our daily tasks, but you have never even lifted a finger to help me with mine."

Once there was an old man, a recent convert to Christianity, who used to come to the mission hospital every day and read the

Gospels to the patients. One day the man was having trouble reading, so he went to the doctor for a checkup and eye examination. The doctor examined his eyes and discovered that he was going blind and would probably be totally blind in a year or two. After this day there was no sign of the man at the hospital; no one knew what had happened to him. Eventually one young man found him and brought him again to the mission hospital. The old man explained to all that he had not been reading to the patients because he had been working very hard to memorize the Gospels while he could still see. "Soon I will be back at the hospital," the old man said to one of the missionaries, "and I will continue my work of teaching the Gospel to the patients."

These three short vignettes present one very important idea that is central to the Christian life — our common call to witness to the whole world of the presence, love, and message of Jesus Christ. All are called to witness; all are called to be missionaries; all are called to venture forth as evangelists. This is not simply a task for the hardy and the strong; all are called through baptism to be Jesus' witnesses. Our witness may be some profound act, but most probably it will simply be our hard work, consciously done with Christian love, to assist others in our common journey of faith.

Saint Luke begins his second volume of scripture, describing the life of the early Christian community and the missionary journeys of Saint Paul, by overlapping a bit with the story he just completed in the Gospel, but now providing greater detail. We are told the story of Jesus' ascension to the Father, but the evangelist equips his readers with more information on what the Lord did before he left this world. Jesus knew that the tasks he was about to assign to his chosen followers would not be easy and, thus, he spent sufficient time, we are told forty days, preparing them for the mission that was ahead. Most assuredly during this post-resurrection period the apostles and other disciples were filled with wonder at what Christ had accomplished, but they must have spent much time in reflection and instruction as well, for they certainly remembered that Jesus told them numerous times that he would one day return to the Father. The Lord most assuredly explained their future mission and his expectations for participation by all who would follow the new way.

The disciples, however, seem to be confused about the whole matter. They ask Jesus when he plans to restore the Kingdom, a significant question for the Hebrews, especially now in the wake of Christ's demonstration of power and, for most, clear proof that he was the Messiah. The Kingdom of Israel had been present on two previous occasions, the Davidic dynasty (1000-583 B.C.E.) and the revolt of the Maccabees (165-63 B.C.E.). It seems that the apostles expected Jesus to lead Israel to sovereignty; it appears they were hopeful Jesus would now lead an active revolt against the Romans. But the Lord quickly corrects this misconception by telling his followers that the Holy Spirit will come to them, and it will be their mission to continue his work, to be witnesses, going to Judea, Samaria (the ancient Kingdom of Israel), and even to the ends of the world. Jesus wishes to make it crystal clear that his mission never was to restore the Kingdom of Israel, but rather was to initiate another Kingdom, the reign of God, in our world. The apostles and other disciples of Jesus are being sent forth, not to restore greatness to the land of Israel, but rather to witness to others, proclaiming Jesus' message to them in word and deed. They are to become Christianity's first great ambassadors, the first evangelists tasked with the duty of building day by day the Kingdom of God in contemporary society. We know that Jesus' commission to his disciples was carried out with Paul being sent to the Gentile world of the Mediterranean region, James serving as the head of the Jerusalem Church, and, according to tradition, Thomas traveling to the region of India to establish the faith in that land.

When Jesus left our world, the Kingdom of God in human society had been inaugurated, but the great work associated with the Kingdom had only just begun. Yes, Jesus' ministry was not completed; he left that task to his followers. People have been completing the work of their masters or mentors since the dawn of human civilization. We recall that King David wished to build a great house for God, but he was told that this task would be done later. Solomon, David's son and successor, was the one who completed his father's dream and supervised the construction of the great Temple in Jerusalem. In the world of music, several master works were left unfinished by their composers before their deaths.

One of the most famous such works is Giacomo Puccini's masterful opera, *Turandot*, which was completed by some of this great composer's disciples after his death. More recently in the political spectrum one could say that people like Lyndon Johnson and the Reverend Jesse Jackson worked diligently to continue the great work of building a more just and equitable society, especially in the realm of Civil Rights, after the assassinations of their predecessors and mentors, John F. Kennedy and Martin Luther King, Jr.

The life, ministry, and message of Jesus Christ were, in their essence, centered about witnessing to God's presence, proclaiming God's word, and, thus, evangelizing the world. Jesus, the Son of God, lived a perfect life; he was without sin. He serves, therefore, as the best model of one who demonstrated a good example to those who heard his words and witnessed his deeds. Christ witnessed to the presence and goodness of the Father who sent him into the world. His example was one of humble servitude. Saint Paul captured the essence of Jesus' example in his famous Christological hymn in Philippians (2:6-8): "Though he was in the form of God, [Jesus] did not regard equality with God as something to be exploited, but emptied himself, taking the form of a slave, being born in human likeness. And being found in human form, he humbled himself and became obedient to the point of death — even death on a cross." Jesus certainly taught by example, but the Gospels also show that he taught by word and deed. Those who walked in the footsteps of the Lord were the first great witnesses of God's eminent presence among us. It would be their task to continue Jesus' work to all peoples at all times.

By observing Jesus and following his lead, the apostles and other disciples were placed on the correct path. The disciples of Jesus witnessed to the power and presence of Christ in their lives, demonstrating how they had been transformed by the message of this simple carpenter. In a similar way the Faith began to spread to countless others who were attracted by what they heard and saw in these first followers of Jesus. Now it is the task of all the baptized to accept our commissions to be evangelists, to go forth, in great ways and small, to be ambassadors to the world of the love of Jesus Christ.

214

The concept of evangelization conjures up some rather challenging and possibly for some rather scary images. Most of us have encountered a street preacher or two in our lives. They stand on street corners, in busy intersections, or in prominent places in parks and, with Bible in hand, proclaim a message of hellfire and damnation to those who will not repent and transform their lives. Some of us might encounter or even participate in evangelization in our neighborhoods. It is not uncommon to observe and talk with folks, often couples or entire families, who walk the sidewalks of our community and share their experience and understanding of the Lord with us. These are obviously overt ways of being evangelists and proclaiming God's message to others. This may not be our method of participation, and we may not feel called to such a ministry, but I think most of us do admire and recognize the courage and strength of conviction that such people have in their exercise of the Faith.

Evangelization is much more than street preaching and sharing in our neighborhoods; our vision and focus on this important action should not be so narrow. Every word and each endeavor of our lives, whether we consciously understand it or not, is a special invitation to others to be like us and, therefore, is in a very true and basic way an act of evangelization. We have, therefore, not only a significant opportunity, but an awesome responsibility to do our best to further the Kingdom, to enlighten minds and hearts to Jesus. We are called through baptism, a great common denominator to all Christians, to witness to Christ's presence and love. In other words, we are all called to be evangelists. We are called to proclaim God's message, minister in God's name, and at least initiate in others a change of heart and mind, what the Greeks call *metanoia*. We are to do this task at all times and seasons, whether the time "is favorable or unfavorable" (2 Timothy 4:2).

We may believe in our highly technological world, a place which affords the best in rapid transportation and almost instantaneous communication, that there is no longer a need for evangelists. We might mistakenly conclude that the world already knows Christ, that few peoples in the world have not at least been introduced to Jesus. This might lead us to think, therefore, that the great

215

mission of the apostles has been completed; there is no need today for evangelization. While it might be true that few people today are not in some fashion aware of Jesus Christ and who Christians claim Him to be, there may be in contemporary society an even greater need to be evangelists than in any time since Constantine accepted Christianity as the official religion of the Roman Empire in 313. Our mission today might more accurately be termed re-evangelization.

Peoples in the so-called first world, especially we who live in the United States, badly need to return to the road that leads to Christ, for we have taken many other roads, which have led us, through the technology, prosperity, and sense of self-autonomy that dominates our society, away from our true destination. Many of us have fallen victim to commercialism and to the abundance that we see all around us. Why should we be concerned about Jesus' message to die to self, to suffer, and to accept challenge when I have the ability today to have almost anything I could possibly desire? Some people today have fallen prey to their own vices and self-centeredness. Unfortunately, it is rare today to see someone who is willing to give up his or her self autonomy so as to promote the common good of all. We prefer, at times even demand, rather, to do what we want to do and when we want to do it. We further our own cause and possibly a cadre of important people in our lives. Many people today are rather unconcerned with the needs of others; they, as they say, "do their own thing." It is truly sad to say, but it is true, that some people in our society of abundance have given up on God. For some, as remarkable as it sounds, God has become irrelevant. Some of these people have become impatient with God, leading them to abandon trust and hope when God does not act on their time table and in the manner they believe is correct. Others believe that they have all the answers they need in the world, through science or other human constructs, and thus have cast God aside. Why believe in a being who cannot be seen and a message that is totally foreign to our contemporary experience?

Human society, especially those of us in the first world, needs to re-discover the message of Jesus Christ and apply it to our daily lives. We, in short, need to be re-evangelized. As Christians we have both the privilege and the responsibility to act and be evangelists. We cannot rest on our laurels and expect others to do our tasks. Evangelization is the work of all people and it is best carried out in our day-to-day lives of faith. Words of encouragement, random acts of kindness, attitudes that demonstrate an inclusive understanding of life — these are the elements of evangelization today. We might stand on the street corner or go door-to-door with Jesus' message, but the simple everyday actions of our lives will speak more profoundly about who we are, the things we believe, and the one whom we follow than all of our great overtures. Let us, therefore, be the copper kettle that reflects God's love to others. Let us be the one who is always willing to lend a hand in assistance. Let us be the one who will go the extra mile to bring Christ's message to those in darkness and ignorance. The task will not be easy and the rewards today will be few, at least as this world would so judge. But our efforts will be witnessed by God, our work will be blessed, and we, through such means, will find God and eternal life.

It's Never Mission Impossible

Many years ago one of the most popular shows on weekly television was *Mission Impossible*. Each episode of the show opened in a similar way. The head of the Impossible Missions Force, or IMF for short, would be found alone in some isolated office, home, or similar space. He would find a large manilla envelope, generally hidden in a desk drawer or possibly in a safe. Inside the envelope he would find materials that described the next mission of his IMF team. There would be lots of printed material, photographs of the principal people involved, and often maps to show various locations. While the IMF chief perused these materials, he listened to a tape recording which described the specifics of the mission. After reviewing the material and describing the mission, the voice on the tape always said, "If you choose to accept this mission and any of your IMF team is captured or killed, the secretary will disavow any knowledge of your activity." The voice then signed off, saying, "Good luck, Jim," and the tape would self-destruct. The credits then rolled on the screen and the episode would begin.

At the outset of each mission the IMF team gathered to plan its strategy. The force chief described the nature of the mission and the objective. Then each team member was assigned specific tasks that needed to be completed in order for the mission to be successful. It was clear in this planning phase that the team must work together and that each person's contribution was significant. The team needed to be complete; the loss of one person or the failure of one assignment could bring disaster to the overall mission. But if the team worked together and if all members of the force successfully completed their assigned tasks, then the mission would be accomplished and the Impossible Missions Force would once again save the day.

Hollywood can, of course, manufacture plots and make things happen in film so that missions can be accomplished. While the program *Mission Impossible* may have aired certain episodes that seemed implausible, the overall concept of what the show was trying to demonstrate, namely that if people work together as a team, each doing his or her specific job well and completely, then absolutely no mission is impossible, was sound.

Realistically speaking, I suppose the apostles of Jesus Christ may have thought that the task given them by their Lord and Savior was "mission impossible." They were present when Jesus told them, "Go therefore and make disciples of all nations, baptizing them in the name of the Father and of the Son and of the Holy Spirit, and teaching them to obey everything that I have commanded you." Certainly such a mission was not to be taken lightly; it would have been a great challenge. Even Jesus' promise, "And remember, I am with you always, to the end of the age" (Matthew 28:19-20), may have been little consolation. Engaging such a mission, in the minds of the apostles, could not possibly have been anything but an uphill battle, possibly an impossible mission. They were to go into a hostile world and speak to many peoples and nations unknown to them. They were asked to proclaim and preach the message of salvation through Christ crucified, a missive that Saint Paul says "is foolishness to those who are perishing, but to us who are being saved it is the power of God" (1 Corinthians 1:18). This was a paradoxical message that was hard to comprehend and even more difficult to accept. The apostles had been given a great, possibly impossible mission, and the leader who presented this significant challenge would not be with them in its daily living. Jesus had returned to the Father; he was no longer physically present with his faithful followers. He had promised the Spirit, but a team with such a difficult mission without its captain and leader is crippled at best.

The apostles were not only hampered by the fact that Jesus was no longer with them, the team itself was now incomplete as a result of the defection of Judas. Thus, during the period immediately after

Jesus' ascension there was a true and immediate need to get the "new way" community ready for the mission that had been inaugurated, but left incomplete. Judas had betrayed the cause, but the work which Jesus gave to his followers and the exhortation and challenge he presented could not be ignored. This process of preparation had to begin with the restoration of the apostolic circle. Thus, we hear in today's first lesson a passage which speaks of leadership in the early Christian community. In fact, the whole second half of the first chapter of Acts describes leadership in the new community of faith.

It was essential before a replacement for Judas was made that the leadership understand and fully acknowledge that the team's fractured existence was destined to be. Peter is clear in his speech that all that happened was necessary to fulfill the Scriptures and the purposes of God. Even tragic events such as Jesus' crucifixion and Judas' betrayal of the Lord must be viewed as part of God's master plan. Peter, the appointed head of the apostles, wants the others to know that no failure or deceit to be discovered in the world in the accomplishment of the mission will not be first encountered in the church. Peter's denial and Judas' betrayal of Jesus were necessary in the overall scheme and plan of God. These events demonstrated the humanity of those who would engage the mission and the failures that would happen. The task which Jesus gave to the apostles and to all who would follow his lead would not be easy, but it would not be mission impossible either. The mission would be difficult, but one well worth the effort expended in its accomplishment.

The need to complete the apostolic circle brought the leaders of the new way together to choose a successor to Judas. The fledgling community did not wish to engage the mission until it was fully prepared and its leadership was whole. We recall from our reading of the Hebrew Scriptures of the importance of the number twelve, beginning with the twelve tribes of Israel. This special number represented unity and wholeness. Thus, as we heard, lots were cast between two men, Joseph and Matthias, and the lot went to Matthias. Now that the leadership team was once again whole, the community was ready to engage the mission as witnesses to the power and presence of God in the world. Together, as a team and

221

guided by the Holy Spirit, their work would be fruitful and the mission which seemed so impossible would be accomplished.

Life today is a struggle which, with the passing of time, only seems to become more complex. Difficult tasks in life, what we might perceive to be impossible missions, are the reality of our daily life. We experience these in the mission of the Church, the charge of society to make the world a better place, and in our own personal lives. We should not lose heart at what seems a daunting set of tasks, for many people and communities before us have faced the same challenges and been successful.

The Hebrew Scriptures are filled with examples of courageous people who accomplished what certainly must have seemed to be impossible missions. We recall how God called Abram, a wandering Semite, to leave all he knew, be the father of a great nation, and follow a path that he would be shown. Moses was given the "impossible mission" of leading 600,000 of his fellow Israelites from bondage in Egypt, through the desert for forty years to the promised land. We remember as well how Samson defeated the Philistines, David slew Goliath, Solomon built the Temple, Jonah converted the Ninevites, and the great prophets such as Isaiah, Jeremiah, and Ezekiel fearlessly spoke God's word to unsympathetic, disinterested, and even hostile crowds. In each case God provided the assistance, words, or actions needed to complete what may at the time have appeared to be an impossible mission.

Jesus also had an important mission on earth, one that he at times might have thought to be mission impossible. He was asked to convert his fellow Jews to a new and higher understanding of God. Jesus was asked to gather all people and tell them that henceforth God's loving plan was for all people for all time. For those with eyes of faith it was clear that Jesus was God, but the Lord's mission was made no easier by this revelation. I am certain in his human nature Jesus must at times have believed that his task was mission impossible. He was accepted by very few; many of those who followed him could not understand his teaching. He was betrayed by one of his inner circle and was denied three times by the one whom Jesus himself hand-picked to be his earthly successor. Yet, through it all, Jesus' life and most especially his passion, death,

222

and resurrection brought salvation history, initiated by the obedience of Abram, to its climax. Jesus' redemptive act of love on the cross brought the possibility of salvation to all people for all time. Jesus completed his mission impossible.

The mission of Christianity today appears to be increasingly more impossible in an environment that is not open to the message of Christ. Our collective mission as God's holy people is not easy. We are called through our baptism, and, thereby, our common vocation to holiness, to evangelize others, to witness through every word and action, and to preach and proclaim God's message of peace and love to an often hostile and unwelcoming world. We are called as well to the service of our sisters and brothers. We cannot sit idly by and think "the other guy will do it." Christians are called to be a leaven in the world, to raise the level of consciousness and action on the part of all peoples. If God's people, the Christian community, work together, share the burden, and assist each other, the day-to-day mission of the church will be accomplished. We will build God's Kingdom stone by stone.

The mission of the church is complemented by the work of secular society. As the Church must be a leaven to the world, so must each Christian who participates in society be leaven to raise the business world, the political arena, and the economic front to higher levels. By maintaining our personal standards at high plateaus and challenging others to follow our lead, we help raise society's contribution to the construction of the Kingdom in our world. This, without question, is a tall order, but society will certainly fail and an impossible mission will exist if we neglect our duty to make the necessary contribution to the whole.

We will face many difficult challenges in our personal lives, tasks that may seem to be impossible missions. In the journey of our working days we will face trying situations. We may face obstacles that will not allow us to work as we want. Coercion, threat, or the temptation of reward may "force" us to do things or take short-cuts which we know might hurt or ill-effect another. We may be required to relocate in order to stay with the company or worse still our job might be lost. At such times we wonder what we will do and what the future will hold. Families experience many difficult challenges.

223

Some people are asked to walk the road of ill-health with a spouse, child, sister, brother, or another relative. Tough love may be required in our relationship with one who suffers from addiction. Many people must suffer the pain of observing a loved one reject God and the church and opt for the things of the world. All of us will one day face the death of one close to us. Our Christian faith will also bring us challenges. We pray fervently to God for our needs, yet our prayers are not answered in the way or time that we want; we might even feel God has abandoned us. Sometimes we lose sight of the road; we move off the track or even reverse course in our journey to God.

We will experience difficult times in our life, with our jobs, our families, and our Christian faith, challenges which may seem to be impossible missions. But if we, like Abram, Moses, the prophets, the apostles, and Jesus, can persevere and continue on the road, then God will recognize and reward our efforts. The task will not be easy; the road to God has pitfalls and obstacles. Saint Paul advised his friend Timothy of this reality, "Join with me in suffering for the gospel, relying on the power of God" (2 Timothy 1:8). But he also assured him, "If we have died with him we will also live with him; if we endure, we will also reign with him; if we deny him, he will also deny us; if we are faithless, he remains faithful — for he cannot deny himself" (2 Timothy 2:11-13).

We must constantly re-evaluate our lives and renew our determination to walk the journey of life which one day will lead to union with God. It will not be an easy journey, if taken seriously, but it is the only path that will one day lead to eternal life. As the Easter season draws to a close, let us be mindful of the Spirit's presence in our midst. Let us believe that if we keep the team intact, if we fully engage the mission, we will be successful. The task will seldom be easy, but then Jesus' victory over death and his inauguration of the Kingdom were won at a very high price. As his followers we can expect nothing better than he received. May we know God's presence in our lives as we go forth to do the Lord's work, fully confident that with his help we can do the difficult today and the impossible will be accomplished tomorrow. Our reward in heaven will be great!

Sermons On The First Readings

For Sundays
After Pentecost
(First Third)

Linda R. Forsberg

"I came so that you might have life, life in all its fullness."
— Jesus, according to the Gospel of John, 10:10

"The glory of God is a human being fully alive."
— Saint Iranaeus

I dedicate these sermons to the glory of God
and to the people of my church
First Evangelical Lutheran Church
of East Greenwich, Rhode Island,
in whose faces I see the glory of God reflected
and in whose lives I see that glory lived.

Foreword

I am a Lutheran pastor. We Lutherans are really big on grace. I am not one for bumper stickers, but there is one I feel no qualms about plastering boldly to the bumper of my aged Volvo. It says simply: "Grace happens." To me it is a wonderful turning upside down of the bumper sticker more popular in our contemporary American culture: "#@%! happens." Bad "stuff" definitely does happen. But God is constantly trying to break through with grace.

We Lutherans believe that this grace comes to us each and every day in many and various ways. But we also teach that it comes to us always and profoundly in two very special ways which we call "the Means of Grace." We define "the Means of Grace" as God's Word and Sacraments. Luther taught that the Canon of God's Word is open and ongoing. In other words, the Word of God continues, living and active. Luther taught that the Word of God continues when it is rightly preached, and also when it is shared in our "mutual conversation and consolation." The living Word, Christ, comes to us through one another, when we speak a word of comfort, a word of hope, a word of encouragement, a word of strength, when we live in such a way that our lives proclaim a word of light in the gloom, a word of justice in an unfair world, a final word of Life even in the face of death.

God's Word is also fleshed out for us in the gift of the sacraments of holy baptism and holy communion. Luther said that every morning when we wash our faces, we should remember our baptisms. Three years ago I baptized a 25-year-old young woman in the ocean. That day, in addition to being her friend and pastor, I also became her godmother. That day, the meaning of our baptisms gripped me as never before. This young woman had been through a great deal of struggle in her life. One day she had come to my office, where — nervous, but with clear, wide-open, yearning eyes

— she said plainly, "I want to be baptized." She ached to die to all the pain of her past, and to rise to new life. As I plunged her three times beneath the surface of a tumultuous sea, "In the name of the Father, and of the Son, and of the Holy Spirit," the words we had just read on the sandy shore came alive: "Do you not know that all of us who have been baptized into Christ Jesus were baptized into his death? We were buried therefore with him by baptism into death *so that as Christ was raised from the dead by the glory of the Father, we too might walk in newness of life"* (Romans 6:3-4). Every day when we wash our faces, we should remember our baptisms. Every day, when the struggles and pains, storms and tumults of this life threaten to overwhelm us, we should remember the One who keeps our heads above water, and helps us rise up to new life.

The One who holds us up also feeds us, daily nourishes and strengthens us. We Lutherans believe that in the sacrament of holy communion, Jesus is truly present, coming to us, feeding us "in, with, and under" the bread and wine. At our church we begin the celebration of holy communion with the invitation: "Here at First Lutheran Church we celebrate open communion because we believe that Jesus invites all people to this table of grace." Many have told me afterwards how they experienced the risen Christ as he came to them through that gracious invitation, and through that sacred meal.

Christ has turned my own life completely around, and inside out. I love God and God's Word passionately. God's Word and sacraments empower every breath of my life. The people of my church have told me that my sermons have helped them to understand God's Word and that they have helped to make God's Word alive and active in their own lives. Thanks be to God! I tried to comply with the editor's request to change all first person illustrations to the third person. In so doing I came to realize that the whole personality of these sermons changed dramatically for the worse. What people say they appreciate most about my sermons is their immediate, "real," down-to-earth, "from the trenches," sometimes almost gritty style. In the third person these sermons became distant, awkward, artificial, and stilted. The editor graciously acquiesced. I do hope that you will be able to share these sermons and/or illustrations, adapting them and making them your own in a way that works for you.

But preaching is a strange thing. It is a kind of participatory, interactive thing. People will sometimes tell me how "such and such," which I said in one of my sermons, helped them to get through a difficult time, changed them, comforted them, challenged them. I frequently think, "I never said that!" I've even scanned through old manuscripts, and concluded, "Yep, I never said that." I have come to believe, however, that that is what they heard. Furthermore I have come to believe that this was not a "mistake," but rather the Holy Spirit at work in the space between. If the Word of God is alive and active, and I fully believe that it is, then the Holy Spirit could ignite some kind of Living Word between the words that leave my mouth and the words that prick your conscience, grip your heart, set your mind on fire, and change the way you live your life.

I foolishly have wondered whether this will happen when an oral/aural, participatory, interactive medium like preaching takes a different form — a visual, written form. I say "foolishly" because I am immediately reminded that that is what the Word of God is all about. An oral and aural tradition written down only to become oral/aural again. Who am I to doubt or limit the working of the Holy Spirit — to doubt or limit the power of the Word of God to become alive and active?

My hope and my prayer is that through my humble offering of this little collection of sermons, God's grace will break through to you, Christ the living Word will speak to you, the Holy Spirit will breathe its empowering breath into your life. My hope and my prayer is that you may know that not only does grace happen, but that it happens *for you*. My hope and my prayer is that you live your life in gratitude and in response, until, as the Scottish theologian George MacDonald, said, "Our lives to Thine are answer and Amen."

In Christ our Life,
Linda R. Forsberg, a.k.a. "Pastor Linda"

Thanks to Elizabeth Fielding for proofreading this manuscript, and for *so much more*, to Paul Verduchi for his wisdom and technical assistance with my computer, and to my children for putting up with me during the preparation of this manuscript. LF

Pentecost
Ezekiel 37:1-14; Acts 2:1-21

The More

In seminary there was a very popular saying. One church even had it written on a huge banner which hung directly beneath the pulpit. It read: "Jesus Christ came to comfort the disturbed/challenged, and to disturb/challenge the comfortable."

Let us pray: O God, this day we gather around your Word and sacrament, and some of us are feeling very disturbed by all of the struggles and challenges of this life. We pray that your Word and sacrament may comfort those of us who are disturbed this day. But God, some of us gathered here this day are much too comfortable. And so we pray that your Word and your sacraments would disturb those of us who are too comfortable — *would challenge us to grow more fully into the people you would have us be*. In Christ our resurrected Lord, we pray. Amen.

It was new members Sunday. As usual, the church had a big celebration to welcome the new members, one of whom was a lovely young woman. This young woman's mother even came to visit that Sunday from out of state, to celebrate the day with her daughter. On the way out of church, the mother introduced herself to me, shook hands, then awkwardly gave me a hug, as she did so whispering into my ear, "Pastor, please call my daughter ... she's very sick ... cancer." I called. I then visited the young woman and her husband in their home. Clear-eyed and straightforward, she explained to me that she had cancer of the pancreas, for which there is no cure. It is terminal.

The young woman and her husband continued to attend worship together. But as the months went by, and her illness progressed, hospice called to let me know that the young woman had now entered the final stage of her illness, to ask if I would come to be with her in these final days, and to ask if some of the members of our church family could take shifts just being there with her when the other family members and hospice workers could not be there.

I went to see her. It was a gloriously sunny, warm day, all the signs of spring's new life bursting into bloom. I entered her room, and was taken aback to see this beautiful young woman now shrunken to half the size she had been ... lying in her bed.

Now you might think that because I am a pastor, I can walk into a room like that and know just what to say and do. That is *not* the case. In fact, I felt a lot like I imagine the prophet Ezekiel felt when he stood in that valley of bones. Like Ezekiel, I felt overwhelmed. Completely inadequate. Like Ezekiel I thought to myself, "What can I possibly say, possibly do?"

Ezekiel was called by God to preach to a people whose hope was as dried up as that valley of bones. Ezekiel was called to proclaim a message of resurrection, of new life, of something *so much more* to a people whose spirit had been crushed when they had been conquered by their most hated enemies, the Babylonians. Their enemies had destroyed Jerusalem, their holy city, had seized their holy vessels as booty, and had rounded up their leaders and marched them into captivity in Babylon, where they lived in exile some fifty years. When called by God to proclaim a message of new life to this defeated, hopeless people, Ezekiel felt as though he were preaching to a valley of dry bones.

That is how the struggles and defeats of this life so often feel.

That is how I felt when I entered that woman's room.

I asked myself, "What *on earth* can I say to this woman? What *on earth* can I do for her?" The answer is: nothing. There is nothing "on earth" we can say. Nothing "on earth" we can do. But one thing that I have learned in this daily walk — this journey through life as a Christian — is that as inadequate as we are, we have One who walks beside us, and within us, every step of the journey — though we frequently fail to recognize it. We have One who leads us through that valley. We have with us One who does have something to say — something to do — which will share strength, comfort, and hope

232

beyond our understanding. One who is powerful enough to bring Life even to dry bones.

So, in times like that I let the Creator of the Universe, the Spirit of Life, Jesus, take over. I sit there and I let the One who is the resurrection and the Life do his thing. I simply take out the Word and the Sacrament. I set the table, and let Jesus be the Host.

The Word I opened to was 2 Corinthians 4:

> *Therefore, since it is by God's mercy that we are engaged in this ministry, we do not lose heart ... But we have this treasure in clay jars [some older translations read "earthen vessels"], so that it may be clear that this extraordinary power belongs to God and does not come from us. We are afflicted in every way, but not crushed; perplexed, but not driven to despair; persecuted, but not forsaken; struck down, but not destroyed; always carrying in our bodies the death of Jesus, so that the life of Jesus may also be made visible in our bodies. For while we live we are always being given up to death for Jesus' sake, so that the life of Jesus may be made visible in our mortal flesh. So death is at work in us, but Life in you. So we do not lose heart. Even though our outer nature is wasting away, our inner nature is being renewed day by day. For this [in comparison] slight momentary affliction is preparing us for an eternal weight of glory which is beyond all measure, because we look not at what is seen but at what cannot be seen; for what can be seen is temporary, but what can not be seen is eternal.* (parenthetical elements mine)

I was cut to the heart, my eyes were opened, and I recognized the resurrected Christ there in that room, in the young woman's luminous face nodding "Yes" to those words.

We broke bread together, our hearts burned within us, and we recognized the risen Christ in the breaking of the bread.

The Church proclaims that God comes to us every step of the journey — every moment of our Christian walk through this life — in all things — everything! *But* the Church also teaches that

God — God's *grace* — comes to us *most powerfully* through two *means*: *word and sacrament*.

This is comforting. This is also disturbing — challenging.

It is comforting because when we face that valley, when we lie in that bed, or sit beside that bed, we know that as inadequate as we are, all we have to do is take out God's Word, set the table for the sacramental meal, and Jesus takes over. God is with us. The Spirit breathes its Life into our dry bones.

It is challenging because ... if you are not breaking open the Word of God every day, throughout each and every day of your walk down this road of life, then you are not "on the road to Emmaus." You have taken a detour, fallen into a ditch, not on "the Way."

Every day in our Christian walk we are to live sacramentally. Luther says every morning when we wash our faces, we are to remember our baptisms — to remember that every day we need to die with Christ to those things we know we need to die to, and rise with Christ to a new beginning — a new way of life. Every day we are to live out our baptisms.

We also are to share in the sacrament of holy communion at every opportunity. Maybe we should offer it daily as the Catholic Church does: bread for the journey of that day. We need Jesus, the living bread's presence, *each and every day*.

I ask you this day, do you live *daily* in God's Word? Do you live sacramentally each and every day?

Today we celebrate the Feast of Pentecost. In ancient times Jews celebrated Pentecost, *Pente* meaning "five," on the fiftieth day after the Passover. The Passover commemorates the people of Israel's escape from slavery in Egypt, the angel of death "passing over" the lives of those whose homes were marked with the blood of the lamb, and their journey through the wilderness of this life — toward the Promised Land. Jews from all over the ancient world gathered in Jerusalem to celebrate the giving of the Law (God's Word) to Moses atop Mount Sinai. In today's text, Acts, chapter 2, Peter preaches that Jesus is the fulfillment of this Word of God — "This Jesus whom *you* crucified."

The people heard this Word of God and they were "cut to the heart." Disturbed. Challenged. Miraculously, they repented. The

Greek word for repentance is *metanoia*, which literally means "had a change of mind, heart, lives," — "turned" from sin and turned back toward God.

God came to them in this disturbing, challenging Word.

"What can we do?" they asked. Their eyes had been opened. "You can receive God in sacrament." We read that 3,000 were baptized that day.

God in Word and Sacrament.

If you look at the context for today's reading from Acts 2, you see that later, in verse 42, after the 3,000 were baptized, "They devoted themselves to the apostles' teaching [Word] and fellowship [Greek "communion"], to the breaking of bread and the prayers [Greek, "Eucharist"]."

Word and Sacrament. *That* is how we grow into the people God desires us to be.

Recently I received a call from a member of the parish, who said he needed to make an appointment to speak with me. He said he'd take me to lunch. I became concerned. The man had a beautiful family, and I hoped nothing was wrong.

There we sat at lunch, and the man said to me, "Pastor, I've been thinking a lot about your recent pastoral letter to the congregation, the one with the headline, 'Challenge for Growth.' Well ... as you know, I responded to your challenge, making a commitment to grow in God's word by reading and praying with scripture daily. So every morning before work, I get up and read my Bible. I've been reading the Gospel of John. Then I pray with the scripture passage. Well ... the more I read God's Word and the more I pray, I feel ... I don't know how to explain it ... but I feel God calling me to something *more*. I don't know yet what the *more* is, but God is definitely calling me to *more* service, to grow *more*, to serve God and the people of God *more*."

A violent, mighty wind of the Holy Spirit blew through the Main Street Grille — and the flame of the Holy Spirit ignited souls on fire as much as it did in Jerusalem 2,000 years ago!

That's what the Christian life is all about. When you are living in the Word of God, as the writer Annie Dillard says, you'd better put on your helmet and strap yourself in, because you are about to be *launched* into a life you never thought possible — into *the most exciting adventure* — into a journey beyond your wildest imagination — into the *more*!

Saint Ignatius of Loyola, the founder of the Jesuit order, wrote a little book of what he calls "Spiritual Exercises." In these exercises Ignatius taught that if we call ourselves Christian, then our lives are *always about the more. Always about growth.*

But church growth — the *more* of the Christian life — is *not* just about growing *numerically.* It is more about growing in God's Word and in sacramental and sacrificial living and giving. How do *you* receive that pastoral invitation to *grow* in God's word by reading scripture and praying daily? What is *your* response? If you think coming to worship once a week is all there is to the Christian life, think about it this way: you are eating just one meal a week. What would happen to your body if you ate just once a week? What would happen if you only saw your partner for an hour and fifteen minutes a week?

Jesus Christ came to challenge the comfortable.

Numerical church growth is *great.* But financial growth frequently lags way behind. Jesus Christ today challenges you who are too comfortable. To live, and give sacrificially.

Today Jesus Christ challenges you and me in Word and Sacrament to walk with him a path which is *so much more.*

Some 125 years ago 41 Swedish immigrants, some families, some individuals, gathered together as a church. They ministered to each other. They met in people's homes. They gathered around the Word of God. They fed each other with God's Word ... and the Holy Spirit blew in and among them in a mighty wind and the flame of the Holy Spirit kindled their hearts ... and they *grew.*

For the first seventeen years of their congregational life they were without a pastor, and they *grew.*

One hundred and twenty-five years later, as they celebrated their anniversary, they said to their newly called pastor, "Pastor, you should have seen us in the year before you came, when we were searching for a pastor. Wow! The Holy Spirit was among us. We followed right along in the footsteps of those original 41 members. We pulled together as a team, each one of us sharing our gifts of the Spirit, and we made it. But I think when you came, a lot of people sat back and said, 'Whew! Now we can relax and let the pastor do it all!' "

That's not what church growth is about. That's not what the *more* of Christian life is about.

Think of the growth that could take place if you continued, each person sharing the gifts of the Holy Spirit, *with a pastor!*

More and more church signs are reading: Ministers of this Church: ALL ITS MEMBERS. The pastor's job is not to be the church for you, but rather to feed the flock with Word and Sacrament *so that you are nourished and strengthened for your ministries!*

The gifts of the Spirit are given *to all of us* for the common good — for the building up of the whole body of Christ (1 Corinthians 12:7).

Church growth — the *more* of the Christian life — is not about a bigger building. As churches grow numerically, there are always those who insist that we need a new building. *Do we?*

There is a possible alternative. In her book *The Call to Commitment*, Elizabeth O'Connor writes about an alternative model, the Church of the Savior in Washington, D.C. The Church of the Savior has no building. It meets in a house, maintaining a low overhead. The Church of the Savior has not relaxed its membership requirements to gain numerical growth. In fact, to join the church you have to be *actively* involved for at least a year. You have to be living in God's Word. You have to be tithing, or at least giving sacrificially. And you have to be an active part of a small group ministry/mission group. As a mission group gets strong, they send it off to start a new, committed community of faith. "As the Father has sent me, even so I send you" (John 20:21).

The Church of the Savior is a model of the Christian life that is disturbing. Challenging. Jesus Christ came to disturb the comfortable. Perhaps churches should think about the alternative of being *intentionally small — a caring family* rather than a megachurch. Perhaps we could be the "Ben and Jerry's" or "Tom's of Maine" of churches.

Instead of expanding a building, how about expanding a ministry?

237

Instead of a $2,000,000 building campaign, how about a $2,000,000 ministry to people in need?

Unrealistic? You bet! Impossible? With God all things are possible!

When my marriage ended, I went through a time where I felt skeptical about marriage. I remember asking a friend, "Do you think marriage is really realistic? Do you think monogamy is even possible?"

I'll never forget his answer. He said. "Realistic? Absolutely not! Possible? Yes!"

He compared it to the ballet. He said when he goes to the ballet, he sits in awe and watches the human body fly through the air in leaps and pirouettes!

Is it realistic for the human body to attempt such things? Absolutely not!

Is it possible? You bet!

Sisters and brothers, on this day when we celebrate the Holy Spirit entering the valley of dry bones and breathing into them the breath of new life, on this day when we celebrate the Holy Spirit coming in a mighty wind and kindling the hearts of all present to go forth in mighty acts of power, on this day when we celebrate the Holy Spirit 125 years ago blowing in the lives of those 41 lay people, the founding fathers and mothers of our community of faith, and kindling their hearts to *grow* as the body of Christ, on this day when we remember the Word and sacrament burning within the hearts and lives of pastors and people, let us pray that the Holy Spirit will blow mightily among *us*, setting our hearts on *fire*, empowering *us* to *grow* in *God's Word and sacraments, in ministry and mission, to grow into the more, together becoming unrealistic with God who makes all things possible!* Amen!

The Trinity

Today we celebrate the Festival of the Holy Trinity. God the Father, Son, and Holy Spirit. God our Creator, Redeemer, and Sustainer. In the Trinity we also celebrate a God who exists "in relationship" — to us, to all of creation, and even within God's very Self. Following the model of a children's sermon, today we will focus on a visual aid for adults: the cross, as a symbol of the Trinity. Maybe you've never thought of the cross as a symbol of the Trinity, but rather as a symbol just for Jesus. But think about it: the vertical beam symbolizing God the Father, the Creator, the transcendent aspect of God, coming down to earth; in other words, the vertical dimension of our relationship with God. The horizontal beam of the cross can symbolize the Holy Spirit, who extends horizontally, living and breathing in all that is. The point of intersection, the heart of the cross, symbolizes Jesus Christ, whose heart loved so much that he gave his life there on that cross for you and for me and for all.

When we cross ourselves, which by the way is okay for non-Catholics to do, we do so as we say, "In the name of the Father, and of the Son, and of the Holy Spirit," or, "In the name of God our Creator, Redeemer, and Sustainer." But I once heard a Lutheran pastor describe it a different way. He said when we cross ourselves, we should pray, "May God be in my mind, in my heart, and in my whole being, Amen."

Raise your hands. How many of you think of God in terms of the first aspect of the Trinity — pray to and relate to God as your Father/Creator? How many of you think of God, relate and pray to

239

God in terms of the second aspect of the Trinity, Jesus Christ? How many of you think of God, relate and pray to God in terms of the third person of the Trinity, the Holy Spirit?

Ah-*ha*! The Holy Spirit always gets short shrift! It is the aspect of the Trinity which we understand the least.

Today, we will briefly explore each of these three aspects of the Trinity, paying particular attention to the often neglected aspect, that of the Holy Spirit.

We see, in fact, the three Aspects of the Trinity — in each of our three readings assigned for this day.

First let us consider the Vertical Arm of the Cross: God the Father, God our Creator. This is the part of the Trinity we focus on in the first article of the Apostle's Creed. Say it with me: "I believe in God the Father Almighty, Creator of heaven and earth."

How many of you remember Martin Luther's explanation to the first article of the Apostle's Creed? When I was in confirmation, we had to memorize it. It begins with, "I believe that God created me and all that exists." God — the Creator — lives in relationship with all of creation, and within Godself.

In today's passage from the book of the prophet Isaiah, it is this first aspect of the Trinity which is revealed: the Almighty God, powerful, transcendent — of which we, like Isaiah, stand in awe. In Isaiah's magnificent vision of our Creator God, God is surrounded by attendant cherubim and seraphim, seated upon a majestic throne, and arrayed in glorious splendor. Before such a God we fall to our knees in fear (Hebrew literally, "awe") and trembling. This Creator aspect of God pours forth in the majesty of creation: the Grand Canyon, depths of the ocean, Mount Everest, moon, stars, constellations, planets, galaxies, and in each newborn child, as Shakespeare said, "So fresh from God."

This is I AM. This is the God who always was, and is, and is to come! Wow!

Young children, I have noticed, connect deeply with this aspect of God, the Creator dimension of the Trinity. They live in constant awe of the mystery and miracle of God coming to us in God's creation. They spend hours watching insects at work, cloud formations moving across the sky, what we would think of as the

240

most ordinary of rocks, wind, rain, snow, sand, dirt. If you want to grow in your relationship with God as Creator, explore God's creation with a young child.

Every year, when our confirmation program begins, I conclude our first class with a time of devotion, focusing on Psalm 8. I take the youth outside, make them lie flat on their backs, and look up at the night sky, as I recite the words: "O, Lord, my Lord, how majestic is your name in all the earth! ... when I consider the heavens, the work of your hands, the moon and the stars, which you have made ... what are we mere human beings that you are mindful of us, and yet you have made us just a little lower than the angels? ... O, Lord, my Lord, how majestic is your name in all the earth!" As these fourteen and fifteen year olds gaze up at the stars, I tell them, "If this is all you remember from confirmation class, it will be sufficient: *that the One who created all of this created you and lives within you — the power that created all of this is within you — and you have access to this power every moment for the living of your life!*"

Ahhh ... God, our Creator.

Let us for a moment skip over Jesus, the second article of the Apostle's Creed and consider the Holy Spirit, the aspect of the Trinity that fewest people relate to. I think this aspect of the Trinity becomes important to us later in life. In Hebrew the Holy Spirit is a feminine word, "she," *ruach*. In Greek the Holy Spirit is a neuter word, but a feminine concept, *pneuma*, "it;" for some reason usually translated "he." In both Hebrew and Greek the same word is used to mean: "wind, breath, and spirit."

Wind. What does that teach us about the Holy Spirit? Can you see wind? Touch it? Grab hold of it? No, but you can feel it and you can see the effects of it. The things it moves. You can see and feel its power. Just like the Holy Spirit. It can be as blasting as a hurricane, or as gentle, subtle, calm, and soothing as a refreshing summer breeze.

Without the Spirit, we are flat and lifeless, like an empty windsock or a sail hanging limp, but with it, we are like a windsock filled with a summer breeze, or a sail, filled with a mighty wind. We are alive, beautiful, full, vibrant, soaring, sailing. There's no stopping us!

In addition to meaning "wind," the word for Spirit also means "breath." Take a deep breath. If Spirit means breath, where is the Holy Spirit?

Inside you! Within you, and every living, breathing creature! It is as close to you as your next breath! In fact, every breath you take is the Holy Spirit living and breathing within you! And breathing out from you into the world all around you! The One who created all of this lives and breathes within you and me, sustaining us every moment of our day.

The third article of the Apostles' Creed, which we say week after week, is all about the work of the Holy Spirit. Say it with me: "I believe in the Holy Spirit, the holy catholic church, the communion of saints, the forgiveness of sins, the resurrection of the body, and the life everlasting." In other words, the church teaches that all that "stuff" is the work of the Holy Spirit. The work of the church throughout the ages; the lives and teaching and example of the saints or holy ones; the forgiveness that is forever sought by aching, repentant hearts, and poured out again and again; the power of the resurrected Christ at work in your life and mine; all this is what the Holy spirit does!

In Luther's explanation to the third article of the Apostles' Creed, to the working of the Holy Spirit, he says, "I believe that I cannot by my own understanding or effort even believe in Jesus Christ my Lord or come to him, but the Holy Spirit has called me through the Gospel, enlightened me with his (her) gifts, and sanctified and kept me in the true faith. In the same way the Holy Spirit calls, gathers, enlightens, and sanctifies the whole Christian church on earth...." In other words, you and I could say that the only reason we are even here today is because the Holy Spirit stirred our hearts, called us here, calls to us through the Word, through the sacrament, working within us to bring us unto Godself.

I can remember one summer when I was about twenty. I lived in Cambridge to attend the summer language program at Harvard Divinity School — "Theological German in ten weeks." That summer, I battled a demon I had battled for many years: the demon of depression. I don't think it was just the "Theological German in ten weeks." I remember being so deeply depressed that I could not

242

even pray. So I journaled — with many sobs and sighs and groans. I had never felt so far away from God. In despair, I reached for God's Word. I somehow stumbled upon Romans 8:26: "We do not even know how to pray as we ought, but the Holy Spirit intercedes for us with sighs/groans too deep for words." I realized that my journaling *was* prayer! I realized that the Holy Spirit was living and breathing and sighing and groaning, and crying out to God for me!

And so the Holy Spirit even leads us back home when we, like the prodigal child, feel that we have wandered too far away.

God the Son: Jesus. The intersection, the heart, of the cross. The living, pumping, breathing, feeling, loving heart of God, the human aspect of God, who wants to live in relationship, as all humans do, who wants to live in relationship with *you*.

The members of our confirmation classes admit, most youth admit, that this human aspect of the Trinity is the one they relate to the most. Partly because, as a contemporary song goes, "Jesus is way cool," partly because Jesus embodies grace, partly because they are at an age when what is most important to them are their peers, and so they can relate to Jesus as a kind of "peer," as a brother, friend, wise teacher or guide, or even as a counter cultural radical — something that's always been appealing to youth!

The second article of the Apostles' Creed is all about Jesus. Say it with me: "I believe in Jesus Christ, God's only Son, our Lord. He was conceived by the power of the Holy Spirit, and born of the virgin Mary. He suffered under Pontius Pilate, was crucified, died, and was buried. He descended into hell. On the third day he rose again. He ascended into heaven and is seated at the right hand of the Father. He will come again to judge the living and the dead."

Those of us who had to memorize *Luther's Small Catechism* remember his explanation to the second article. I can remember these words moving my heart when I was a teenager struggling to memorize them for my confirmation: "I believe that Jesus Christ — true God, Son of the Father from eternity, and true man, born of the virgin Mary — is *my Lord*. At great cost he has *saved and redeemed me*, a lost and condemned person. He has *freed me* from sin, death, and the power of the devil — not with silver or gold, but with his holy and precious blood and his innocent suffering and death. *All this he has done that I may be his own."*

I can remember being cut to the core, and thinking, "Wow! I sure must be important. For Jesus to do all that *for me."*

Jesus did all that *for you.* Grabbing hold of that radically changes the way we look at ourselves, and the way we live our lives.

Many years ago, a teenager named "Hannah" was in my confirmation class. I remember her making an appointment to come and speak to me privately. Her face was chalky white with anxiety. She stuttered and stumbled as she told me of a party she'd gone to recently, of drinking at the party. Of drinking way too much at the party. Of getting so drunk that she lost her sense of good judgment, and went into a room with a boy, and wasn't quite sure what happened in that room with that boy.

Hannah was a wreck about what she had done. She was a jumble of guilt and tears, remorse and embarrassment. In gulping sobs she asked if I thought God would forgive her.

"Hannah," I spoke gently, "remember all the stories about people coming to Jesus, people who had made mistakes, people who had done things they wished they hadn't, people who had sinned, people who had regrets, people who felt guilty?" She sniffled and looked at me. "Yes ..." she said tentatively. "Well, if they were truly sorry for what they had done, and asked Jesus to forgive them, did he ever turn anyone away?" Her eyes caught on, like a trapped animal catching a glimpse of escape. "Hannah, if they were truly sorry, Jesus said to them, as he says to you right now, 'My child, your sins are forgiven, go in peace.' "

We all screw up. We all say and do things we wish we hadn't done. We all hurt others. Sometimes on purpose. Sometimes without intending to. "No one is righteous, no not one," God's Word reminds us (Romans 3:10). We are all in need of God's forgiveness ... and of God's grace.

When Jesus walked this earth, again and again, he engaged people, inviting them into relationship with him. Sometimes in those relationships he comforted the disturbed; sometimes in those relationships he disturbed the comfortable. He related to each one, knowing what lay in the heart of each.

Then and now Jesus embodied grace.

Grace is a peculiar concept in our world where nothing is free, and strings are always attached. We Lutherans need to realize that the greatest gift we have to share in our world today is the major belief/tenet of the Lutheran Church: justification by *grace* through *faith*. I emphasize this concept of grace at each new members' class, where people from all different church backgrounds, and many with no church background, find it difficult to comprehend. In our world we stress working hard, striving to achieve, getting what you deserve, making your own way, self-help. At our new members' classes I begin teaching the basics of Lutheran theology by saying, "Here at First Lutheran, we like to start by giving you a free gift."[1] You wouldn't believe the looks of suspicion! I then hand each new member a beautifully wrapped package, in which are a prayer book, an introduction to Lutheran theology, a pen with Luther's rose on it, etc. I then joke with people, acknowledging their suspicion of my "free gift." But I go on to illustrate that that is precisely the heart of Lutheran theology — the heart of the gospel — the Good News of what God has done for us in Jesus Christ. God comes to us in Jesus, offering us the free gift of forgiveness, offering to save our necks from the messes we've gotten ourselves into, offering to turn our lives around and let us have a completely new beginning. Offering to live in a deep, intimate, passionate, exciting relationship with us. Offering this to us not because we've been perfect and deserve it, but because God desires this fullness of life for us. Because *grace happens.*

This is the grace in which we stand.

So ... what do these brief and cursory ponderings of the Holy Trinity tell us about God?

That God is Mystery — unfathomable — deeper and wider than our minds can ever comprehend.

That God — even within Godself — within God's very nature — exists in community — in relationship — and so wants to be in relationship with you and with me.

One of the ways "sin" is described in contemporary theology is as whatever separates us from God, from one another, and from creation. "Sin," therefore is whatever it is that isolates us and fractures the relationship between us and God, between you and me, between us and any other part of creation infused with the breath of the Spirit.

In the passage from Isaiah we see Isaiah struggling with the sin of "I'm not good enough." You and I, like Isaiah, often feel a sense of low or no self-worth. We think, "Who am I, God, that you would want to send me? I can't share your message of hope with others. I'm not good enough. I'm in bondage to sin and I cannot free myself." The sin, the guilt, the addiction, the shame, the missing the mark, the failure although you tried really hard. All of this separates us from God, blocks us from living in intimate relationship with God.

But God Almighty, our Father/Creator, who made us in God's own image and likeness, who wants to be in relationship with us, reaches out to us, touches our lips — our hearts, our minds, our hands, our lives — and sets us free from the sin of not feeling good enough — and makes us worthy. So Isaiah, and you and I, can stand before God Almighty and say, "Here I am, Lord, send me."

In the passage from Romans 8:26 we see that the Holy Spirit comes to us when we are groaning in a prison of anguish, sadness, grieving, depression. The Holy Spirit comes to us when we feel so isolated that we cannot even pray as we ought, and the Holy Spirit intercedes for us, prays in us and for us with sighs, with groans too deep for words. When we groan and cry out to God in anguish, that is the Holy Spirit who has been within us all along, praying *for* us, and showing us the way out of ourselves. The Holy Spirit calls us through the Word, through the sacraments, through the church — that is, through one another — working to bring us home to God, and back to the One who is as close to us as our next breath.

Finally, we've learned that Jesus invites us to live in relationship with him, just as Jesus, in the famous, pivotal story of Nicodemus, invites Nicodemus to live in relationship with him. Nicodemus was a Pharisee, a "religious one," a "churchgoer," like you and me. In fact Nicodemus was a leader of the temple, a member of the Sanhedrin (the Council of seventy religious elders), the one whom everyone looked at and said, "Now he's got his life all together." This guy, like you and me this day, was in the prison of "there's got to be more to life than this." Do you know that prison? You come to church. You sit here. You've always done it. You're a "good Christian," but something's wrong, something's missing, you can't put your finger on it. "There's got to be more to life than this" is what's separating you from God, and others, and from God's creation.

Nicodemus, we read, comes to Jesus "by night." In other words, in secret because, you see, he doesn't want all those other "churchy" people to to know he's living a life separated from God and others. It's okay. Jesus doesn't mind. We can come to him in secret. It can be just between him and you as you come to him in secret ... now ... in your heart. The people sitting beside you don't even have to know that you are coming to him. Come to him, with whatever it is that is separating you from God and others, with whatever prison you are living in, and ask him to set you free.

This day he promises you and me, as he did Nicodemus, that in him we can be set free from our sin, our separation, our prison — no matter what that prison is. This day, like Nicodemus, like person after person whom the living Christ has encountered, we can be born anew, born again, born from above. "For God so loved *you* that God gave God's only Son, that whoever believes in him should not perish but have eternal life" (John 3:16).

Come to Christ now, touch the waters of baptism to your head, and make a cross, asking the Triune God — the Father, the Son, and the Holy Spirit, the Creator, Redeemer, and Sustainer — to be in your mind, in your heart, and in your whole being. Then come forward, receive his body broken on the cross *for you*, his blood shed *for you* in order that you might be set free, forgiven, and given the gift of new life. In order that you this day might be born from above. Come, receive the gifts of grace, the gifts of new life. Amen.

---

1. This idea was given to me by my friend, Reverend Jim Hazelwood, pastor of St. Andrew Lutheran Church, Charlestown, Rhode Island.

God Calling *You!*

One Friday I had kind of a rough morning. The usual: making sure three children are dressed and fed, with homework done, projects for the day ready to go, lunches made, or one dollar, two quarters, a nickel and a snack if they're buying. A monkey-wrench thrown into the routine was when my older daughter said she didn't feel well. She had all kinds of legitimate symptoms, so I let her stay home. The symptoms all miraculously disappeared. In the meantime, I had to make a whole series of phone calls to arrange child care for a supposedly sick child, which made me run late in getting my youngest child to school. I looked at the clock. "I'm gonna be late." I looked down at my pajamas and slipper socks. "I guess I could just drop her off at the door," I reasoned with myself. "No one will see me. I don't have to get out of the car." I hopped into the car, hair and teeth unbrushed, in my pajamas. I think I need to describe the pajamas. They were a joke gift from members of our church family who had just gone to Disney World, who know I do morning prayers outside in my backyard each day. So ... as a joke they gave me these wild, funky pajamas, in a lovely box, with a note: "For your morning prayers." Specifically, the pajamas are a big white jumpsuit, covered with brightly colored Mickey Mouse and friends. As I'm driving toward the school, I'm repeating the litany, "Oh, but I won't see anyone. I'll just drop her off at the door." But as she's getting out of the car, there, walking into the elementary school, is a tall, curly-haired woman, looking very sleek and professional with her business suit and briefcase. Could that be? It IS! My college roommate, now a successful engineer, whom I see once every several years at our college reunions. She glances in my direction, she recognizes the car, she sees me, she jogs over to the car, in her shiny black pumps. She opens the door, takes one look at me and says, "Oh! It's 'The Reverend'!"

The truth is, I'm *both*. I am both a sometimes frazzled, overwhelmed, but conscientious single mom, and a "Reverend." Which is why I prefer the word "pastor." I find it hard to live up to that "Reverend" title. But I *am* a woman of God.

When I was first ordained, I tried to fit the mold, to look like other pastors I had known. This was especially difficult because I'd never known a woman pastor. I wore my hair tied back, no make-up, gray suits. One of my best and oldest friends came to visit me. She walked in and said to me, "Girl, you look awful! What's with the suit?" It just wasn't me, and you see, God called *me*!

Today we see how God called a mere boy, Samuel, and how God called Philip and Nathaniel. We know God called Peter and Paul, and all the other disciples, and they were all so different from each other. But God needed each one of them with their unique personalities and gifts, because Peter could reach people Paul could not, and Paul could reach people John couldn't, and you, because of who you are, can reach people I cannot. God is calling each of us to respond, like the young boy Samuel, "Here I am!" God is calling *you* to share the unique and particular gifts that only you have to share with the body of Christ — the Church — in our world today, which badly needs all of us. Then God calls you and me, in our own way, to invite others to come along. Like Philip invited Nathaniel to "come and see."

You don't have to try to fit somebody else's mold. You don't have to be like some saintly person you know or read about. You just have to be the best *you*, for as you grow more and more in your relationship with God, you will grow more and more into the person God would have *you* be.

Thomas Moore wrote that God's call is *arresting* and *disrupting*! Think of Samuel. Life will never be the same if you say, "Yes," to God's call! Life will become a never-ending adventure! Just when you get it all figured out, God will call you to something new. But, oh, it will be *grand* ... and *glorious!*

It's like the movie *Godspell*, a modern retelling of the Gospel of Saint Matthew. In the contemporary rendition, the story takes place in New York City. You see the crowds milling at an intersection of two major avenues. It's all in black and white. Then you hear God calling, and one face in the crowd, one person, says, "Yes," to being a disciple, and is colorized amidst all the black and white.

At the end of the film there is the scene of Jesus' crucifixion ... and resurrection ... and then the disciples go back into the crowds — into the world. The world is still black and white, but now the disciples, you and I, are in technicolor. *That* is what saying, "Yes," to God's call is like. Others will see something different about us, will be attracted to what we have that they don't have, and then we will be able to call them. God will call them through *you* and *me* to "come and see."

There is a quotation which I have up in my room at home. I have it up in my office as well. I have sent copies to most of my friends. It is a quote by Nelson Mandela, the first black president of South Africa. After years of battling against the evil of apartheid in South Africa, after spending most of his life in a prison camp for speaking out against apartheid, finally after the dismantling and collapse of apartheid, Mandela is released from prison, and miraculously, elected President of South Africa. We cannot begin to imagine how he felt as he makes his inaugural speech to his people. To black South Africans who have been oppressed, beaten, humiliated, tortured. He says to them, and I hope you can hear him speaking to you as well:

Our deepest fear is not that we are inadequate. Our deepest fear is that we are powerful beyond measure. It is our light not our darkness that most frightens us. We ask ourselves, "Who am I to be brilliant, gorgeous, talented, and fabulous?" Actually, who are you not to be? You are a child of God. Your playing small does not serve the world. There's nothing enlightened about shrinking so that others will not feel insecure around you. We were born to make manifest the glory of God

251

that is within us. It's not just in some of us; it's in everyone. And as we let our own light shine, we unconsciously give other people permission to do the same. As we are liberated from our own fear, our presence automatically liberates others.

This day God is calling *you*. What is your response?

Proper 5
Pentecost 3
Ordinary Time 10
1 Samuel 8:4-11 (12-15), 16-20 (11:14-15)

Our Solution ... God's Solution

A familiar Yiddish folk tale goes something like this: a man goes to his wise and revered rabbi for advice. He complains: "O, Rabbi, my house is too small for my wife and my children and myself. We get on each other's nerves and drive each other crazy. What should I do?"

The rabbi sits pensively for some time, then asks the man, "Do you have a dog?" Puzzled, the man replies, "Yes." The rabbi continues, "Do you keep your dog inside or out?" "Out," the befuddled man answers. After another long moment of silent deliberation, the rabbi utters his profound verdict: "My advice to you is to go home, bring the dog to live inside the house with you and your family, and come back to me in a week." Confused, the man went home, and did as the wise rabbi said.

A week later the man returned. "O, wise and venerable Rabbi, may I dare say it is only worse." At great length the man moaned, groaned, whined, and complained about the state of affairs in his home. The rabbi, again, spent a great deal of time pondering the man's situation in silence. Finally, he spoke, "Do you have any sheep?" The man's brow furrowed, "Yes, we have four sheep." Nodding wisely, the rabbi pronounced, "My advice is for you to go home, to bring the sheep inside the house to live with you and your family, and to come back to me in a week." Shaking his head, the man departed from the rabbi.

So the folk tale goes. Goats. Pigs. Cows. Horses. Chickens. Finally, after the man, his wife, and his children have been living with an Old MacDonald menagerie week after week after week, the man returns, "O wise and venerable Rabbi, I am at my wit's end. We cannot live like this any longer. There must be something else we can do!"

After a ponderous silence, the rabbi said calmly, "Go home, take all of the animals out of the house, and come back to me in a week."

A week later, a relieved and radiant man returned, "O wise and wonderful Rabbi, you are brilliant. We have never been so happy and content in our house. True peace reigns there."

Sometimes we do a lot of complaining, when in fact we need to be reminded just how good we've got it.

Sometimes we look for solutions in all the wrong places, rather than to the One who *is* the solution.

The Story of the People of God, the people of Israel, *our* salvation story, is a story of a people who, again and again, think we have the solution to our every problem. Think we have the answers. Our story is a story of you and me, like the people of Israel, like the man who visits the rabbi, moaning and groaning, and whining, and complaining about the state of our lives, and about the solution God gives us in the beginning. It is a story of human wandering, taking the circuitous path, looking for answers in all the wrong places, foolishly trying to take things into our own fallible hands, rather than leaving them in the hands of God.

Biblical scholars say that the story of the people of God, our salvation story, is the Exodus story. The people of Israel had been living as *slaves* under the brutal and tyrannical rule of the Egyptian slave masters, making bricks, some say to build all those pyramids. They cry out to God. God amazingly, miraculously *sets them free* through a series of amazing acts of power and miracles on God's part: the ten plagues, the parting of the Red Sea, the pillar of cloud by day, and the pillar of fire by night. God is leading them toward the Promised Land, the Land flowing with milk and honey, but the way there leads through the wilderness. In several commentaries, Bible scholars estimate that it's about a forty-day journey through the wilderness. That's right, forty *days*. But the people try to take the situation into their own hands. I don't know, I think I'd trust the guy who'd just made a pathway for me through the

Sea, but no, they decide to take things into their own hands. Their solution is to moan and groan and whine and complain. Their solution is to bicker and fight. Their solution is to rely on their own power and wisdom, the result being that it takes them not forty days to get to the Promised Land, but forty *years*! Talk about not stopping to ask for directions!

In great and small ways they wandered far from the path. In great and small ways they moaned and groaned, whined and complained, and tried to come up with their own solutions rather than looking to the One who *is* the solution. For example, the story shows them complaining about the food in the wilderness. "Gee ... back in Egypt we had good meat with onions and spices. Here we just have this boring, tasteless hardtack." Their solution: "We want to go back to Egypt." Moses tries to remind them, "Yes, but you were *slaves* in Egypt. Remember the whip, the oppression, the abuse, the killing of all of our baby boys, the slaving away, brick after brick after brick, the crying out to God for rescue?" Nevertheless the *whole congregation* (and I thought I had it bad with just a few complaining) — *the whole congregation* — complained against Moses and Aaron for leading them into the wilderness! Was it Moses and Aaron who had led them there anyway? No, it was God, the One who just turned the Nile to blood, who turned day to night, who parted the Sea, who provided an Exodus — *a way out!*

Moses goes to God. I imagine he too complained, "These people you gave me. They're driving me crazy! We're camping and they want fine dining! You rescued them, and they prefer the ruts they were living in! You got me into this. What do I do now?"

God's solution: "Tell them I have heard their complaining. I will send them quails every night and manna every morning." Literally, food from heaven. But the human memory is pathetically short. Almost immediately they complained again, this time about the food God showered from heaven: "This manna — it's so boring, day after day after day. And there's only so much you can do with it." They also tried to take things into their own hands again. They'd been told to take only what they needed for each day, but they hoarded it, trying to come up, once again, with their own solution: "Maybe if we save up a bunch of it, we can do more with

255

it." The hoarded manna turned rotten and bug infested. God's little reminder to us every time we try to take things into our own hands or come up with our own solutions. God creates a situation where we have to come back to God each day for what we need to get through that day.

In our confirmation class we have been studying the story of the people of God, the people of Israel, our salvation story. We have studied Genesis, Exodus, Leviticus, Numbers, Deuteronomy, Joshua, and are now finishing up Judges. There is a pattern in the book of Judges: the people turn from God, try to come up with their own solutions, try to rely on their own power and wisdom, and everything in their lives falls apart. The people repent, (which literally means, "turn"), turn away from their foolish ways and ridiculous solutions, turn back to God, cry out to God for help, and God gives them God's solution. God raises up a leader to help the people. This God-appointed leader, or judge, leads the people in the ways of God. Things go well for a period of years. The judge dies. The people turn away from God, try to come up with their own solutions, try to rely on their own power and wisdom, everything falls apart, people cry out to God, God gives them God's solution. God raises up a judge to be their leader, and so on and so forth. The pattern repeats itself.

Finally, the story of the people of God, the people of Israel, our salvation story, your story and my story, comes to a climax in today's lesson from 1 Samuel. "We're sick of these judges, who only rule for a little while. We want to be like everybody else. Why can't we be like our neighboring nations? They have a king! We want a king!" Moan, groan, whine, and complain. Wah, wah, wah! Developmental psychologists say that the people of God, psychologically, are adolescents. "They have pierced ears; why can't we have pierced ears? They have pierced noses; why can't we have pierced noses? They have tattoos; why can't we have tattoos? They wear their pants ten sizes too big with their boxers sticking out, why can't we? Their curfew is midnight, and ours is only 10 p.m." Moan, groan, whine, and complain. The people of God, like adolescents facing peer pressure. Wah, wah, wah! "Look at all our neighboring nations! They have a king. We want a king! We want to be like them!"

One girl in confirmation class asked: "Why does God keep helping them? Doesn't God get sick of it?"

Yes, God does. And, I think God gets *angry* too. The more you enter the story of the people of God, the more you understand the "wrath of God." The "wrath of God," a concept prevalent in the Hebrew Bible, always troubled me. Just a few years ago, when it fell upon me to preach on a passage that was all about the wrath of God, I researched it. In one of those eye-opening, soul-opening moments, I discovered, as some biblical scholars put it, that the word "wrath" could actually be translated, "the burning love of God." God was compared to a mother lion who roars with protective, burning love when her cubs are threatened or endangered in any way — even by their own stupidity or foolishness. God is like us parents who burn with angry love when our children hurt each other, when they turn away from us, their fathers and mothers who love them, and foolishly wander down a wrong path, a path we know to be dangerous. In the Hebrew Bible God's "wrath" is displayed whenever God's children hurt each other, fail to treat each other as children of God, turn away from God, or turn from the Way of becoming the people God created and desires them to be.

The solution of the people of God, again and again, our solution, is to take things into our own hands, to look for answers in all the wrong places, to look for power and wisdom in mere human beings. Our solution is to think another human being, a flawed and mortal human king, is the solution to all our life's problems, rather than letting God reign in our lives.

In what ways are you in your life like the people of Israel? How often have you tried taking the situation into your own hands rather than trusting in God? How often have you complained, forgetting the One who acted powerfully in the past to bring you out of whatever bondage you were living in to a land flowing with milk and honey, the One who rescued you and showed you a way out, the One who will bring you to a new and promised place if you just trust? If you just realize how good you've got it compared to where you used to be.

Or how about us as a church? Yes, God has led us out toward a new place, and we're not there yet, so it sometimes does feel a bit like the wilderness. And all of us, myself included, sometimes look back at the small cozy little church family we used to be, and complain that things don't always taste as good here. We need to trust that the One who is leading us forth, is the same One who led us mightily in the past. We need to remember that if we pray for and sincerely seek God's solution and not our own human solutions, we could reach the Promised Land in closer to forty days than forty years. Although our house does sometimes feel a bit crowded, we could realize just how good we've got it.

Our solution could be to choose bickering, fighting, and division within the Christian community rather than God's solution of the unity of the Spirit and the bond of peace. God's solution of unity, oneness, many different gifts all meant for the growth of the body of Christ, building itself up in love.

The very first church I served as pastor was blessed with healthy leaders. One of the first activities we did together as a Church Council was an outdoor Group Obstacle Course. Twenty-six years old at the time, I was the youngest member of the group. The eldest was a man in his mid-eighties. We were about half male and half female. Some of us were very thin, even frail. Some of us were very large. There were a couple athletic types, but the vast majority were *not*. The goal was to get the entire group through or over several obstacles, from point A to point B. For example, each and every member of our motley crew had to cross a "poison" river, Tarzan style on a rope; as a group we had to lift each other's various size bodies through openings in a giant spider web; we had to hoist each other over a sheer ten foot wall. The miraculous thing is, *we did it*!

I must say I've been having a lot of fun fantasizing about our current Church Council doing this same activity together.

The goal is *not* for one or two — the young or athletic — to make it. Not that one or two could make it on their own anyway, for the course is designed in such a way that even the wisest, strongest, most athletic person needs to rely on others to make it through. Besides, the goal is to get *everyone* from point A to point B. If one person is left behind, you've failed your mission.

So it is with the people of God, the community of faith, the body of Christ. Sometimes in this life you or I try to make it on our own, only to realize that there are some obstacles that we cannot overcome unless we do it together.

Sometimes in the church, the body of Christ, we take things into our own hands, come up with our own, human solutions. The result is fighting, divisions, or getting so aggravated with each other that we think of leaving someone behind or of dropping out of the course. In either case, the whole, the mission, would fail.

So somehow we have to figure out how to put up with each other, how to carry the one who can be really heavy, how to help others overcome their fears, how to deal with the headstrong or the soloists — the kingly types who think we should look to them for a solution. Together we need to pray and seek God's solution, let the Way of God reign.

Each week we are given a powerful reminder of the way we try to handle a situation. Each week we begin our worship with the words, "We confess that we are in bondage to sin, and cannot free ourselves." Each week we begin our worship confessing our foolish and faulty solutions, all of which fall flat on their faces. But each week we then admit our need for God, and are reminded of, and granted, God's solution: forgiveness, freedom, the promised land, the unity of the spirit, the bond of peace, one body, one Spirit, one hope, one Lord, one faith, one baptism, one God of all, who is above all, and through all, and in all. Each week we are reminded of something the Twelve Step programs point out for us, "That there is a God, and we're not it, thank God!" Amen.

259

Out Of Control!

Recently some 900 teenagers and adult advisors from all over New England gathered at Hammonasset State Park in Connecticut for a giant camp out weekend, the theme of which was "2001: A Faith Odyssey." We gathered for fun and fellowship, to camp and to swim, but mostly to spend time together in the Word of God, learning how to apply that living Word to the faith journeys of our lives. There was a nationally renowned speaker and a band the youth love. There was dancing and tie-dying, jam sessions, arts and crafts. There was lots of awesome worship, most of it led by the teenagers.

I had been asked to serve on the planning team for this event. As it turns out, I was the only clergy person on the planning team, so when it came time to open up the Bible, everyone automatically looked to me. "Can you think of a biblical character we could focus on for the weekend, perhaps a young person whose faith journey was really interesting, something the kids could relate to?" I immediately thought of David. David, who went from humble shepherd boy to King of Israel. David, poet and musician, who went on to compose most of what is now the Book of Psalms. David, who went from fighting off wild animals who threatened his flocks, to fighting the notorious Philistine giant Goliath, to being one of the greatest military commanders in Israel's history. David, ruddy and handsome, with some twenty wives and concubines, and a love life that makes the most popular soap operas pale in comparison. David, a beloved and honorable king, a man of courage and bravery and integrity, who followed God's way and always struggled to do the right thing. Except for one time. David, whose most famous sin was so wretched, it was hideous. Lust, greed, abuse of his kingly power and authority, adultery, deception, trickery, and murder. But David, who afterwards agonized over his sin, was grievously sorry for what he had done, repented, and begged God for forgiveness. David, a beloved and faithful friend to Jonathan. David, who above all loved God with his whole heart and soul and mind and strength, through the many incredible high points of his life, but also when he was in the depths of despair. David, whose life indeed was a Faith Odyssey.

As those 900 teenagers gathered for their weekend camp out, our opening devotions Friday night were today's passage from 1 Samuel. Try to enter into the mind and heart and life and spirit of a teenager. What is the world of a fifteen, sixteen, seventeen, eighteen year old all about? Sadly, so much of it is about "outward appearance." "Am I too fat? Too thin? Too short? Too tall? Wearing my hair in the right style? Wearing the right clothes? The right make up? Is my complexion good enough? Am I athletic enough? Popular enough? Do I have the right job? The right parents? Come from the right neighborhood? Listen to the right music? Hang with the right crowd?" Unfortunately so much of who I am depends on what others say about that, how they judge me.

Into the struggling, striving for approval, aching hearts of those 900 teenagers breaks the Word of God. "Do not look on his outward appearance or the height of his stature ... for the Lord sees not as human beings see; human beings look on the outward appearance, but the Lord looks upon the heart" (1 Samuel 16:7). It doesn't matter what you're wearing or how you part your hair; God doesn't care about your skin or even your report card. God looks upon your heart.

When God sent the prophet Samuel to the town of Bethlehem to the house of Jesse to anoint one of Jesse's sons to be the next king of Israel, even the great prophet Samuel thought surely it would be one of Jesse's elder sons. For they were big, strong, manly men. They fit the image one would expect of a "king." But God kept whispering to Samuel's spirit. "No, this is not the one. This is not the one. This is not the one." Finally, Jesse had paraded all of his big, strong, manly sons before Samuel. "Are all your sons here?" he asked their father, Jesse. Jesse replied, "There remains the youngest, but behold he is keeping the sheep." In other words, he's only a boy. Just a kid. Wet behind the ears. A mere scraggly shepherd boy. Surely *that's* not what you have in mind for our next king?

The anointing of the scraggly, young shepherd boy, David, is dear to my heart. Because it brings me reeling back to that hot, lazy summer day, when I was a teenager, fifteen to be exact. I had just turned fifteen that June. It was my summer vacation, and I can remember that day vividly. I was bored, as teenagers often are on their summer vacations. I had been reading. I went into my parents' bedroom, and threw myself down on their bed. I can clearly recall the picture of Jesus hanging on their bedroom wall. I also still can see clearly the view out their bedroom window. It was one of those brilliantly sunny days, when the sun shone through the leaves of the maple and oak trees in the woods bordering our backyard, and the sunlight was so bright the leaves glistened, dazzled, looking like silver and gold. The sky was a vivid blue. From the time I was a little child I can remember experiencing God most profoundly through God's creation. So it was that summer day. As I gazed out my parents' bedroom window, I was filled with awe. When we are faced with the vastness of God, we cannot help but feel tiny, minute, like a speck of dust in that whole huge scheme of creation.

But just then, the sun's rays shifted, and fell through the leaves in such a way that it fell like a spotlight upon the place where I was lying on my parents' bed. In that instant, I knew. I knew that in that vast scheme of things, little, insignificant, fifteen-year-old Linda was to play a significant part. I knew that the Creator was calling me to be a pastor.

After a time the sun shifted, the experience ended, but I stand here today because of that experience which happened "when I was only a youth" — a scraggly young girl.

Weeks after that experience my parents invited our vicar (intern pastor) over for dinner. After dinner my mother said, "Linda, why don't you tell the vicar your good news?" I did. He sat there, and then his red, rotund face broke into hysterical laughter. He pounded the wooden arms of the chair with his fists, as he commanded, "You can never be a minister! You're a girl!"

Human beings look on our outward appearance, but God looks upon the heart.

Not only was I "only a youth," I was also "only a girl youth."

Yet I knew without a doubt in my fifteen-year-old soul, that *God* had called me, so *God* would make a way. The one who made the earth and sky and sun — the Creator of the universe — could make a way. For others look at our outward appearance, but God looks upon the heart. The vicar could not see beyond the outward appearance of a fifteen-year-old girl. The sad thing is, that when we look at others' outward appearance, and make our judgments, and put them in a box, we are really putting God in a box. When we limit others, we really are limiting God. We are in effect saying, "I don't believe you are big enough, God, to work in this person's life." We need to explode the boxes we have put others in.

The Greek word for God-like love, Christ-like love, is *agape*. The more we grow in God, in Christ, the more we are able to see others as through God's eyes — with *agape*. To see beyond their outward appearance, to look upon the heart. We need to explode the box we have put God in.

Many, many years ago I preached a sermon called "God in a Box." I remember thinking it was not the greatest sermon. One woman, however, still mentions that sermon to me. It helped her to explode the box she had put God in, and realize that God is so much bigger than that little box to which she had confined God. She went through a radical transformation in her life. One night at Bible study she talked about how suddenly she looked at life through different eyes, and could see God in all things. She told our Bible study group about a box-exploding experience she had had early one morning when she was coming around an entrance ramp onto Route 95, and suddenly, this mist — this incredible mist — filled her vision, and she knew that God was in the mist. She knew that she had been keeping God in a little box, but that God, the Holy Spirit, was really more like that mist — uncontainable, limitless, out of our control!

"Out-of-control" can be a very scary thing. If you have a person in your life who is out of control, that is a scary thing. That vicar found it a scary, threatening thing that a young girl felt called to be a minister! That was outside his parameters and rubrics; he must have felt out of control!

Parenting is an example of being out of control. For many of us, parenting can be a very scary thing, but I think no experience in this life has expanded me more than the experience of parenting.

One of my favorite parts of worship is "Just for Kids," the children's sermon time. But parents have confessed to me that they become very nervous because they never know what their child is going to say or do! That's what I love about it! They expand us because they are forever exploding our boxes!

I know a man who was very conscientious about raising his children in the church. When his daughter graduated from college, she — his beautiful, young pride and joy — felt called to be a missionary in a part of our world that has been torn by war and violence. Her father confessed that when he had brought his children to church all those years, it had never occurred to him that truly following Jesus is not always a safe thing! That if we truly raise our children to be Christian, that if they truly become Christians — followers of Jesus Christ — then they most definitely will be "out of our control." Then we have to take, as that father had to take, that frightening, threatening, out of control step of trusting — of entrusting them to God's care.

Jesus was clearly out of the box, out of control, out of bounds. A perfect example is when, at the beginning of his ministry, Jesus enters the synagogue, and reads the Torah. The people love Jesus' words, his teaching. "How nice," they say. But when Jesus challenges them to respond to it, to live it out, to change the way they are living, they respond with, "Who does he think he is? Isn't this Jesus? The carpenter's son?" I remember a poignant bulletin cover which said with regard to this text, "They had wanted Jesus to grow up, but not beyond their expectations or control."

We are in the story. We are those people gathered in the temple, who hear the words of Jesus and say, "Isn't that nice!" But we have selective hearing! This week someone spoke to me about tithing.

That's a part of the Word of God a lot of us don't want to hear! Or how about radically changing our lifestyle — changing all those things which we know are inconsistent with being a follower of Jesus: letting go of our addictions, our judgment of others, reading the Word of God daily, forgiving? How *dare* he ask us to do these things! Who does he think he is? Calling us to change! Calling us to follow him! Calling us to let our lives be out of our control and in his control? That is scary! Who does he think he is?

The God of the universe! The One who does not see as we see. The One who does not look upon outer appearance, but who looks upon the heart.

Someone gave me an explosive little paperback book called *Mister God, This Is Anna.* It is a true story about an English man in his early twenties, named Fynn, who is living in London in the early 1900s. One day Fynn finds a little girl, orphaned, living on the streets. He brings her home to live with him and his mother in their home, which seems to collect homeless people. The book is a collection of conversations and experiences which this young man has with this little girl, four, then five years old, named Anna, who has exploded my box that I have put God in, as children always do.

Anna told Fynn how everyone looks at life as through what she calls "colored bits o' glass," judgments or prejudices that "color" the way we look at things.

One day, Fynn asked Anna, "Have you gotten rid of your pieces of glass?"and she said, innocently, matter of factly, "I have." Fynn thought of all those things he should say to her like "pride cometh before a fall," but then he realized that those judgments were *his* "bits of glass." So he said to her, trying to bait her a bit, "You reckon you know more than Rev. Castle?" "Nope," she said. "Has he got bits of glass?" Fynn asked her. "Yes," she answered. "How come you haven't got bits of glass?" "Oh, 'cos I ain't frightened."

Fynn says, "Now that's probably the most missable sentence that can be uttered. Missable because that's what it's all about. Missable because it is too damned expensive. Missable because the price of not being frightened is *trust.* And we know what a word *that* is!"

Fynn is a mathematician. To him mathematics is beautiful, poetic, perfect in every way. He had a mathematical toy, a kind of geometric puzzle he carried around and played with. It was, quite simply, two copper rings, linked together like links of chain. One day, as he sat pondering this life, he held the two circles at right angles to each other. Anna came upon him where he sat, pointed to one of the circles and said, "I know what that is — that's me. And that's Mister God," she said, as she pointed to the other circle. "Mister God goes right through my middle and I go right through Mister God's middle."

Now of course, we can discredit all this because, after all, Anna is only a child. David was only a shepherd boy. I was only a girl. Jesus was only Joseph the carpenter's Son.

Or we can say, "Yes," to the Creator of the universe. "Yes, I will trust you. Yes, I will let my life be out of control — out of my control, that is, and in your control, O God. Yes, I will throw away my bits of glass. Yes, I will begin to look not upon the outer appearance, but to look upon the heart. Yes, I will let you explode the boxes I have put you in. Yes, I will let myself accept the fact that you, O God, are much bigger than the box I've put you in. Others are much bigger than the boxes I've put them in ... and O, so scary is the thought ... I am much bigger than the box I have put myself in. For you, O God, go right through my middle, and I go right through your middle. You are *agape*, *love*, and we all know how out of control *that* is."

Let us pray: Creator God, God of the universe, you who look upon our hearts, help us to say, "Yes." Amen.

267

Proper 7
Pentecost 5
Ordinary Time 12
1 Samuel 17:(1a, 4-11, 19-23) 32-49

What Are *Your* Goliaths?

I chaperoned a fourth grade class on a field trip to the Olde Mystic Village and Seaport. Five children, ages nine and ten, were entrusted to my care for the day. At one point we sat in the bandstand, a large gazebo-type structure in the center of the Village Green, for a demonstration of nineteenth century music that sailors aboard the sea vessels might have enjoyed: peppy tunes on the banjo and concertina, jigs and reels on the fiddle. Spontaneously, the five children in my group stomped their feet to the music, then looked at each other, arose from their seats, clasped hands, and danced! Heads thrown back, radiant smiles lighting their faces, whirling and twirling, they captured for me in a kind of visual and visceral snapshot what childhood should be: freedom, unself-consciousness, beauty, abandonment, joy! They whisked me into their exultation as I joined them in their dance.

Just hours later I opened my Sunday newspaper (okay, so I didn't have time to read it on Sunday), and saw the faces of five older youth on the front page. Cold, hardened faces. Angry, glaring, insolent faces. Faces of five youth, ages nineteen to 21, who were responsible for the execution-style death of a beautiful young man and woman — also youth — that very weekend.

How is this possible?

I could not help but see these two snapshots in all their shocking juxtaposition: the joyous faces of the five younger youth dancing. The stone cold faces of the five older youth.

What happened between ten and twenty? Or did it happen long before that?

And how is it possible for us as people of faith to walk through this world, and to send our children forth — to grant them the freedom — to walk through this world of such incredible beauty and joy, and such horrifying and random acts of violence?

How is this possible?

This life often feels much as I imagine it felt for the people of Israel, struggling to plant their vineyards, raise their families, and instill in their children faith-based values to help them navigate through the challenging terrain of life. Just when we think we'll have smooth sailing for a spell, the "Philistines" rear their ugly heads. Just when we relax for a bit, lean back and sigh to savor the moment, just when we think we've finally got it down, we're blind-sided by something huge, something terrifying, by ... *Goliath*.

As a parent and pastor and youth leader it was as though the five youth on the front page bore placards with *Goliath* smeared in blood across their fronts. Like Goliath they showed utter disdain for all that we hold sacred. Like Goliath they taunted us to fight against their enormous embodiment of hatred, fear, evil. Or, perhaps, they taunted us to back down, to give up, to fall to pieces before something so horrifying.

Confronted with the giant Goliath, the Israelites, like us, were understandably in a quandary as to what to do. So ... they did nothing. They wrung their hands and hung their heads, and allowed their fear to incapacitate them. Day after day, Goliath taunted: "I am bigger than you are. I am stronger than you are. Evil is greater than good. Darkness is stronger than light. I defy the armies — the forces — of your living God! Look at the front page! Random acts of violence crush your foolish little random acts of kindness! Look at Columbine! Look at Santana! Look at Oklahoma City! Look at your World Trade Center! Look at your Pentagon! Look at the so-called 'Holy' Land! Look at the KKK! Look at your addictions! Look at organized crime! Look at racism and sexism, and every other 'ism' I use to divide and conquer! Look at divorce! Look at custody battles! Look at marriage and family and our most primary relationships broken and defiled! Look at cancer! Look at death! Look at depression! Look at your crippling, paralyzing fear."

"Goliath" is that which threatens to overwhelm us and undo us. We all have our "Goliaths."

I ask you this day, what is your "Goliath"? What is it that throws you into a quandary so that you wring your hands, and hang your head, and do nothing? What is it that makes you most afraid? What is it that cripples you, paralyzes you? What is it that threatens to overwhelm you and undo you? What is it that defies the power of the living God in your life?

What is your "Goliath"?

And how can we possibly combat such a mammoth foe?

The answer lies in the last place we'd expect to find it.

We would have expected Saul, the king and military leader of Israel, who stood, scripture says, a head and shoulders taller than other men, to go head to head with Goliath. Or we would have expected one of the Israelite army's biggest and strongest, bravest and best soldiers to step forward. Or maybe even some brilliant military commander to come up with some wise maneuver, some shrewd strategic game plan — some clever mastermind who could anticipate every possible move the Philistine army could possibly make, as in a giant military chess game.

But a kid with a sling shot ... well ... go figure.

Something so small, so insignificant, so seemingly powerless, so everyday and ordinary. A telephone call from a friend. Knowing that grandfather figure is praying for you, as he said he would. A smile from a compassionate stranger. That quiet co-worker who had the courage to act with integrity. The matter-of-fact bravery of those who live with physical challenges every day of their lives. Second marriages. Wisdom in the lyrics of a rap song. Public servants who are truly committed to helping and serving others. The discerning spirit of a four year old. The hit-the-nail-on-the-head advice of a four year old. A daisy in the crack in the solid stone wall. A trickle of water that ends up blasting through rock. A small, living shoot from the stump of Jesse. A shepherd boy with a few smooth stones. A baby born to poor parents, lying in a manger. A simple, total trust in the power of the living God.

God's ways are not our ways.

The giant Goliath is conquered by someone very small, who lived every moment of his life in communion with Someone, Something very big. With the Spirit of the Living God.

Martin Luther identified his greatest sin as despair. Perhaps it's a Lutheran thing. Like Luther, depression or despair is a Goliath I have battled on many occasions. Recognizing the taunts of this Goliath, I know I need to be prepared for battle. I consult my "military advisors": children. Just being with children renews my strength. The way they face life head on, fearlessly. The way they are unburdened from the past, and not anxious about the future, completely present to the moment. There is a little girl, Ellie, who lives a few doors down from the church. Just to chat with her for a few minutes as she learns to ride her bicycle with training wheels in the church parking lot rejuvenates my spirit. Just to spend a few minutes looking at this life through Ellie's eyes as she kicks her way through the fallen leaves on the way to the corner bus stop to wait for her brother, kicks *me* out of the dumps I'm down in and makes me look at life more simply, and with a lot more hope. There *are*, after all, things in this life that we can count on. Ellie is certain of that. She knows that one season follows another. She knows that if she practices a lot, the bike riding will get easier. She knows that the leaves are beautiful, and that God is trying to get our attention through their colorful beauty. She knows that her brother will get off the bus and greet her with an understated shrug, but she also knows that deep down he loves her just as much as she loves him. She knows that the Lutheran minister is down in the dumps today and needs a little encouragement. Yes, the Spirit of the Living God ministers to my spirit through Ellie. A little child can tackle a Goliath any day.

Last year a ten-year-old member of our extended church family died of cancer. I visited him in the hospital frequently in the months before he died. "Isn't it depressing?" I would often be asked. It was, in fact, exactly the opposite. Bobby met his cancer and his death with the same equanimity with which he met the different hospital personnel or visitors who came to his room. He met all with his eyes wide open, and a gentle smile on his face. When he was in pain, he would wince slightly, as you would when swallowing a spoonful of bad tasting medicine, then he would continue playing with his toys, talking with his friends and visitors, reading his books. Cancer, and death, were not dreaded enemies, but parts of his life which he faced calmly, as calmly as the shepherd boy faced the giant. A child can disarm a Goliath by his simple lack of fear, and conquer evil and hatred by her complete purity of spirit, the perfect purity of Love.

God's ways are not our ways. When confronted with our Goliaths, we must be open to the power of the living God coming to us in unexpected places, and small yet mighty ways. We must never underestimate the small, the simple, the ordinary, because for some strange reason, that is how God often chooses to come to us.

Many years ago I worked with a phenomenal group of adult advisors, as part of a church's Youth Ministry Team. One of the adult advisors was a beautiful young woman, not too much older than the youth with whom she worked. She was a mother of three preschool aged children, the youngest of which was an infant. The youth adored her. She spoke their language, related well with them, was "on their level." I became concerned, however, when she, who was slender to begin with, began to look almost anorexic. I became even more concerned when her family, who did not have much money to begin with, seemed unable to feed their children. Late one afternoon, she came to my home. She looked haunted, ravaged with fear. She confessed to me that she was battling the Goliath of a cocaine addiction. She had plunged her family into debt through this addiction, and so, had borrowed several thousand dollars from her husband's parents to pay the debt. But Goliath's taunting had gotten the better of her, and she had spent the thousands of dollars borrowed from her in-laws on cocaine as well. She wrung her hands. She hung her head. She didn't know what to do.

Frankly, I didn't know what to do either. So I prayed for her, with her. Feeling as puny as David, we faced Goliath in the name of the Living God. Goliath was struck down and conquered by a few smooth stones. We got her into a good rehab program. With her permission, the team of youth advisors told the youth the cold, hard truth. Together, the youth and adult advisors, and other caring members of her church family, rolled up their sleeves and cleaned up a long-neglected apartment. We set up a daily child care schedule for her three children for the months she was in rehab. We made meals. We helped pay the bills. Small, insignificant things. We changed diapers and cleaned closets. We paid an electric bill and made a casserole. We prayed. We loved. We healed. Goliath fell dead.

Never underestimate something small in the name of the Living God.

Because in the Word of God, again and again, we see that, for some strange reason, that is how God chooses to act. God's ways are not our ways.

The biblical world was no less violent or frightening than our own. How did the people of God navigate their way through this world? How did Jesus journey through this world? Did he say, "There is suffering and strife down that path, so I think I'll take this other path"? No. Did he say, "Evil Goliaths are taunting the children down that path, so I think I'll wring my hands and hang my head and turn away"? No. He courageously journeyed through it all. We cannot choose what befalls us. But we can choose our response to it. Our response can erupt from our lower nature — meeting violence with violence, hate with hate, uncertainty with fear and anxiety, difference with judgment and superiority, beauty with jealousy, freedom with shackles of control, joy with the poison of negativity, the Spirit of Life with a spirit of evil and death.

Or ... we can choose the way of the Living God. The way of Christ. The way of the Spirit of Life. Courage. Freedom. Childlike abandon. Beauty. Radiant light. Joyous exultation.

Recognizing that the powers of darkness, evil, violence, and death loom large and real, we can let them and our fear of them cripple us, overwhelm us, and undo us. Or we can journey through this world knowing who journeys with us through it all, knowing that the final word is not death but resurrection, and therefore, with our heads thrown back and our faces radiant, we can join the children in the whirling, twirling victory dance of Life! Amen.

Proper 8
Pentecost 6
Ordinary Time 13
2 Samuel 1:1, 17-27

The Light Shines In The Darkness, And The Darkness Cannot Overcome It

Lament. What a powerful biblical word. Lament. To cry out to God from the depths, aching, grieving, yearning, mourning the loss of that which you cannot even imagine living without.

In today's lesson, great and powerful King David laments the loss of King Saul and of Saul's son Jonathan, David's beloved friend from the time of his youth. One thing about David: he does everything passionately, from the core of his being. He celebrates passionately; he worships passionately; he loves passionately; he prays passionately; he mourns passionately.

"Your glory, O Israel, lies slain upon your high places! How the mighty have fallen! ... You mountains of Gilboa, let there be no dew or rain upon you, nor bounteous fields! For there the shield of the mighty was defiled, the shield of Saul, anointed with oil no more ... How the mighty have fallen, and the weapons of war perished!"

David calls all creation to join his lament of Saul and Jonathan.

David's lament for King Saul is striking because the history of the relationship between Saul and David was fraught with tension. A kind of love/hate relationship on Saul's part. Some biblical scholars have wondered whether King Saul was manic depressive. One moment he loves and appreciates David. The next minute he tries to kill him! Somewhat understandable in that God called the prophet Samuel to anoint the shepherd boy David as King while Saul still reigned. David started his military career off with a bang with his amazing victory over the Philistine giant, Goliath. After that first battle with the Philistines, as the Israelite army marched home in

275

joyous celebration, the women sang, "Saul has killed his thousands; and David his ten thousands!" In other words: "Rah! Rah! King Saul is great! Rah! Rah! The shepherd boy David is greater!" It's no wonder King Saul found David to be a threat. So much so that later he and his troops sought David's life.

But there is another thing about David. He had integrity. He fought fair. He had honor, whereas King Saul applied every under-handed, sneaky tactic to try to get David's head. David, on three different occasions, had the opportunity to take King Saul's life, but would not, because he would not slay God's anointed one. In fact, I think David lamented the fact that Saul was jealous of him, and sought his life, for deep down, I think he loved Saul, and wished that there were peace between them.

So perhaps David's lament for Saul was also a lament for that which would never be — for the loss of that hope, that potential, of a future wherein he and Saul could make amends. David mourned the death of King Saul on many levels.

David mourned another death as well, that of his beloved friend, King Saul's son, Jonathan. The friendship between David and Jonathan is one of the most profound examples of friendship we find in the Bible. They were friends from the time of their youth. One of the most remarkable things about their friendship was the complete lack of jealousy and competition between them, particularly on Jonathan's part. For Jonathan, as King Saul's eldest son, was the one slated to be the next king of Israel. If anyone should have been jeal-ous of David, it should have been Jonathan. But we see none of that. Quite the opposite. At the beginning of their friendship, in fact, we read: "The soul of Jonathan was bound to the soul of David, and Jonathan loved him as his own soul ... Then Jonathan made a cov-enant with David, because he loved him as his own soul. Jonathan stripped himself of the robe that he was wearing, and gave it to David, and his armor, and even his sword and his bow and his belt" (1 Samuel 18:1-4). In this symbolic action Jonathan gave up his succession to the throne, and bestowed it upon his friend David in his place. Talk about selfless love! I think the friendship between Jonathan and David is one of the most remarkable examples of friendship you can find. On another occasion, when Jonathan knew that his father Saul was feeling obsessed with jealousy toward David, and feared that his father would kill David, Jonathan actually defied his father, King Saul, and risked his own life to help David escape. Thus was the love between Jonathan and David.

In today's text we see David's deep, painful remorse at the loss of his most beloved, faithful friend: "Jonathan lies slain upon your high places. I am distressed for you, my brother, Jonathan; greatly beloved were you to me; your love to me was wonderful, passing the love of women. How the mighty have fallen, and the weapons of war perished!"

In today's text David's soul aches with passionate lament. But what does David do in his grieving? He creates from it the beginning of new life. With his words of lament which we just heard, he composes a song, a song which he plays upon his lyre, a stringed instrument like a guitar. Only a heart large enough to know great joy can feel such deep sorrow. But in turning his lament into a song, David shows us that, even as he grieves, he hopes. Even as he laments, he knows, that "The light shines in the darkness, and the darkness cannot overcome it" (John 1:5).

Today we as a church family, like David, lament. I as a pastor lament. A pastor's life is both incredibly difficult and incredibly awesome. Again and again and again you are with people in the most overwhelmingly painful times in their lives, and also in the most sublime, joyous, beautiful, awesome times of their lives. All Christians are ministers — so really, that is what all of our lives are to be like in this mystery and miracle called the body of Christ — the church family.

Even as we lament, our souls proclaim the refrain. Say it with me: "The light shines in the darkness, and the darkness cannot overcome it!" Even in the midst of the dark storm of our grieving, we have that peace which surpasses all our understanding. That peace is like the calm eye of the storm. God never said we will not have storms, but that somehow in the midst of them, we will know that God is with us.

For those of you who have not heard, just a month ago, we lost seventeen-year-old Sara in a tragic car accident. Then this week,

Wednesday, we lost Dan, who just celebrated his eighteenth birthday, in a tragic train accident. Dan's mother works in our church office as our Activities Director; his family lives in our parsonage. Wednesday was probably one of the most difficult days in our life as a church family. All that dark day we were with Dan's family. And yet ... and yet the way you have gathered up his family and ministered to them, and to one another, has been incredible. It has shown that even as we grieve, we hope. Even as we lament, we remind one another, say it with me, "The light shines in the darkness, and the darkness cannot overcome it."

Thursday, the day after, I asked Dan's grandfather, "How can I be most helpful to you and your family this day?" He said something remarkable. He said, "Go about your pastoral duties. Continue to live life, as a pastor and as a mom. Go home, and hug your children." In other words, life is stronger than death. Say it with me: "The light shines in the darkness, and the darkness cannot overcome it." In the midst of our suffering we experience that peace which passes all our understanding.

So Thursday I did as Dan's grandfather said. One of my pastoral duties that day was to serve at God's Galley, our soup kitchen here in town. During my opening announcements, I asked for their prayers for Dan's family. We then said grace, and people filed through the line for their meal. Total strangers came through the line, reached out, grasped my hand, tears filling their eyes, and said, "I've been praying for that mother since I heard." "We've been praying for that family all day." They sent me off with dinner for Dan's family. "The light shines in the darkness, and the darkness cannot overcome it." In the midst of our pain, we are somehow flooded with that peace which passes all our understanding.

Thursday night, we had our monthly Church Council meeting. As a Council we unanimously voted to establish a Sunday School Memorial Fund to the glory of God in Dan's honor and memory, since Dan *loved* kids. We signed up to bring dinners to his family. One of our members who owns a landscaping company gave a beautiful, flowering dogwood as a living memorial. We decided that we would use the memorial money to put up basketball hoops in the church parking lot, and build a playground for young children in the yard of our Christian Life Center. In other words, even as we grieved, we hoped for the future. Even in the midst of the storm, we knew that peace which surpasses our understanding. Even in the face of death, we chose signs of new life. Even as we lamented, we proclaimed, "Life is stronger than death." And "the light shines in the darkness, and the darkness cannot overcome it."

Friday afternoon I celebrated the sacrament of holy baptism for two teenagers, John and Mary, brother and sister. Because John and Mary are Native Americans, they share my feeling that the most beautiful cathedral there is, is God's creation. So I baptized John and Mary at the home of their uncle, on a beach. The setting was sublime. God's Word, which their mother and I had selected for their baptismal day, was sublime. John and Mary are two gorgeous, incredible, strong, young people, embodying in their beauty and their youth hope, promise, potential. Do you know that every time we have a death in the family of faith we also have a baptism? I know that is God's way of proclaiming to us that life is stronger than death. "The light shines in the darkness, and the darkness cannot overcome it."

Today, we celebrate Andrew's baptism. We celebrate the awesome beauty of this child, this family, of the gift of God's grace in baptism. Indeed "the light shines in the darkness, and the darkness cannot overcome it."

Today our children will plant bulbs at the conclusion of our children's sermon, and learn the Bible verse, "Because I live, you will live also" (John 14:19). Because Christ lives, we shall live also. "The light shines in the darkness, and the darkness cannot overcome it."

A few years ago, Lent was especially difficult for me. I confess that I just wasn't up for Lent. I confess that in my core I hungered to skip over the darkness, the struggle, the suffering, the cross of Lent and jump straightaway to Easter. Then I had a kitchen sink realization. As I stood washing dishes at my kitchen sink, it struck me that Jesus did not say, "Pain and suffering are down that path, so I think I'll take the other path." No, Jesus took a deep breath,

279

and went down to meet darkness head on, and by so doing, overcame it. There at the kitchen sink, it struck me that as Christians, that is our task as well.

It's not easy. I admit sometimes, I'll be having a good, an "up" day. Frankly, I don't feel like calling those who are facing death, those who are in deep grieving, those who are suffering. But then I remember the kitchen sink realization about Jesus, so I do. I take a deep breath, call them, and say, "I just want you to know that I'm thinking about you. Would you like to get together some time?" As Christians, that's all we need to do. We don't need to say all the right words or do all the right things. We just have to be willing to show up. To be there. Not to turn away when everyone else does because it's just too heavy. Our very presence as a brother, a sister, in Christ will proclaim, "The light shines in the darkness, but the darkness cannot overcome it."

Years ago when I was a student at Harvard Divinity School, I went to a Billy Graham Rally. I looked at it as a learning experience. I have to say, I was very impressed. During the altar call, when they invite everyone who is ready to make a commitment to Christ, everyone who is willing to let Christ take control of their life, to come forward to the altar, they had hundreds of counselors mingled in with the crowds to talk with/minister to those who came forward during the altar call.

This afternoon a lot of hurting young people are going to be here at Dan's funeral. Many of them were here for Sara's funeral just a month ago. I have a vision of all of us being like those Billy Graham counselors. I have a vision of all of us, even though it's hard, taking a deep breath, and sitting beside some kid who looks in real pain, reaching out and grasping his hand, talking to him afterwards, sharing with him some comfort, strength, or hope in your own words, in your own way, or with no words at all, just by your presence, your caring, proclaiming to him that "the light shines in the darkness, and the darkness cannot overcome it."

Thursday, the day after Dan's death, I walked my children to school. Then I walked home with four-year-old Kaitlin and her mom. Kaitlin was reveling in the fact that it was the first warm day, her first day in shorts and in a tee-shirt. She kept begging her mother, "Please can I take my sweatshirt off? Please?" Finally, her mother shrugged her shoulders and said, "Okay." Kaitlin threw off the clothes of winter, and danced in the breeze, in the sunshine. "Dance with me, Mommy!" she laughed. "Yeah, right," her mom said, hesitating.

I didn't hesitate. I joined her. I danced because "the light shines in the darkness, and the darkness cannot overcome it."

Yesterday, I had a dilemma. My daughter Victoria and I had been signed up for eight months for a Brownie Girl Scout overnight at the Boston Aquarium. My daughter, of course, had long been looking forward to this mommy/daughter field trip. But sleep on the floor of the Boston Aquarium with a dozen little girls and their moms the night before church, before I preach, the night before a baptism, the night before First Communion, the night before Dan's funeral? Try to write two sermons there at a Brownie Girl Scout overnight? The insanity of it all!

But Dan's grandfather had told me and you to "continue to live life in all its fullness." He had, in so many words, told us to dance in the breeze and in the sunshine, even in the shadow of death. To turn our mourning into a song. *Not* to let death have the final word. Rather in our words, in our presence, in our living, to proclaim, especially to those who dwell in darkness, in grief, in pain, in the shadow of the valley of death, that "the light shines in the darkness, and the darkness cannot overcome it." Amen.

281

By What Power Did You Do This?

When I was growing up, my family belonged to St. Paul's Lutheran Church (Missouri Synod) on Elmwood Avenue, in Providence, Rhode Island. Actually, in the very poor, rough neighborhood of South Providence. As a teenager, I helped out with something called "Saturday Group," which was a program designed for the children and youth of that inner city neighborhood. It involved recreation (believe it or not, we had bowling alleys in the church, along with pool and ping pong tables!); a free lunch; a thrift shop — free clothing program; and Church time, led by a lady named Josie. Josie was as wide as she was tall. I have no idea how old she was. Being a wisdom figure, she seemed quite old to us youth. I know she was "retired." And I do know her job beforehand had been as a hat maker, because each week this pious "church lady" would wear the most wild, colorful, outlandish hat. We used to like to go to Saturday Group just to see what hat she would have on that week!

Josie in her retirement was one of the most active people I have ever known. She was like a godmother to all of the children of that neighborhood. Her door was always open. Her pantry was always shared. So was the wisdom and experience of her long, rich life. Josie's life and teachings *all* connected with the Bible. No matter what a child was dealing with — a fight at school, a drunk parent at home, gangs, violence — Josie had a lesson from the Bible that directly applied.

During "Church time" at Saturday Group, Josie would do a little preaching. She would also do a little singing in her high,

283

operatic voice which made all of us look at each other and giggle. Then always, *always* we would end with the Twenty-third Psalm. At first, I confess, I did not have it memorized. But then one day Josie told all of us that there in the Twenty-third Psalm was everything you needed to get you through this life. For example, you never knew when you were going to be in a valley someday, with the shadow of death breathing down your neck, and you would need to know that "Yea, though I walk through the valley of the shadow of death, I will fear no evil: for thou art with me." You never knew when you were going to come face to face with your enemies someday, and then you could remember that line: "Thou preparest a table before me in the presence of mine enemies!" Josie convinced me that everyone should memorize the Twenty-third Psalm. So I memorized it. Today my children know it as well. Thanks to Josie.

Josie knew the Lord as *her* shepherd. Knowing that empowered her to live out her life as the godmother to so many children in that South Providence neighborhood.

By sharing her image of "The Lord is My Shepherd" Josie helped others to become empowered for the living of their lives. Including me. I have shared "The Lord is My Shepherd" with my own children, and with all of the children and young and not so young people with whom I have worked over the years, helping them, I hope, to become empowered for the living of their lives. And on it goes.

This gem, this priceless treasure of simple yet profound wisdom for the living of our lives, is attributed to King David. In today's text we see that the Israelites loved David. "Then all the tribes of Israel came to David at Hebron, and said, 'Look, we are your bone and flesh. For some time, while Saul was king over us, it was you who led out Israel and brought it in.' " They acknowledged that David was a powerful leader of the people because he lived his life in deep, passionate communion with Yahweh, his beloved Lord God. David was lavishly blessed with many gifts: he was handsome, brilliant, creative, musical, poetic, courageous, charismatic, a great military leader, a wise ruler, a powerful king. But I think David's greatest gift of all was that, blessed so abundantly with all

284

these gifts, he had the gift of humility. He knew that his power was not from himself, but from God. He knew he was a great king only because God was with him. "All of the tribes of Israel said to David, 'The Lord said to you: It is you who shall be shepherd of my people Israel, you who shall be ruler over Israel.' So ... King David made a covenant with them at Hebron before the Lord, and they anointed David King over Israel. David was thirty years old when he began to reign, and he reigned forty years ... And David became greater and greater, for the Lord, the God of Hosts, was with him."

The thing I like the most about David is that David, shepherd boy made king, when he was at his best, knew his place. He always gave God the credit for his "success," for his power, for his greatness. He knew from where his power came. Therefore, in poetic imagery rising up from his core, his roots, his youth as a shepherd boy, King David writes, "The Lord is *my* shepherd." This day, as we reflect on the life of David, we need to apply the lessons of his life to our own lives. We need to ask ourselves, by what power am I living *my* life? Am I living my life in deep, passionate communion with Yahweh? Do I look at all that I have and all that I am as my own achievements? Or as the result of the fact that God is with me. Can I truthfully say that the Lord is *my* shepherd? Have I been letting God be the shepherd of my life?

Today I would like us to look more closely at the Twenty-third Psalm, and how it can be applied to the living of our lives. For as David knew, and as Josie knows, we have in the Twenty-third Psalm a simple yet profound "manual" of everything we need for the living of our lives.

Today we will look at this beloved Psalm as having three major parts.

First we will focus on what we shall call the "power-up" part — the part that gives us power for the living of our lives: "The Lord is my shepherd; I shall not want." David knew, and Josie knows, that if we truly let Yahweh be the shepherd of our lives, we shall lack nothing that we truly need. I can remember a high school biology teacher, Miss Kelly, who said to us students, "If I had children I would give them everything they need, but nothing that they want." When questioned as to what she meant by this, she explained,

"Sometimes a toy, an ice cream, a party dress is something a wise and discerning parent would know his/her child really needs." "The Lord is my shepherd; I shall lack nothing that I truly need."

Frequently God is blamed for what is lacking in the lives of God's people. The Twenty-third Psalm challenges us, therefore, that if anyone lacks anything, it is not because God has not created enough abundance. It is because some of us have more than we need, and so are to share with those who have not. "How does God's love abide in anyone who has the world's goods and sees a brother or sister in need and yet refuses to help?" (1 John 3:17). Sometimes Josie, whose life was empowered by the Lord, her shepherd, provided food, sometimes a safe place, sometimes advice, sometimes teaching, sometimes a word from the Bible, sometimes recreation, sometimes much needed discipline, sometimes comfort, always love.

Do you, like David, like Josie, let the Lord shepherd — lead, guide, and empower — your life? Do you give thanks and gratitude to God in whom you lack nothing that you truly need? Do you share with those who are in need so that they too may come to know the Lord as the shepherd of their lives?

"He maketh me to lie down in green pastures; he leadeth me beside the still waters; he restoreth my soul...." In other words, he supplies everything, in beauty and abundance: food and drink, beauty, and that peace which restores us. When we spend time daily with the Lord it is like grazing in green pastures, like drinking from cool, peaceful waters. It fills us, nourishes us, strengthens and fortifies us, rejuvenates us, restores our souls. It is so clear when we immerse ourselves in the book of Psalms, so many of which are attributed to David, that David spent time throughout each and every day in God's Word, in prayer and meditation, in communion with the Lord. "Blessed is the one ... who delights in the law of the Lord, and on this law he meditates day and night. He is like a tree planted by streams of water, that yields its fruit in due season, and its leaf does not wither. In all that he does, he prospers" (Psalm 1:2-3). Martin Luther is famous for having said, "I have so much to do every day that I can't get by without anything less than two hours of prayer!" With all of the hectic, busyness of our lives we need to make sure that we have spent time with our Shepherd, being fed, being at rest, finding our peace within, getting our souls restored so that we can go out there and face all that we must do in the world. Which leads into the next line: "He leads me in paths of righteousness for his name's sake." Treading down paths of righteousness is not easy. In fact, if we walk in our own power, it is impossible. But if we let the Lord, our shepherd, lead us, we will be fueled with all the power we need.

Part Two can only follow after Part One. For Part Two is all about when the going gets tough: "Yea, though I walk through the valley of the shadow of death, I will fear no evil: for Thou art with me." It does not say there will be no valley, no shadows, no death. It does say, "Even there ... 'Thou art with me.' "

So many visual representations of the Twenty-third Psalm show a meek, mild shepherd, sweetly holding a cute, fuzzy little lamb. It all looks so gentle, calm, and pastoral. But I remember seeing a painting of the Twenty-third Psalm that blasted that image of a meek, mild shepherd to smithereens! In this rendition the shepherd was large, strong, and muscular, resembling Atlas. His clothing was ripped and smeared with blood. Clearly the lamb he was clutching to his breast had been in some grave danger before its rescue. The setting was dark, stormy, gloomy, ominous. The terrain looked treacherous — jagged, rocky crags, and dangerous, jutting precipices. The shepherd's muscles were strained as he climbed up out of a steep ditch overgrown with dark, entangled branches bearing sharp thorns. Ferocious shadowy beasts could be seen in the distance. One could not be sure whether the shepherd had just rescued the sheep from one of the wild beasts, from the entangling brambles of one of the deep ravines, or from falling off the edge of the cliff. But the resolute, determined look on the shepherd's face made you know without a doubt that that sheep was now safe. That that shepherd had gone, and would continue to go, to the limit to rescue that sheep and bring it to safety. The shepherd was reminiscent of a front page newspaper photograph of a firefighter rescuing a small child from a fire. Total devastation loomed behind them, but there was not a doubt in the viewer's mind that that child would be safe. The painting of the shepherd was reminiscent of another newspaper photograph of a mother, her baby on her hip, fording a raging river. You knew that mother would give her life to get that baby to safety. *That* is the kind of shepherd who walks with us through the valley of the shadow of death. The Lord is my *strong, courageous, tough shepherd.* The Lord is my rescuer when I've wandered too far, when I am in a place of danger, when I am attacked by ferocious beasts, when I am lost in a lonely, desolate, frightening place.

"Thy rod and thy staff they comfort me." When the former Bishop of the New England Synod of the Lutheran Church, the Reverend Robert Isaksen, came to our church to visit, some of us were intrigued with his Bishop's staff. "It looks like a shepherd's staff," several people said to him. "It *is* a shepherd's staff," he responded. Then in his sermon, he talked about it. Admittedly, most of us had never seen one before. One end of it, he said, is the "rod." The "rod" part is used to poke or prod the sheep when they need it. For example, when they are straying from the fold, when they are headed toward a ditch. It doesn't take too much imagination to apply that to you and to me. Sometimes *we* need to be poked and prodded. The crooked end, he said, was the staff end. A shepherd would use it as a giant hook, to lasso the sheep when they started to meander too far, or sometimes to scoop them out of traps they'd fallen into. Just like God our shepherd scoops us out of harm's way.

"Thou preparest a table before me in the presence of mine enemies." Again, it does not say we will have no enemies. It *does* say, "Thou preparest a table before me in the presence of mine enemies." In other words, "Thou provides strength and nourishment for me to contend with my enemies. Thou art present to me in the bread of new life and in the cup of Thy salvation. My enemies will see this, and will tremble because they will know that my power is not from myself, but from you, the Lord. They will see the One by whose power I do what I do, the One who empowers my life." "Thou anointest my head with oil...." In other words, "Thou baptizes me, anoints me, sets me apart as sacred, puts your own seal upon my brow *even* in the presence of mine enemies!" So I can live my life boldly, despite my enemies, fearing no enemies, for "Thou art with me."

David, as king, had many enemies. David, as a military leader, ventured again and again on military exploits which marched him smack into the valley of the shadow of death, which brought him face to face with the presence of his enemies. Over 1,000 years after David we see Jesus' disciples empowered even in the presence of their enemies, who asked them, "By what power did you do this?" Peter, filled with the Holy Spirit, said, "By the power of the resurrected Christ." By the power of Easter. By the power of the One who raised Christ from the dead. That same power is within you and me and *that* is the power with which we walk through our valleys, past our shadows, through our deaths, feasting at the table in the presence of our enemies!

This week my devotions have been excerpts from a book called *The Mothers of the Disappeared*. The Mothers of the Disappeared is a movement that began in Argentina, when young men and women who worked for justice, fed the hungry, clothed and educated the poor, and worked to provide housing for those living in poverty, began to "disappear." Some would eventually return and tell horror stories of their imprisonment, their torture, and the deaths of many in their movement.

The mothers of the disappeared began their own movement; bearing white handkerchiefs, and the words, "The resurrection lives!" they would gather in the Plaza de Mayo.

"Yea, though I walk through the valley of the shadow of death, I will fear no evil." It doesn't mean there will be no evil. It means we will not be overcome by it. It doesn't mean we may not face death. It means. Even there "Thou art with me." Reverend Vernon John, who served as pastor at Ebenezer Baptist Church in Montgomery, Alabama, just before the Reverend Dr. Martin Luther King, Jr., began his pastorate there, paved the way for Dr. King by his own courageous witness. He said: "If there's nothing in this life worth dying for, then there is nothing worth living for."

Thou preparest a table before me even in the presence of the Philistine army, seeking my head; even in the presence of the Roman authorities, seeking to put Christians to death; even in the Plaza de Mayo; even in Montgomery, Alabama, in the 1960s; even in the poor, dangerous community of South Providence; even in

289

the presence of mine enemies; even in the valley of the shadow of death, "Thou art with me."

The third and final part of the Twenty-third Psalm we shall call "A New Place; Beyond the Valley; the place of empowerment — of power within; Dwelling in the House of the Lord." This is the place David was in when he had the courage to face Goliath. This is the place where Josie dwells when she dares to open her home and her heart to all of the young people who need a godmother in her neighborhood in South Providence. This is the place of power the disciples were living in when they faced those same authorities who had crucified their Lord and said: "We have the courage to stand before you today because the one who raised Christ from the dead is on *our side*, is within us." This is the place inhabited by every martyr who stood resolutely in the Coliseum facing the lions. This is the place of power in which the mothers of the disappeared live and hope. All of these witnesses had arrived at a New Place. A place of empowerment. A place of power within, fueled by the Living God. A place where our cups runneth over. A place where "Thou art with me" is a constant state of existence, so "surely goodness and mercy shall follow us all the days of our lives, and we will dwell in the house of the Lord even beyond that — forever!"

It is in *this* power that you and I can live our lives. It is in the power of the Great Shepherd who rescues us, frees, us, walks through every valley with us, laid down his life for us. It is in the power which on the third day raised Christ from the dead. It is in the power of Easter that we live. It is in *this* power that you and I can go forth from this place for the living of our lives, and someday for the facing of our deaths, knowing that we will dwell in the house of the Lord forever. Amen!

Proper 10
Pentecost 8
Ordinary Time 15
2 Samuel 6:1-5, 12b-19

True Worship Turns Us
Upside Down And Inside Out

"To worship is to quicken the conscience by the holiness of God, to feed the mind with the truth of God, to purge the imagination by the beauty of God, to open the heart to the love of God, to devote the will to the purpose of God" (William Temple). "To worship is to change. To stand before the Holy One of eternity is to change. If worship does not change us, we have not truly worshipped." So begins the chapter on worship in Richard Foster's book, *The Celebration of Discipline.*

During the children's sermon, when the children are having a tough time with a question, and I turn around and ask you to tell me, say, the Ten Commandments, do you get nervous? Uncomfortable? Many of you have said that you do. That's because most of us come to worship to sit back and relax, not to work! To receive, not to give! To be entertained, not to participate!

Maybe we need to turn our whole understanding of worship upside down and inside out. The word "liturgy" does not mean "the work of the pastor." Nor does it mean "the work of the worship leaders." The word "liturgy" literally means "the work of the people." To worship is to change. To stand before the Holy One of all eternity is to change. If we leave worship and we have not been changed, we have not truly worshiped.

One of my seminary professors said that true worship is fully living out the Sh'ma, the prayer that Jews pray three times a day, "Hear O, Israel, the Lord our God, the Lord is One, and you shall love the Lord your God with all your heart, with all your mind, with all your soul, and with all your strength; and you shall love

291

your neighbor as yourself." It was this prayer which Jesus turned into his "Greatest Commandment." True worship, therefore, would be to live out Jesus' commandment to love.[1]

Are you ready to *worship*?

To let the living God turn your life upside down and inside out?

King David knew how to worship! He worshiped with his whole being — poured out the deep, passionate love he had for his Creator with all his heart, soul, mind, and strength. As David and the 30,000 chosen men of Israel carried the ark of God into the holy city of Jerusalem, "David and all the house of Israel were dancing before the Lord with all their might, with songs and lyres and harps and tambourines and castanets and cymbals ... and when those who bore the ark of the Lord had gone six paces, he sacrificed an ox and a fatling. David danced before the Lord with all his might; David was girded with a linen ephod. So David and all the house of Israel brought up the ark of the Lord with shouting, and with the sound of the trumpet."

David was so fully immersed in worshiping the Lord, in fact, that he did not realize that his linen ephod, the small ceremonial apron in which he was attired, was leaving him fully exposed to the whole company of Israel! King David in all his naked glory!

It is for this reason that his wife, Michal, "despised him." In the passage immediately following today's text, we read that after this festal worship celebration: "David returned to bless his household. But Michal the daughter of Saul came out to meet David, and said, 'How the king of Israel honored himself today, uncovering himself today before the eyes of his servants' maids, as any vulgar fellow might shamelessly uncover himself!' "

David said to Michal, "It was before the Lord, who chose me in place of your father and all his household, to appoint me as prince over Israel, the people of the Lord, that I have danced before the Lord. I will make myself yet more contemptible than this, and I will be abased in my own eyes; but by the maids of whom you have spoken, by them I shall be held in honor."

Michal was not truly worshiping. True worship is not a spectator sport. She wanted to sit in her comfortable choir loft and critique David's performance as he worshiped. By comparing and contrasting David and Michal, let us explore true worship as that which turns us upside down and inside out.

First, what would it mean for us to let worship turn us upside down? For a children's sermon I once asked all of the children to stand on their heads, and to tell me what they saw. Metaphorically speaking, worship changes our perspective. It should turn us upside down because, as another seminary professor said, "True worship, like true prayer, is *God*-ward."[2] Our worship is toward the Lord of heaven and earth, toward the Holy One, toward the One who is beyond us, toward the transcendent One. Worship is *God*-ward, upside. My worship is not addressed toward you, but toward God; your worship should not be toward one another or toward me, but toward God. David was so caught up in worshiping God (upside) that he didn't notice his revealing ephod. Michal was so caught up in watching David and his revealing ephod (down, human-ward) that she forgot to worship. David worshiped with his whole heart, mind, soul, strength, and body! Michal seems not to have worshiped at all. David refuses to accept Michal's critique. You can almost hear the aching, pleading in his voice, as he challenges Michal to get over herself, and join in worshiping the Lord.

How about you? Is your worship God-ward? Or are you sometimes focused on a lower plane? For example, I confess that when I was a child, I would sit in my pew and watch the members of my congregation filing up for holy communion. They would kneel at the altar, about twelve at a time, receive the sacrament, then walk back to their pews. As I child I would focus on the different hats the ladies were wearing! But once God's Word grabbed hold of me, once God's Word cracked me open, my focus became Godward. The mystery and miracle of the sacrament was what I would ponder as we celebrated the sacrament of holy communion.

David worshiped in spirit and in truth. Michal noticed peoples' hats. True worship flips our normal human focus upside down. True worship is Godward.

The Word of God is alive and active. We are never to dare to approach the living Word of God by sitting back and relaxing! It is *alive* and *active* and sharper than a two-edged sword. It was written for you and me today every bit as much as it was written for those who lived thousands of years ago. It is not a children's sermon where you can sit back and relax. It's a children's sermon where you as a child of God are expected to participate. Nor is worship a place where we come to have our minds stimulated, and are given something to think about. It's a place where we engage the living God — the Holy One of all eternity — and so we leave and we change and our whole lives are turned upside down.

Let's get specific. This day, do we dare to enter the text about David and Michal and let it change us? Do we dare stand on our heads and see things from a different angle? Do we dare to let ourselves be turned upside down by God?

True worship is to love the Lord your God with all your heart, soul, mind, and strength. True worship is to let the power of the living God live in you.

Remember the movie *Jurassic Park*? One of the best parts of that movie was when the funky, bohemian scientist said: "Your theme park idea won't work! The life force is too great — too powerful — too explosive! It will find a way to burst out of the boundaries — out of the bindings you've constructed for it!"

That's what happens when we worship the living God! I always sign my letters "In Christ our Life," with a capital "L." God, Christ, the Holy Spirit *is* the Way, the Truth, the Life. In the resurrection we see that all the Force, the Power of Life, is in Christ breaking through the bindings/cloths of the grave, bursting out of that cave, rolling that stone away, exploding all of the boundaries we had constructed for him — for Life.

My father's mother was a woman who, like David, worshiped God with her whole being. My grandmother, like David, was full of Life, lived life passionately. She loved to eat and drink and celebrate life. She had a gentleman friend till the end of her life. She dressed vibrantly, with colors and flowers, and hats. She loved flowering gardens. After she died, my parents moved into her home for a time. Each spring, in the strip of grass in the middle of her concrete driveway, bright, vibrant, colorful lilies would burst into life. My father, like Michal, would complain because he wanted to park in the driveway, and the foolish flowers got in the way! But I loved it, because like the funky, bohemian scientist said, like David said to Michal, you cannot stop the unstoppable power of the One who is Life!

Like David, I sometimes worship God with dance. One Lent the Clergy Association in our town hired a dancer and choreographer to work with a group of volunteers on a dance for our community worship service on Good Friday evening. I was one of the participants. As the scripture immersed us in the story of Christ's Passion, so we entered the dance of death. At the conclusion of the Passion story, all of us dancers wound ourselves into a long piece of fabric symbolic of the grave cloths — the cocoon of the tomb. There was a pause. Silence. Darkness. We then slowly began unwinding from our chrysalis in the dance of new birth, like butterflies, like spring, like resurrection. I am not certain what those sitting in the congregation experienced, but for us who danced the experience was so moving that Holy Saturday I felt much like David bringing the ark into Jerusalem. I could not stop dancing! My children and I were decorating Easter eggs, blasting old rock and roll music on the stereo: "Wild Thing!" As we often do, we began to dance around the kitchen and the dining room. My youngest child reached up, "Mama, spin me, pick me up, swing me, dance with me!" Our dance was Godward. Our dance, like David's, was with our whole hearts, minds, souls, and strength. We danced the victory dance of Life — the dance of Easter.

I hope someday, when my children are old, and I am in my grave, that as they prepare their dinners, set their tables, wash their dishes, and decorate their Easter eggs, they play music, and start to dance. I hope they scoop up their children's children and dance wildly the victory dance of Life, and remember me, and know that I'm still dancing! I hope that they remember David, and know that he's still dancing!

Today the victory dance of Life bursts forth in music, flowers, children's excitement, beauty, springtime, the love of family gathered, of this family, the Christian family, the family of the One who burst the bonds of death, the One who explodes in you and me in unstoppable Life!

Saint Francis said to the almond tree, "Sister, show me the love of God," and she bloomed! And so should we. So should we.

Do we, like David, dare to let God turn us upside down?

How about inside out? Remember, true worship is to live out the love commandment. The love commandment has two parts: the Upside Down part — that is, loving God with our whole heart, soul, mind, and strength — *and* the inside out part — loving our neighbors as ourselves. "For if you cannot love your sister or brother whom you have seen, how can you love God whom you have not seen?" (1 John 4:20).

True worship will change us from the inside out. God's explosive new life will burst forth from us toward others. This, I think, is why the people of Israel loved David. Because his worship was pure, it changed him from the inside out. As he loved his God, so he also loved the people of God, his neighbor as himself. Because Michal did not truly worship, she despised David, her husband, her "neighbor."

"So if you are offering your gift at the altar and there remember that your brother or sister has something against you, leave your gift there before the altar and go; first be reconciled to your brother or sister, and then come and offer your gift" (Matthew 5:23-24). You cannot worship God in spirit and in truth and mistreat or despise your neighbor in whom God dwells.

An old man sat riding a bus, a gorgeous bouquet of vibrant, colorful flowers upon his lap. A young woman, visibly sad, upset, got on the bus. For the entire ride, she could not take her eyes off those flowers. Finally the old man rose to get off at his stop. He thrust the bouquet in her lap. "I noticed you couldn't take your eyes off these. I think my wife would like for you to have them. I'll tell her about it. I know she'd want me to give them to you." He stepped off the bus and walked a short way through the gate of a cemetery, his gift of beauty, of color, of Life, turned from the inside out, helping to unbind the young woman from her wrappings of death.

This turning inside out was taking place yesterday at the clean-up of our church grounds. As we raked away dead, brown leaves we helped to set free the green shoots struggling toward life beneath. As we pruned, and untangled, and dug out all of the dead stuff of winter, we helped to clear the way for the new life beneath it all. Let us this day begin to be about doing that for each other.

This turning inside out can be seen gently and explosively in a man I've known for many years. He has grown children. He has a beautiful, bright, professional wife. He is a pillar of his church. When I was his pastor I loved and respected him, but suspected that he might have an alcohol problem, for alcohol could be detected on his breath early in the morning at church when he shook my hand. He had always functioned. He was a successful, productive member of the community. He was a committed leader in the church. We never talked about it.

He came to see me recently. He showed up at my office, sat down, and stared at me with a smile that was uncontainable. "Guess what?" he burst out like a child who couldn't wait for me to open a gift he had made. "What?" I asked. "I've quit drinking." He poured out his story without stopping. "This past Christmas was the first Christmas I've celebrated with my family sober since the children were small. It's like I've been reborn. It's like our marriage has been reborn." The grave cloths of alcoholism have been thrown aside, rolled up and tossed away. The power of the resurrection has been made possible by others who helped to roll the stone away, who helped to unbind him, who helped turn him inside out. "I want to make you an offering," he said. "If there is ever someone in your church, or in the community, who is an alcoholic and wants to stop, give them my name and number. You have my permission." True worship turned him inside out. True worship means that we, like this man, love the Lord our God with all our hearts, souls, minds, and strength; *and* that we love our neighbor as ourselves.

So often when people leave church they shake hands with the pastor and say, "Good sermon, Pastor." But remember, true worship changes us. Saint Francis said, "Preach the gospel at all times; if necessary, use words." If we have truly worshiped, then our lives, like David's, will be turned upside down and inside out. Our lives will preach the gospel. Our lives will reflect our worship. Our lives will embody our love for God and for our neighbor.

297

To worship is to change. To stand before the Holy One of all eternity is to change. If we leave worship and we have not been changed, then we have not truly worshiped.

So today if you say to me, "Good sermon, Pastor, " I will respond, "That remains to be seen."

---

1. Dr. Phil King, Professor of Old Testament at Boston College, in the class, "Eighth Century B.C. Prophets," spring, 1983.

2. Dr. Krister Stendahl, Professor and Dean, Harvard Divinity School, in the class, "Worship and Prayer," spring, 1983.

God Is God And
We Are Not, Thank God

In Twelve Step programs there is a popular saying, the origin of which is unknown: "God is God, and we are not, thank God." That is a saying we frequently need to be reminded of. That is a saying that David, in today's lesson, needed to be reminded of. David meant well. After being on the road non-stop during the course of his various military campaigns, David finally gets to rest, to kick back for awhile, to settle into the holy city of Jerusalem. One day he says to his most trusted advisor, the prophet Nathan, "See now, I am living in a house of cedar, but the ark of God stays in a tent." Probably because David's love for Yahweh was undeniable, and because David sincerely meant well, Nathan said, off the cuff, "Go, do all that you have in mind; for the Lord is with you." As the Lord has always been with you.

But that night the Word of the Lord came to Nathan: "Go and tell my servant David: Thus says the Lord: Are *you* the one to build *me* a house to live in? ... I took you from the pasture, from following the sheep to be prince over my people Israel; and I have been with you wherever you went, and have cut off all your enemies from before you; and *I* will make for *you* a great name, like the name of the great ones of the earth. And I will appoint a place for my people Israel and will plant them, so that they may live in their own place ... Moreover the Lord declares to you that *the Lord* will make *you* a house. When your days are fulfilled and you lie down with your ancestors, I will raise up your offspring after you, who shall come forth from your body, and I will establish his kingdom.

He shall build a house for my name, and I will establish the throne of his kingdom forever. I will be a father to him, and he shall be a son to me."

In other words, "Remember, David, I am God, and you are not, thank God." Now that you have some rest, now that you're not fearing for your life in the thick of battle, now that there's smooth sailing for a few days and you don't need me as much as you did when you were at war, now you forget who's God. *You* want to build *me* a house? I cannot be contained in a house! Remember your place, David. *I* will build *you* a house. There is a pun going on in the Hebrew. David says, I will build Yahweh a "house," meaning a "dwelling place" — a house made of cedar. God says, "I will build you a "house," meaning a "dynasty" — a house made of flesh and blood, a dynasty which will climax in the Messiah.

Remember, God is God, and we are not, thank God.

After the terrorist attack on the United States of America on September, 11, 2001, I don't think any of us will ever be the same. In the weeks that followed, churches were left open day and night truly as sanctuaries in the midst of a dark, difficult, and frightening world. We pastors spent our time just being with people in their grieving, listening to them as they poured out their feelings, and praying with them.

In terms of preaching, what can we possibly say in the face of such tragedy?

At such times I find my sermons follow a pattern Jesus used in his preaching and teaching. Bible scholars describe it as a style of preaching where short vignette follows upon short vignette, like simple beads strung together on a cord.

I offer these simple "beads."

The first bead is a realization that came when I arrived for a day's work at the church office on September 11. Our church sexton ran toward me as I made my way across the church parking lot. She pulled me into our Christian Life Center, where she had the television on. Together we sat and watched the horrifying, terrifying images of first one tower, then the second, crashing down ... then of the Pentagon falling under attack. She clasped my hand, and we prayed.

How mortifying to realize that even the most powerful nation in the world is not immune. That even the most powerful nation in the world can be shaken.

Ironically, all that kept coming to me was what I had read during my devotions just that morning, "That which cannot be shaken will remain" (Hebrews 12:27).

As my eyes watched the shocking images, again and again, underneath it all I had this sense that "There is One in Whom we believe, in Whom we dwell, who can never be shaken, who remains: God."

God is God and we are not, thank God.

A second bead is that God dwells not in a house of cedar or a tower of steel, but within flesh and blood. A lovely business woman stopped by the church. She looked me straight in the eye and said, "All my work, and appointments, my 'to do' list suddenly seem so irrelevant. I just want to call up everyone I love and tell them that I love them."

She reminded me of a piece of wisdom on life I learned many years ago from a fifteen-year-old young man battling leukemia. He said, "We spend so much time and energy running around after things which, in the grand scheme of things, are irrelevant. My facing death taught me that there are really only two things in this life that are ultimately important: our relationship with God and our relationships with those we love."

Would that we would live that way every day.

The third bead is a bead that is hard to swallow. I think the thing many of us found the most difficult was to see the incredible hatred with which so many in our world look at us "Americans." Rationally we know that that is always the case when you are the biggest and the brightest and the most beautiful and the best. The underdogs will often hate you for that.

But then the big question arises: "How are we going to respond to such hatred?" As we wrestle with how to respond, feelings of anger and revenge are completely understandable. But I always think of what Martin Luther King said: "If we respond to hate with hate, we are only contributing to the force of hate in this world. If we respond to evil with evil we are only contributing to the force of evil in this world." Martin Luther King, of course, was trying to live out Jesus' mandate: "Love your enemies, and pray for those who persecute you, so that you may be children of your Father in heaven" (Matthew 5:44-45).

Grant us wisdom, grant us courage, for the facing of this hour, for the living of these days.

Ironically the morning of the attack I'd been journaling on a very personal level. I had been feeling hurt by someone close to me, and had been frightened by the amount of violence and evil which dwells within each human heart. At first, in light of the attack, I thought to myself, "That all seems so trivial now," but then I realized, "It's not trivial. It all starts *here*: in your heart and my heart."

Some years ago the Irish rock band, U2, whose own country has been torn apart by religious war, wrote a song with a line that is striking: "I can't change the world, but I can change the world in me."

God is God, and I am not, thank God. Change the world in me, O God, create in me a clean heart, and renew a right spirit within me.

Grant us wisdom, grant us courage, for the facing of this hour, for the living of these days.

A fourth bead is how God's ways are so completely different from our ways. We see this revealed to us throughout God's Word. Now some may say that the God revealed to us in the Hebrew Bible is a God of violence and revenge. Look at all those passages about the "wrath" of God. But one time when I had to preach on one of those "wrath of God" passages, I did a little research. One biblical scholar said the "wrath of God" could be translated more accurately as "the burning anger of love." He said it was similar to the *roaring* of a mother lion when her cubs are threatened. "Yes," God must be saying, "look at their warring madness. I regret that I ever made them. They've failed so miserably to live up to what I created them to be." God's wrath at this time is God's burning anger of love for us as a planet, as a human community, knowing that we were created to be *so much more*.

God's ways are *not* our ways. God is God, and we are not, thank God.

Some people, as they struggle to try to live out their faith in the face of such evil, have asked, "Pastor Linda, is it okay to pray for the perpetrators of this awful, violent, evil act?"

Absolutely! We can pray, in fact, for a complete change of heart within those responsible for the tragedy. If such a change of heart seems impossible to us, we need only to look at the Word of God, which reveals to us, again and again, the complete transformation of the heart which God has brought about in life after life after life.

One of the most dramatic examples is Saint Paul. Before his conversion Saint Paul, then "Saul," had been a perpetrator of violence and evil. He was personally involved in hunting down Christians, having them arrested, tortured, and killed.

God transformed Saul, changed his heart, and changed his name to "Paul" to mark the beginning of a completely new life. On a number of occasions Saint Paul says that he thought God must have chosen an extreme case like him to serve as an example. Paul said, in effect, "If God can change my heart, God can change *anyone's* heart." God's ways are not our ways. God is God and we are not, thank God.

On September 11, we saw the trough of human ways: complete lack of reverence for Life. In the Gospels, in Jesus, the living Word, we see the complete opposite — the apex of God's ways which emphasize the awesome value of each individual child of God. Jesus even uses sarcastic humor to emphasize this. "What shepherd would not leave the 99 in the wilderness to find the one, wayward, lost sheep?" Christ's hearers, many of whom were shepherds, would have been laughing boisterously at this point. For not a single shepherd would do such a thing; that would be ridiculous!

Jesus' point is that God is *that* extravagant — seeking even one who is lost. Like a shepherd seeking that sheep, like that woman sweeping out the house until she finds that one lost coin, like the father of the prodigal son, who did not rejoice until the one who was lost had been found. This same God seeking each one of us who is lost, not resting till each one who is lost is embraced in the arms of our shepherd.

God's ways are far from our ways. God is God, and we are not, thank God.

As we string together the beads from the week of the tragedy, some of those beads were priceless pearls. The most extraordinary pearl of all was an eighteen-month-old child of God named Lucy, whose name means "light." Lucy was adopted from China. Lucy's family had been living in a place of deep grieving because of the tragic, sudden death of her mother's brother, a handsome young man only 38 years old. Then Lucy arrived — a beacon of light.

The first weekend after the terrorist attack, our congregation celebrated the grace of God in Lucy's baptism. Even in the face of our huge national tragedy, Lucy was a beacon of light in our grieving church family. Indeed it is a fact that every time we experience a tragedy, we also celebrate a birth or the new birth of baptism. I think it is God's way of reminding us that Good will always be victorious over evil, and Life over death. God reminds us that God's ways are not our ways. That God is God and we are not, thank God. God reminds us that God comes to us, again and again, in the midst of the darkness, in startling and surprising ways. "You who walked in darkness have seen a great light; you who have lived in a land of deep darkness — on you light has shined ... for unto us a child is born" (Isaiah 9:2).

Indeed the week of the terrorist attacks, the darkest week in our history as a nation, there were many other beads — many other beacons of light. So many volunteered to help that they had to send people home. Americans gathered for strength and prayer, lighting candles in vigil, uniting as a nation as never before. The proliferation of flags reveals a deep sense of gratitude for America and for the freedom it represents as never before. On a global scale, even some of those nations who have been considered our enemies are praying for us! The United Nations has never been as united as in its stand against terrorism.

Another bead of light came from a man who hasn't set foot in our church in the five years that I have been the pastor. He showed up the week after the attack. I was surprised how passionately he spoke. He said we must not be immobilized in our fear, but instead must *live boldly*. "Otherwise they will have won."

304

A final bead of light came in a letter to all of us pastors from the Bishop of the New England Synod of the Evangelical Lutheran Church of America, the Reverend Margaret Payne. She wrote:

All of us are wrestling with the enormity of this event. Our nation is changed forever. Yet God is the same. [That which cannot be shaken will remain.] And the path through the pain and damage caused by these evil terrorist acts — the path through — is charted by our faith in the God revealed to us in Jesus Christ ... God is close to us, suffering with us ... and giving consolation during this time of anguish. Jesus Christ is the light of the world and not even this darkness can overcome his power. Especially now ... We are the keepers of this light of Christ and we must hold it high. (parenthetical element mine)

At the end of Lucy's baptism, we did what we always do. We took Lucy's baptismal candle and lit it from the large Christ candle which stands front and center in our sanctuary. We quoted the baptismal liturgy: "Jesus Christ is the light of the world. But Jesus tells us that in him *we* are the light of the world. Lucy, may your light so shine before others that they may see your good works and give glory to your God in heaven."

This day, let us go forth as lights in a dark world in the power of Christ, the light of the world, who not even *this* darkness can overcome. May our light so shine before others that they may see our good works and give glory to our God in heaven. Amen.

305

Sermons On The First Readings

For Sundays
After Pentecost
(Middle Third)

Timothy J. Smith

To Donna,
Becca, and Matt

Thanks for your love and support

Foreword

At one point during the sermon our eyes met. She and her friend were guests sitting near the back of the sanctuary. She smiled at me as she and her friend stood up and walked out during my sermon. I never heard from this couple, so I do not know why they walked out. I do not know their names or where they live or what they expected that summer Sunday morning. I've thought about them often, especially as I confront a biblical text.

I wonder if the reason that young couple left as they did was maybe, just maybe, I was giving a little too much background information on the Old Testament text that morning. I readily admit that over the years I have struggled with being relevant while at the same time being true to the scriptures. We are, after all, people of the Book. It is my belief that we need to be firmly grounded in God's word and resist preaching the "feel good about yourself" messages that are sometimes preached in an effort to speak to the needs of people.

With those thoughts stated, I offer these ten sermons as my honest attempt to be both true to the scriptures while at the same time offer a message of hope to persons living in the first decade of the twenty-first century.

Introduction

"Where do we go from here?" are the words from a popular song a couple of decades ago. "Where do we go from here?" is a question that we ask at various times in our lives when we face difficult decisions or when faced with new challenges or when we or a loved one face serious illness. Where do we go from here?

We ask that question after we confront a major failing in our lives. How do we pick up the pieces of our broken lives and allow God to make them whole again? In the first sermon in this collection David has a moral failing, which leads to deception and ultimately to murder. Where is God in the midst of our failings? Sometime later David was confronted with his sin, which led to a humble confession. Confessing our sin is the first step toward reconciliation with God. Only God can take the broken pieces of our lives and make them whole again.

Parents reach that point when their children begin to act in less than healthy ways and ask, "Where do we go from here?" David also reached that point. He failed to intervene in the lives of his children, which led to more pain and heartache. At such times we need to be "in your face" with our children.

Where do we go from here in times of uncertainty? We ask ourselves, "Is this where God wants me to be in my life?" We seek God's direction in our lives. Solomon at the beginning of his reign looked to God for guidance. Solomon wanted to get off to a good start. Likewise in times of doubt we seek God's presence. At times of uncertainty or doubt we discover that God is indeed present with us in our struggles.

"Where do we go from here?" might be a question young couples ask as they contemplate marriage. The Song of Solomon is a celebration of being in love. In this message we will explore the importance of being in relationship with other people and ultimately with God.

Three sermons from the book of Proverbs explore the themes of how we treat other people, how we build a firm foundation, and what it means to state that our lives belong to God. The way we treat each other is a reflection of our relationship with God. With a firm foundation we are able to weather any storm that might happen upon us.

Where do we go from here when we find ourselves in a place we never expected to be? Esther found herself in the unique position to save her people. In spite of the risk involved, Esther was responsible for saving her people from death. The message affirms that God is able to use each and every one of us to God's own glory.

This collection of sermons ends with Job, who also asked that same question, "Where do we go from here?" In one horrific day Job lost everything he had, his livestock, his property and later, his children in a terrible accident. Job eventually lost his health. Still, Job clung to his relationship with God, trusting that somehow or another God would see him through those difficult days. In the end Job discovered that God is good all the time!

This past year as I've been working on these sermons, two of our elderly members were involved in a serious car accident in the church parking lot. One woman broke both arms and both legs and had a broken nose. The day after the accident when I visited her in the Intensive Care Unit of the local hospital I was touched by her strong faith. Like Job she clung to her relationship to God, believing that God would see her through this mishap. She never once blamed God for the bizarre accident. Throughout her lengthy recovery her faith and positive attitude made a big difference.

Six months after the accident she was back in her apartment. She was now able to walk with the aid of a walker. She shared with me that the doctors were afraid she might never walk again. "I showed them," she said with great confidence.

When we ask that question, "Where do we go from here?" we realize that our faith gives us the strength and that God is with us and will never desert us.

Timothy J. Smith
September 1, 2001

God Knows

It's the sort of thing that yields high ratings on television and high volume of sales of supermarket tabloids. Relationships destroyed by unfaithful acts. You can see it on almost any given weekday afternoon on television. One person reveals that he or she has been unfaithful to the obvious delight of the studio audience. The more outrageous the love triangle the more the audience laughs and cheers. What a sad commentary that so many find such programs entertaining. What they teach our young people about relationships can be far more damaging.

Television and movies have made light of acts of infidelity, seemingly taking the sting out of it. Such movies are advertised as great love stories. In a recent *Woman's Day* magazine, the author laments the number of movies making adultery a source of slapstick humor, or romantic hilarity, or a heart tug. Then asks, "When we romanticize adultery or use it as a slapstick tool to provoke laughter — as if the hurt and betrayal are inconsequential — what kind of values are we teaching?"[1] Unfortunately we have become numb to such movies and programs calling them entertainment.

Famous persons have been caught in sex scandals from the President and other elected officials to celebrities, and ordinary people. Apparently no one is exempt. As a result countless persons have been hurt.

We try our best to soften the impact, rationalize all sorts of excuses as if that will make it all right. We have become good at placing the blame on other persons, our spouse's lack of attention, our parents who did something to us while we were growing up, our overly demanding children, our flirtatious co-workers, our seductive neighbors, or whomever. We label it a boo-boo, a mistake, an error in judgment instead of calling it what it truly is — a sin. While we might not want to call sin a sin, God certainly knows it is a sin. While it might seem like conquest or a game to some, we need to remember how much such acts hurt other persons especially children. Too many take lightly the fact that they have damaged their marriage often beyond repair as if it were of little consequence or somehow acceptable behavior.

Our lesson opens in the spring of the year when kings normally go off to battle. Instead of leading troops into battle, David remained content at the palace. His general was out fighting a battle while David secluded himself within the safe confines of his home. David used to lead by example. He used to be out in front, leading his troops into battle. But that was in the past. The thrill of victory did not thrill David as it once had. Besides all that David was older, in mid-life. Some suggest that the reason David did not go to battle was because he was experiencing a mid-life crisis.

David arose one day after his afternoon nap, after lunch, and decided to stroll on the rooftop of the palace. Perhaps in looking out over the city, he felt a sense of pride. He was, after all, responsible for uniting the northern and southern kingdoms, and establishing the new capital in Jerusalem, as well as the prosperity the people enjoyed. He took a deep breath as he looked out over his kingdom. Then it happened. He saw a beautiful woman bathing on a nearby rooftop. David inquired about this woman and a servant soon returned to tell him that the woman in question was "Bathsheba, daughter of Eliam, the wife of Uriah the Hittite."

It was not love that compelled David to act. That much needs to be made clear: it was lust. Messengers were sent to bring this lovely woman back to the palace. Mighty King David, who was at the height of his popularity, who thought he could do no wrong, committed adultery with Bathsheba. To make matters worse David showed no remorse whatsoever for what he did. Perhaps he thought his status and his power would shield him from anyone pointing the finger at him. Who would dare accuse the king of wrongdoing?

We do not know whether David thought about Bathsheba in the subsequent days and weeks or if she was a forgotten conquest. What we do know is that sometime later, Bathsheba sent word to David that she was with child. It was obvious to David that he was the father of the yet unborn child.

David launched a full-scale cover up. He devised a plan he thought would be foolproof. If Bathsheba's husband, Uriah, would come home for a visit and spend some time with his wife, then no one would suspect anything out of the ordinary. He sent a message to Joab on the battlefield, "Send me Uriah the Hittite." You have to feel sorry for Uriah as he reported to David without suspecting the real reason he was summoned to the palace. David quizzed him, asking how everything was going in battle, and how the men were doing. After giving his report, David instructed Uriah to "Go down to your house." The thoughtful king even sent a gift along with him. Problem solved — at least that's what David was depending on.

What David did not count on was Uriah's deep sense of loyalty and duty. Uriah would not go home to visit his wife. Instead Uriah spent the night among the king's servants at the entrance of the palace. The next morning David was informed that Uriah did not go home, which totally frustrated David. Flabbergasted David called Uriah in a second time; "You have just come from a journey. Why did you not go down to your house?" It is at this point that we discover Uriah's moral character and strong sense of duty. "The ark and Israel and Judah remain in booths," he tells David, "and my lord Joab and the servants of my lord are camping in the open field." No Uriah did not go home and would not go home under such circumstances. Uriah was a Hittite, not a native Israelite; he was from a proud race of mercenaries, now comprising an elite military unit. "As you live, and as your soul lives," Uriah tells David, "I will not do such a thing."

Uriah spent another day in Jerusalem. Meanwhile David had to devise another plan, but he was not about to give up. David would invite Uriah to have dinner with him that evening. David made sure to give Uriah just a little too much to drink. Certainly in his intoxicated state he would forget about his duty and go home to rest with his wife. However, once again Uriah did not go home, but slept among the king's servants.

The next morning, after hearing this news David became even more desperate. He tried his best to remedy the situation, but repeatedly failed. Now it was time for a more drastic solution. It was obvious that Uriah would not break his oath as a loyal soldier. Maybe the most tragic aspect of this entire episode was that Uriah unknowingly returned to the front carrying his own death warrant. In the letter to Joab, David wrote, "Set Uriah in the forefront of the hardest fighting, and then draw back from him, so that he may be struck down and die." Joab carried out David's order and Uriah was killed in battle. Finally after much effort David thought he had taken care of the problem. What he had forgotten all the while he was scheming was that God knew what he had done and was not pleased. David had broken several of the Ten Commandments. He committed adultery, and in trying to cover up his sin he ordered the death of an innocent man. The king who thought he could do no wrong had sinned. This event would signal the beginning of the end for David. Life would never again be the same for him, either. There would be consequences for his action for many years to come.

While we might be intrigued by this story of David and Bathsheba, of sin and its consequences, we need to realize that we, you and I, are susceptible, on the right afternoon, after a good lunch, to great sin.

In 1987, Donna Rice rose to notoriety in a scandal with presidential hopeful Senator Gary Hart. Remember the famous picture of her sitting on Hart's lap that appeared in newspapers and magazines? Aboard Hart's yacht aptly named *Monkey Business*, they sailed to the Bahamas and did not return until the next day.

Donna and her sister grew up attending Sunday school and church. When she was in ninth grade a friend took her to a Cliff Barrows crusade where Donna knew she wanted a personal relationship with Jesus. During high school she enjoyed singing in the choir, participating in youth group, going on mission trips, and bringing friends to church so they, too, could experience the love of Christ.

Donna speaks very candidly about the subtle compromises she began to make as a Christian. While in college she began partying and dating young men who weren't Christians. Various decisions, she admits now, edged her toward a lifestyle that in her own words, "Wasn't God-honoring." After college she fell in love with a drug dealer. The relationship ended when he was sentenced to jail.

It was a New Year's Day party in 1987 when she met Senator Hart. She remembers he called her the following day, but she never suspected that he was married. Eventually one of her friends tipped off the media, which broke the scandal she was unprepared and ill-equipped to handle. "My life was falling apart," she admits, as the media camped out in front of where she was living, as well as her parents' home. As a result she soon lost her job.

It was during this period that one night she turned on the television and began watching the movie, *Jesus of Nazareth*. "Suddenly I was struck with how far off course I'd gotten," she says, "and I knew I couldn't continue with my current lifestyle." With the support of family and friends, Donna recommitted her life to Jesus Christ.

Recently Donna Rice Hughes is back in the spotlight as a leading national spokesperson in the fight against pornography and for making the Internet a safe place. Donna is now in her mid-forties and is former Director of Marketing and Communications at Enough Is Enough!, a non-profit organization dedicated to stopping illegal pornography, assisting victims, and making the Internet safe for children. She currently serves on the advisory board for Get Net Wise, an industry initiative to keep the Web safe for families. She's also written a book, *Kids Online: Protecting Your Children in Cyberspace*, which offers practical tips to parents in the hope of preventing easily accessible pornography from being available to children.[2]

Sin arises when we try to base our lives on false notions and lies. It's easy to succumb to sin and it's hard to acknowledge it, but we can get our lives back on course with the help of our Lord Jesus Christ.

1. Barbara Bartocci, *Woman's Day*, November 1, 1997.

2. "Enough Is Enough: Donna Rice Hughes," Ramona Cramer Tucker, *Today's Christian Woman*, September/October 1996.

The Power Of Confession

A man wrote to Dear Abby admitting an affair with another woman that cost him dearly. A co-worker began to flirt, flatter, and confide in him. He allowed himself to be convinced an affair was justified, since his wife was so busy raising his children. After the affair was exposed, this man had to leave his home and family.

Realizing his mistake he wrote: "Abby, I traded everything important in my life. Although I never strayed before, my reputation is ruined. My children will never again respect me." He shared his story as a warning to others. He concludes his letter, "I wish I could change everything I have done ..." knowing that he could not. He signed his letter, "Sadder but Wiser."

Abby replied, "If you don't value what you have, you're sure to lose it."[1] David would soon realize the truth of those words. While David thought he had the perfect cover up and had gotten away without anyone suspecting his affair with Bathsheba, he would be in for a rude awakening.

David must have breathed a sigh of relief. His extensive and frustrating cover up worked; no one suspected him of doing anything wrong. David had acted on his impulses in having an affair with Bathsheba, who was married to Uriah. When word reached the king that Bathsheba was with child, David arranged for her husband to return home from battle for a short stay. What David did not count on was Uriah's deep sense of duty and loyalty. Uriah would not under any circumstances return to his home while other soldiers were in battle. It just would not be right. In a desperate, despicable act, David ordered Uriah's death; he would be killed in

319

battle. Again no one would suspect anything out of the ordinary —
soldiers die in battle all the time. David thought he had solved the
problems he created.

Bathsheba mourned the death of her husband before marrying
David. No one would ever surmise anything was wrong, and the
few who might have known or heard about David's indiscretion
would never say anything. At least that was what David was counting on.

The temptation for those in power is to define power in their
own terms, so that whatever they do is all right. Taking unfair advantage of another person by someone in power would be called
an abuse of power. David thought he had gotten away with something that deep down he must have realized was wrong. Before too
long, Bathsheba "became his wife, and bore him a son."

While David thought he had gotten away with his deceit, God
knew what had taken place. While we might be able to convince
others of our innocence or goodness, we cannot fool God. At the
time David was anointed king, the Lord God explained to Samuel,
"For the Lord does not see as mortals see; they look on the outward appearance, but the Lord looks on the heart." God knew what
had transpired and was not at all pleased.

Not long afterwards God sent Nathan to pay a personal visit to
David at the palace. Nathan was a prophet who was in tune with
God. It was not unusual for a prophet like Nathan to visit David,
after all kings often acted as judge in disputes over property. David
did not suspect anything out of the ordinary when he greeted Nathan.
The prophet told him a story about two men, one wealthy and the
other poor. The wealthy person had much livestock while the poor
person had only one lamb. The lamb became a pet to the poor
person's children. The children gave the lamb a name; when they
called, the lamb would come to them. The lamb slept with the family, ate food from their table, and drank from their cup. Everyone
in the family loved this little lamb. It was almost as though the
lamb was a part of the family the way they treated it.

One day an out-of-town traveler visited the wealthy person.
Instead of taking one of his own livestock for dinner the wealthy

person seized the poor family's pet lamb. The children were distraught over this outrageous act; they were crying their eyes out having lost their pet.

David, having been a shepherd boy, was caught up in this story. He was outraged that anyone would do such a thing. David told Nathan, "As the Lord lives, the man who has done this deserves to die." He then issued a judgment, "he shall restore the lamb fourfold, because he did this thing, and because he had no pity." What enraged him so was how the rich person took something that belonged to the poor family without a thought of the family's feelings and how later the wealthy person appeared generous by treating his guest to a feast.

Then came the moment of truth. Nathan might have taken a deep breath before telling David; "You are the man!" It was a risky business to speak the word of the Lord and Nathan knew it. David could have just as easily ordered him killed as he did Uriah. Be aware of persons telling you stories. Stories have a way of pulling you in, hook, line, and sinker. A good movie is one that draws you into the story at some point. The parable Nathan told had that effect on the gullible but guilty David. David was filled with outrage over the rich person who took unfair advantage of the poor family. Then Nathan turned the story around to him. David was the man! He was the man with power who took the wife of a poor man. He was the one who acted so cruelly. He was the one responsible for an innocent man's death.

Before David could say a word, Nathan launched into what God laid upon his heart. "Thus says the Lord...." It was God who gave David his power in the first place. Everything that David had, all his victories, were because God willed it. And Nathan speaking for God said, "If that had been too little, I would have added as much more." David would be punished for what he did. Nathan concluded by asking, "Why have you despised the word of the Lord, to do what is evil in his sight?"

David remained silent. There was no arguing with a prophet who spoke the word of the Lord. When Nathan finished David humbly admitted, "I have sinned against the Lord." David admitted and confessed his own sin. In the Psalm attributed to this experience

David pleads, "Create in me a clean heart, O God, and put a new spirit within me" (Psalm 51:10). Even though David sinned he could still pray and find God with him.

Even at those moments when we know we have sinned, we can still pray with the assurance that God will hear us. No matter what we do or where we find ourselves, God is still present with us. Even in the valleys of life it is still possible to experience God's presence.

There is a healing power in confessing our sins as Charles Axe relates: "All I could think of is how I had failed everyone — friends, church, God." He thought all his friends would abandon him after they learned what he did. He thought about this while he sat in a prison cell. After a brief but destructive bout with gambling, Charles was arrested for stealing.

As the months passed while he was awaiting trial, members of the church had blessed Charles with their friendship. While he appreciated their friendship, he was afraid that if they knew what he had done they would no longer be his friends. Out of fear Charles continued to claim his innocence.

Charles began praying and seeking God's guidance. Eventually he came to understand what he had known all along: "To experience God's forgiveness," he says, "I needed to plead guilty and to begin apologizing to everyone I had hurt." It was an emotionally charged moment when he began telling others of his wrongdoing all the while praying for forgiveness. God answered his prayers, and as time passed he felt the burden of guilt finally being lifted from the depth of his heart.

Charles recognized that through his ordeal God never abandoned him. God has forgiven and blessed him with comforting friendships. "Through God's eternal presence, the truth has set me free," he claims quoting Jesus. "The truth will make you free."[2]

Nathan was not trying to make David feel guilty over what he did, rather he wanted him to confess and experience God's forgiveness. David realized the error of his ways and made his humble confession, "I have sinned against the Lord."

Sin does have consequences that are hard to escape and David's sin would continue to haunt him for many years to come. The prophet Nathan speaking the word of the Lord told him, "The sword shall never depart from your house, for you have despised me...." What David did and tried to cover up in secret would spell disaster in the future. Instead of being secret what would transpire in the future would be out in the open for the entire world to see. Nathan speaking the Word of the Lord told David, "I will raise up trouble against you from within your own house." This would be the beginning of the end for David.

Confessing our sins is the first step toward our reconciliation with God. It was an ordinary afternoon for David Daniels. Weeks before he had made the commitment to take a prayer retreat once a month. He envisioned it as a whole day of "basking in the presence of the Lord." Full of anticipation, David arrived early. He prayed for God to "open the doors of heaven so that I could enjoy him in prayer and worship." David read from the scriptures, quoting verses and memorizing new ones. He prayed and sang hymns aloud.

Five hours later David was angry with God because he says, "Though I was drawing near to him, he seemed so far away from me."

God's message was undeniably clear: "My child, I'm not hiding from you. You've been hiding from me. And before you can enjoy fellowship with me, you must uncover the hidden places of your heart."

Those words struck David. He knew they were indicting but true. As he admits, "I harbored sin — habits, words, actions, attitudes — that I had tried to conceal." Rather than admit his own sin, he had counted on "spiritual" activities to cancel it out — or at least to cause it to be overlooked. That afternoon David realized that it was time to be honest with God.

The most dangerous result of unconfessed sin is the inability to relate rightly to God. To confess involves stripping away layers of disguise to expose what is really at the center of who we are. "That day," David says, "I learned that communion with God must be preceded by confession before God."[3]

As in all episodes from the Bible, this one forces us to consider if we are the ones who have sinned against God. If so, then we need to acknowledge our sins in the hope of being forgiven.

Only when we make our humble confession to God are we able to experience forgiveness. When we claim the error of our past we are given a new future that does not look back.

---

1. "Dear Abby," Abigail VanBuren and Jeanne Phillips, "Man's affair cost him family's respect," June 28, 2001.

2. "Truth or Consequences," Charles Axe, *The Upper Room*, July/August 2000, p. 27.

3. "Coming Clean," David Daniels, *Christian Reader*, January/February 1998, pp. 70-73.

Before It's Too Late

Actress Melanie Griffith candidly writes of her painful experiences while growing up. When she was four years old, her parents broke up and she believes this contributed to her life-long feelings of insecurity.

As a teenager she hid her fears behind a rebellious streak. She was barely fifteen when she met the 22-year-old actor Don Johnson and announced that she wanted to live with him. "I didn't have to put up a big fight," she says.

Reflecting on her life, Melanie states, "What I really needed was to be sent to boarding school to give me the chance to grow up."[1] This serves as another reminder that parents have a responsibility to their children. It is important for children to feel the love and support of their parents. There might be times when parents need to intercede when a son or daughter is acting in inappropriate ways.

David's life must have seemed like a recurrent nightmare. Nothing seemed to be going right. David's life and that of his kingdom would never again be the same as a result of his affair with Bathsheba and the subsequent murder of her husband, Uriah. The prophet Nathan confronted David with his sin. Speaking the Word of the Lord, Nathan told David that the consequences of his sin would be played out in his own family. One reason we might be hesitant to admit our sin is because we are afraid of the consequences. David confessed his sin, admitted the wrong he had done, and was forgiven. God promised David that he would not die.

Much had happened to David and his family in the years since the prophet confronted him. David's oldest son had attacked one of his daughters. While David knew what had happened, he did nothing. Another son, Absalom, was livid over this attack on his sister and two years later had one of his servants murder the brother who attacked his sister. In his grief David still did not seek to intervene in any way.

Absalom then fled and would not return to his family for three years. When he was allowed to return to Jerusalem he undercut his father's authority. This continued for four additional years. During that time Absalom gathered an army and claimed to be king, which forced his father to depart abruptly from the capital city of Jerusalem. The fighting continued, "The battle spread over the face of all the country." The result was many lives lost in battle.

David was in a difficult position. On the one hand, he was the ruler and had to deal effectively with anyone who challenged his authority. On the other hand, David was also a father who did not want to see any harm come to his son. David called his military advisors instructing them, "Deal gently for my sake with the young man Absalom." Alas, victories are not won by dealing "gently" with the enemy.

"All the people heard when the king gave orders to all the commanders concerning Absalom." This is an interesting note, everyone including the soldiers knew they should not harm the prince, Absalom. If the soldiers captured Absalom they would obey the king's order and not harm him.

The battle took place in the forest and surrounding countryside. The fighting was heavy with casualties on both sides. At one point in the battle Absalom unexpectedly met up with some servants of David. Trying to escape capture, Absalom rode away on a mule as fast as he could, but somehow he managed to get snagged by a low branch. Absalom was left dangling "between heaven and earth" as his mule continued without him. He was stuck and could not free himself. He was alone in the forest; his soldiers were not around to free him or protect him either. There he was defenseless in the heat of the battle.

Word soon reached the commanding field officer, Joab, that Absalom was caught in an oak tree. Joab questioned the soldier, "Why then did you not strike him there to the ground?" Joab would gladly have paid anyone who took care of the rebellious prince "ten pieces of silver and a belt" to be rid of this troublesome young man. The soldiers had heard the king's command not to harm Absalom so they would not strike him. So Joab decided to take matters into his own hands. Going against the king's orders, he thrust spears into Absalom's chest. Only then did the others join in. Absalom was killed and buried in the forest.

The victory belonged to David. The insurrection was over. Now he could claim his rightful place as king. One thing remained however. Who would tell David that his son was dead? Messengers bringing bad news to the king have been known to be killed. They decided to send a foreigner to tell David of his son's demise.

Like the father in the Parable of the Prodigal Son, David is anxiously awaiting word on his son. With a sentinel David waited between two gates. Off in the distance he spied a messenger. His heart pounded. Would this be the one to tell him that his son was alive? The first messenger arrived to inform David that "all is well." When asked specifically about his son the messenger was silent.

The second messenger arrived telling David the news, "Good tidings for my lord the King! For the Lord has vindicated you this day, delivering you from the power of all who rose up against you." This was all well and fine but what David really wanted to know was if his son had survived the battle. The only thing he wanted to hear was news about his son. The messenger broke the news to him as best he could that his son had been killed in the battle.

David was heavyhearted with the reality of his son's death. Retreating to his chamber David wept over the death of his son. Down through the ages we can hear David cry out, "O my son Absalom, my son, my son Absalom! Would I had died instead of you. O Absalom, my son, my son!" David was undone by the news of his son Absalom's death. In that moment everything else became irrelevant, the battle, the rebellion, the throne, everything but his deep grief.

A message from this tragic episode might be that when we face difficulties or even open conflict with those we love, our family or circle of friends, we need to intercede as soon as possible.

Was David's grief intensified because he felt responsible? After all, his sinful act set in motion all that transpired. Or, was David grieving in part because this sad chain of events might have been prevented had he intervened earlier with his son?

For this passage to mean anything to us we have to ask ourselves how we would respond when a loved one is in serious trouble. How might we intervene to prevent potential tragedies? We live at a time when there are more books about creating successful, happy marriages and raising children to reach their potential than at any other time in history. Besides books and tapes you cannot walk past a magazine display without noticing articles which offer all sorts of help for our troubled relationships. Why is it that if there is so much available that so many people are hurting?

Perhaps what is missing is our willingness to confront wrong, to talk problems out when someone we love hurts us. The longer we wait the more difficult it becomes and the more time that passes the more resentment grows.

One day Misty was cleaning her teenage daughter's bedroom when she happened to find some letters which she found quite disturbing. The letter was from her daughter's best friend, who wrote about murdering a teacher she did not like. There were other letters decorated with monkeys with vampire teeth, axes, and knives that told of death.

When her daughter came home from school, Misty confronted her about the letters. At first her daughter tried to play it down: "Oh, we didn't mean anything bad." Things would get worse before they would get better. Her mother described this difficult time with her daughter. "When she wasn't raging, she was seething and moody, and she continually taunted us with threats of running away." Her daughter was becoming more and more difficult to communicate with. Misty reached the point that many parents reach. "Part of me was so angry that I almost didn't care," she admitted. "Here was this girl, this child I had carried for nine months and loved with all my being, telling me that she hated me."

Misty and her husband knew that they had to do something. They realized that if they did nothing things would only get worse. Their daughter repeatedly threatened to run away from home or commit suicide. Over Christmas break they enrolled their daughter in a private Christian school. They began regular searches of their daughter's room and backpack, monitored her use of the phone, and forbad her to leave the house without permission. Naturally their daughter was angry and wrote a note to a friend saying she had the dumbest parents in the world.

Fortunately this family received the love and support of their church during this time. They tried to involve their daughter in the youth group. At first it was a struggle. That spring their daughter attended a youth retreat where she made new friends and that helped turn her life around. She recommitted her life to Jesus Christ. As time went on Misty could not believe how her daughter had completely changed. Their daughter seemed like a totally different person.

Through all her trials, Misty discovered that "despite the best efforts of parents and relatives, teachers and friends — a good kid will go bad, and there is little more you can do than admit your shortcomings and start picking up the pieces."[2]

It is especially important to intervene when a person we love is acting in destructive ways that could cause harm to themselves or others. Whether we like it or not, there are times when we need to be "in your face" with those we care about.

It's easier to see someone else's faults than to identify our own and work toward resolution. It's easier to ignore the problem, hoping it will go away by itself or our loved ones will grow out of it, rather than dealing with it in a loving, forgiving way to restore the relationship.

We cannot help but wonder what might have happened to David and his family had he intervened earlier. David did nothing and look how badly things turned out: he had two dead sons and his kingdom was in turmoil.

Alica walked in front of the lights and cameras at a Pennsylvania high school and calmly spoke her lines as part of a public service announcement. "My daughter, Natashia, was killed in a single-car, drug-related accident. She was sixteen. Please learn from this tragedy. You have a life. Be there for it."

As Alica spoke those heart-felt words she was surrounded by some of her daughter's classmates along with a framed picture of her daughter. Her daughter's friends and other students wanted to be involved in the project. Between 200 and 300 ideas had been submitted and then the students picked five to be filmed.

While it was hard for Alica to say those words in front of a camera, she wanted others to view her personal tragedy as a warning to parents and others in the community to reach out to other young people who are in trouble. Alica's daughter had died just three months earlier.

"Natashia made a terrible mistake," she said. "She was a wonderful kid; she just made a very bad choice." Then this grieving mother said, "You hope and pray that you're never in my place. If I could just reach one child, then I feel like my daughter's death was not in vain."[3]

May David's grieving cry, "O my son Absalom, my son, my son Absalom! Would I had died instead of you. O Absalom, my son, my son!" serve as a wake up call for us that we do all in our power to prevent misfortune from happening to those we love and care about.

---

1. "I Took A Chance On A Normal Life," Melanie Griffith, *Parade*, August 6, 2000, p. 4.

2. *She Said Yes*, Misty Bernall, (Farmington, Pennsylvania: The Plough Publishing House, 1999), p. 38.

3. "Hempfield Students Deliver Message," Alyssa Roggie, *Intelligencer Journal*, Lancaster, Pennsylvania, May 8, 2001.

Proper 15
Pentecost 13
Ordinary Time 20
1 Kings 2:10-12; 3:3-14

Where Do We Go From Here?

It was a critical time in the life of the people. Their beloved king had died. In spite of all David's shortcomings and failures, he was still popular in the eyes of the people. The royal throne would be passed down to a young son, Solomon. Solomon was the second son of Bathsheba and David. Whenever there is a change in leadership, there is a sense of uncertainty, of not knowing what life will be like in the near future. Will the new leader follow in the steps of the old one? Or will the new leader initiate new programs and focus in new directions? There might even be some anxiety; not knowing what path the new leader will follow. The people might have wondered, "Will our lives ever be the same again?"

In times of uncertainty or even crisis it is important to seek out God's direction. That's exactly what Solomon did. He left the hustle and bustle of the city and traveled some seven miles to a place called Gibeon. Gibeon was a place where people went to offer sacrifices to God. Being one of the highest spots, it was a place where people came to worship God. In the silence of worship Solomon would pray, seeking God's guidance in his life.

Ian Frazier traveled to Nome, Alaska, to cover a story for a magazine, but bad weather made his task impossible. The rain fell constantly that August. There was nothing for Ian to do except sit in his lonely hotel room for several days. During that time he read "obscure books to the sound of the rain." He saw no one for a couple of days. When he needed a break he would look outside the window as "Bering Sea waves the color of wet cement landed on the riprap shoreline with thuds."

After three or four days, he says, of being "completely bummed out," he went to the airport and flew home. By the time he arrived back home he says of his experience he felt "wonderfully refreshed."[1]

Time away from the busyness and stress of our lives can revive our souls. We are nearing the end of summer, a time when people enjoy vacations. People enjoy the beauty of water or mountains or desert. Away from all the distractions of daily life, people find rest and feel refreshed.

For people of faith it is a natural reaction in times of uncertainty or when facing new challenges to seek out God's direction. Solomon loved God and God loved Solomon. Still young Solomon couldn't help but feel overwhelmed at the enormous responsibility that was thrust upon him. As the ruler he was responsible for many people. Maybe he felt he was in over his head.

After offering a sacrifice of "a thousand burnt offerings" Solomon decided to spend the night in that tranquil setting. It was while he was sleeping that God spoke to him in a dream. In the dream God asked the young ruler, "Ask what I should give you." Solomon's response has become a model prayer for us. First he acknowledged God's grace in his life, even though he was undeserving of such favor. "And now, O Lord my God, you have made your servant king in place of my father David, although I am only a child." Second Solomon readily admitted his own sense of inadequacy, "I do not know how to go out or come in." It is a humbling experience to admit our shortcomings before anyone yet alone before God.

Next Solomon prays for God's gift of wisdom, realizing that he cannot rule the people without God's help. He prays, "Give your servant therefore an understanding mind to govern your people, able to discern between good and evil." He knew deep down how much he needed God's help. He wanted to be the best possible ruler of God's people, and he must have realized that he could not do it alone. Solomon knew that he could not acquire wisdom by his own effort. He also knew he was not born with wisdom either. Rather, wisdom was a gift given from God. Solomon was wise enough to seek God.

Too often our problem is that we do not seek out God's guidance until we are in over our heads. Our prayers tend to become selfish shopping lists of all the things we think we need or want instead of asking for God's direction for our lives. The starting point must be to seek out God's direction for our lives.

Josh enjoyed working in the family-owned car repair shop. Being part of a family-owned business, Josh never really thought about any other career. It was always assumed he would help manage the shop.

At the annual church picnic at a local park, Josh volunteered to help with the games for elementary-aged children. That day at the park Josh had a wonderful time with the children. Afterward several people commented how well he related to the children and how the children responded to him.

This caused Josh to do some soul searching. He would pray seeking God's direction. Then the idea came to him that he should be a schoolteacher even though that would require going back to college at age thirty. Josh was surprised at how supportive his wife and family were of his decision. He prayed some more. He spoke with his pastor. It seemed everyone responded in a positive way, encouraging him to pursue his new goal. A friend told him he wondered what took him so long to decide to become a teacher. As is often the case, other people recognized the gift before Josh even realized he possessed it.

Josh continued working full-time while attending classes in the evening. After a couple of years Josh had enough credits and was certified to teach elementary school. He was hired as a fourth grade teacher.

Before too long, "Mr. G." as he was affectionately called by his students was one of the most popular teachers at that school. He won the respect of his students and their parents as well as his colleagues.

In asking for wisdom, Solomon pleaded with God. In the dream God continued speaking to Solomon, "I give you a wise and discerning mind; no one like you has been before you and no one like you shall arise after you." Solomon's wisdom has become legendary. One of his first acts as ruler was to decide a case involving two women both claiming to be the mother of an infant. The women continued arguing back and forth over which one was actually the child's mother. Finally Solomon had heard enough. He asked one of his attendants to "bring me a sword." He would cut the child in half and give half to each woman.

As Solomon held the sword in the air ready to strike the child, one of the women pleaded, "Please, my Lord, give her the living boy; certainly do not kill him!" The other woman could gladly take the child. Solomon with his great gift of wisdom ordered that the child be given to the woman who was willing to give the child to the other woman just as long as the child was not killed. "She is the mother," Solomon exclaimed, because no mother would want to see harm done to her child. At the end of chapter 3 we find that "All Israel heard of the judgment that the king had rendered; and they stood in awe of the king, because they perceived that the wisdom of God was in him" (1 Kings 3:28).

At those times of uncertainty or confusion or when crises arise we need to seek God's direction in our lives. When we do we come to an amazing discovery. While we think we have looked for God, in truth, God has been looking for us. We did not choose God, rather, God chose us as the Apostle Paul reminds us, "God chose you ..." (2 Thessalonians 2:13). It was God's invitation, God's initiative when he appeared to Solomon in a dream.

Anne Lamott tells of her long and painful journey to faith. She says it wasn't a leap of faith but more like a "lurch of faith." While she was growing up, her parents showed little interest in matters of faith, at times they even seemed antagonistic to Christianity. While in high school Anne became friendly with a girl whose whole family was Christian. In college Anne took a course on religion which stimulated her longing for faith. She took the course, she says, "In deference to this puzzling thing inside of me that had begun to tug on my sleeve from time to time, trying to get my attention." She found herself in the chapel trying to pray.

Then came some troubling years for Anne. Tragedy struck as her father was diagnosed with a terminal illness. She became involved with alcohol and drugs, and one destructive relationship followed another. "Then one afternoon in my dark bedroom," Anne says, "I believed that I would die soon from a fall or an overdose." At that low point in her life she remembered hearing about a new pastor in town. She realized she needed to talk with someone and called him. He offered her words of hope that would begin the long process toward faith and wholeness. As Anne spoke of her pain she shared that she did not feel loved and found it hard to believe that God could love her. "God has to love you," said the pastor. "That's God's job."

Next Anne began attending church but always left before the sermon. "I loved singing, even about Jesus, but I just didn't want to hear about him." Eventually she would stay for the message. She experienced and felt love from that congregation that brought her to faith in Jesus Christ. "No matter how badly I am feeling, how lost or lonely, or frightened, when I see the faces of the people at my church, and hear their tawny voices," she says, "I can always find my way home."[2]

Finally, God promised Solomon, "If you will walk in my ways, keeping my statutes and my commandments ... then I will lengthen your life." Solomon awoke from his dream. He returned to Jerusalem and "stood before the ark of the covenant of the Lord." Again he offered sacrifices and then treated his attendants to a feast.

Solomon began his rule in an acceptable way, seeking and following God's direction. Trouble would find Solomon when he lost his focus, his desire to follow God's objective, and the same is true for us whenever we think we can make our own decisions excluding God. The starting point in our lives is to seek God's direction.

---

1. "Woe Is Me," Ian Frazier, *The Atlantic Monthly*, March 2001, p. 25.

2. *Traveling Mercies*, Anne Lamott (New York: Anchor Books, 1999), pp. 23-55.

Proper 16
Pentecost 14
Ordinary Time 21
1 Kings 8:(1, 6, 10-11) 22-30, 41-43

Promises, Promises

George recalls the time many years ago when he and his wife were about to have their first child. Neither of them attended church. George says, "I didn't consider myself a Christian at all, but we decided it might be a good thing to go to church to raise our child to be a moral, ethical human being." They thought they could go and not necessarily believe what others did. They would just go to church and receive the benefit of that moral teaching.

They went to an Episcopal Church near their home, neither having been raised Episcopalian. They sat near the back that first Sunday. As the service began there was a procession of the choirs, worship leaders, and pastor. They noticed someone carrying a large cross. The procession of the cross began in the front, moved along the side of the sanctuary to the back and finally up the center aisle. At one point during the processional, the cross passed right next to the pew where George and his wife were sitting.

"I experienced something that day," George explains, "I would call a baptism of the Holy Spirit. I didn't have any name for it at all — it was as if both of us were hit by lightning and filled by the very presence of God." They both began weeping and fell to their knees and prayed. Suddenly they realized that there were people all around them praying, "like a great cloud of witnesses or heavenly hosts gathered around in prayer with us."

It was at that moment, George says, that he became a Christian. There were no words spoken, no four spiritual laws, no preaching had been done. The power of seeing the cross in procession, recognizing the honor that had been given to it, left George speechless. As George later explains, "I understood what the cross really was about and really meant — it communicated everything I needed to know."[1]

King Solomon's desire was for the Temple to be a place where people could come to worship God. In the beauty and grandeur of the newly constructed Temple, people would be able to feel the presence of God in their lives.

For Solomon and all the people the completion and dedication of the Temple was a major accomplishment worthy of celebration. It was a defining moment as Solomon stood before all the people as the famed Ark of the Covenant was brought to its new home. It was one of those rare times when everyone felt good, we might say proud, to be present for such an historical event.

Solomon's father David was responsible for bringing the Ark to Jerusalem after it had been out of sight and out of mind for nearly forty years. The Israelites believed that the Ark was holy and somehow contained God's presence, which could be felt in powerful ways. As Moses led the ancient Israelites in the wilderness for forty years the Ark of the Covenant traveled with them. A special tent housed the Ark. Years later the Ark would have a permanent home in the newly completed Temple. Solomon hoped that the new Temple would symbolize God's favor just as the Ark had for the people in the wilderness. In Solomon's eyes the dedication of the Temple was just as momentous as Moses leading the people across the sea on their journey to freedom and the Promised Land.

The Temple was completed in just seven years and consisted of three parts, an open air vestibule, a Holy Place or nave which contained a table for the "bread of the Presence," and finally the Holy of Holies which was where the Ark would be housed. The Holy of Holies was a perfect cube, unlit by any natural light. The walls and floors of both the Holy Place and the Holy of Holies were overlaid with gold. Access to the Holy of Holies was limited for priests only on special occasions.

The day of dedication contained much pageantry as the priests marched several hundred yards carefully carrying the Ark of the Covenant while the king and other officials and all the people looked on in astonishment. It soon became apparent that God was present with them that special day. "When the priests came out of the holy place, a cloud filled the house of the Lord." The priests quickly exited, "for the glory of the Lord filled the house of the Lord." Clearly this was a decisive moment that would be remembered and retold for generations to come.

If only in our moments of doubt we could feel God's presence in such a powerful way, as the people did that day when the Temple was dedicated — then we would no longer question our faith. There are times in our lives when we wish we could sense God's presence in our lives. There are other times when we make major decisions and look for God's direction and guidance. We question over and over whether we have done the right thing. We wait for some sign of approval and often do not perceive it.

The last years of Robert Buker's mother's life were filled with questioning whether she and her husband's first missionary assignment in Burma had made any impact on the people. "There is nothing left of our work in Burma," Bob remembers his mother saying over and over. "It was wasted effort, wasted years, all in vain," she would tell her children. Her despair surprised Bob. His father had been a missionary doctor while his mother was a nurse. They set out for the mission field in 1926.

A few years after World War II, Burma closed itself to missionary work. His parents tried to keep up with the news, but the reports were never good. During the war under enemy occupation, many people renounced their faith.

Bob along with fifteen family members decided just months after his mother's death to visit Burma, which the government finally opened to outsiders. It was there that Bob says, "We found our parents' work had produced results they could never have imagined."

"Mother and Father never knew the rest of their story, but now in glory they do. And their children and grandchildren have seen it with their own eyes. A strong, growing, indigenous church — self supporting, self-educating, and evangelizing, even under difficult circumstances — has blossomed from a seed planted long ago."[2] Their work was not in vain, as Bob's mother thought in her later years, but did touch many lives.

We discover that God has indeed been present in our lives in fact even at those difficult times when we have a hard time discerning God's direction for our lives. The truth is that we might not ever know the impact of our words and actions on other people. The Apostle Paul reminds us: "I am confident of this, that the one who began a good work among you will bring it to completion by the day of Jesus Christ" (Philippians 1:6).

Perhaps Solomon and the people gathered around the newly completed Temple wanted to know if their work pleased God. "The glory of the Lord filled the house of the Lord." Having experienced the cloud of God's presence filling the Temple, looking out at all the people, some of whom might have been crying tears of joy, it might have been difficult for Solomon to find the proper words to speak at such a momentous occasion. "Solomon stood before the altar of the Lord in the presence of all the assembly of Israel, and spread out his hands to heaven." He began his prayer praising God, "O Lord, God of Israel, there is no God like you in heaven above or on earth beneath."

Solomon with great confidence, standing with his arms outstretched, led the people in prayer, "Hear the plea of your servant and of your people Israel when they pray toward this place; O hear in heaven your dwelling place; heed and forgive." The Temple would be a powerful symbol not only of God's presence, but also of God's omnipotent power. Yet Solomon in his wisdom realized that God cannot be contained or limited in any way. While the people would worship in the newly dedicated Temple for generations to come, God could not be limited to one place. "Even heaven and the highest heaven cannot contain you," Solomon humbly prayed, "much less this house that I have built!" God could not be contained or limited to one specific place for all time. God was grander, bigger, more powerful than any human could ever imagine.

While it is comforting to know that God hears our prayers and loves and cares for each one of us, sometimes we are tempted to define God by our own limited experiences. That way of thinking only gets us into trouble, when we think that God must be like us and hold the same likes and dislikes as we do. As Solomon prayed that day, he understood that God could not be contained or limited to one place. Nothing human hands could ever construct would hold God.

For people searching for God, the Temple was a good place to begin. In the same way today, people seek refuge from the many stresses of their daily lives in the sanctuary of churches. The church is a quiet place where people can come to pray. Sitting in the sanctuary in silence provides persons with the opportunity not only to pray but also to listen for God's still small voice away from the many daily distractions. Solomon hoped that the Temple would be a starting place for people on a journey to faith.

Solomon in his wisdom realized that God was the God of all people, not just the Israelites living near the Temple. Continuing with his prayer, Solomon prayed, "Likewise when a foreigner, who is not of your people Israel, comes from a distant land ... and prays toward this house, then hear in heaven your dwelling place...." Solomon imagined the day when a traveler from a far away land would visit Jerusalem and be taken in by the grandeur and beauty of the Temple. Perhaps viewing the Temple would elicit a prayer or the realization that there is a God. Again the Temple might be a starting point for a person's journey to know God. Our God is an awesome God whose saving presence can be felt all over the world. "So that all the peoples of the earth may know your name and fear you," Solomon prayed.

Our lesson once again reveals that God is trustworthy. Above all else, God keeps God's promises. Solomon prayed, "The covenant that you kept for your servant my father David as you declared to him; you promised with your mouth and have this day fulfilled with your hand." God entered into covenant relationship with Noah, Abraham, Moses, David, Solomon, and others.

Even when sinful humanity broke the covenant with God, God still kept the promise. Remember how Abraham and Sarah were promised a son. As Abraham waited he decided to take matters into his own hands by having a child with one of Sarah's servants. Even that willful act did not break God's covenant promise. Despite all odds Abraham and Sarah did have a son in their old age. While there might be times when we fail God, when we do things that we know deep down are wrong, God is still faithful to us.

341

Throughout the pages of the Bible, we discover how God keeps God's promises. From the promise made to David concerning the building the Temple by his son down through the ages until the promise of another son was fulfilled, in our Lord Jesus Christ. God remains faithful to that promise today.

---

1. *Ancient-Future Worship* video tape, Robert Webber, Institute for Worship, Wheaton, Illinois 60189, 1999.

2. "Wasted Years?" Robert H. Buker, *Christian Reader*, January/February 2001.

Proper 17
Pentecost 15
Ordinary Time 22
Song of Solomon 2:8-13

Where Have All The Flowers Gone?

The Song of Solomon is a collection of some of the world's greatest love poems. The Song of Solomon is different from other Old Testament books. Instead of concentrating on tribal conflict or political or religious disputes, the focus is on personal relationships. While we live in a world filled with people experiencing the pain of broken relationships, the Song of Solomon is a celebration of being in love. May these verses remind us once again of the importance of being in relationship with other people and ultimately with God.

Most couples are nervous as their wedding day approaches. Perhaps as the day gets closer some couples are filled with second thoughts, wondering if getting married is the right thing for them. Martha Manning remembers all too well those apprehensive feelings prior to her wedding day. She specifically recalls the vows she and her husband took 22 years ago. "The vows worked then and they still work now," she says. However, she admits that her wedding vows mean something different to her now than they did when she was 21 years old standing before friends, relatives, and God on her wedding day. Candidly she says, "When I said those words at 21, resisting recipe cards, avocado appliances, and a boring life were the challenges I anticipated." Then she acknowledges, "When I first said those words, I never envisioned that they would have to stretch so far — over times of tremendous pain and suffering, over the wonderful and awful stages of parenthood, over advances we never expected and losses we'd always feared." Those vows carried her through the "I hate you and anyone who looks like you" times as well as the "I love you completely" times. "All I knew was that I meant them then," Martha says, "and I want to mean them for the rest of my life. And the best thing is that I still do."[1]

We do not know anything about the young couple in today's lesson who were so passionately in love. However, I see an older, more mature woman sitting by herself on her porch reminiscing about the past when she was young and in love. It was obviously a very special time in her life. Maybe the years have added pain to her life. Perhaps she is older still and is grieving the recent loss of her "beloved."

She remembers with vivid detail the time she first met her beloved many years before. Clearly this was a turning point in her life. It was an ordinary day, when she met the one person who would forever change her life. It was springtime when the earth seemed to come alive with new life. As she is sitting on the same porch, she closes her eyes and remembers the day long ago when her beloved came "leaping" and "bounding over the hills into her arms." He was young then, so healthy, athletic, and good-looking, with the strength and energy of a "gazelle or young stag."

We remember the ordinariness of the day when we met our "significant other." There might have been times when the other person caught our attention as well as those times when that special person went unnoticed.

Mike and Amy occasionally ran into each other while attending college, but neither felt drawn to the other. The summer before Amy's senior year she got a job at the local mall where Mike worked. "After a week," Amy says, "he asked me out on a date." Amy soon discovered that Mike was different from most of the other guys she had dated. She discovered that Mike "was serious about living for God."

Mike grew up without his father so he never knew what would make a good marriage. He remembers, as a boy watching the adults around him, the couples always seemed to be fighting, and always struggling. He hoped eventually to get married but was gearing himself up to grit his teeth and endure the hard stuff.

It did not take Mike too long either to realize that Amy was right for him. "Amy is so easy to love," he recalls. Three months later they were married.

Soon after Mike and Amy were married, he says, "The biggest surprise was that marriage is so much fun." Candidly but truthfully he says, "I didn't expect marriage to be such a blast."

Friends and family ask Mike and Amy what has made their marriage so successful. Both viewed their first couple of years as critical. "We were so poor," Mike remembers, "all we had was each other. No money for a television, no money to go out to dinner or the movies." Amy adds, "It was a good time for us to learn to depend on each other." Through good times and tough times Mike and Amy's relationship remains strong.[2]

The woman in our lesson remembers her first encounter and those first feelings of love stirring inside her. She remembers the sound of his voice as he called her, "Arise, my love, my fair one, and come away." No one would deny the euphoria of being in love, but we must add a word of caution to our young people. A host of recent movies depicts persons falling in love at first sight. This love is described as the love of a lifetime, before sufficient time is spent nurturing the relationship. This might make blockbuster romantic movies, but it is not the way people enter into loving relationships with each other. In other words, it's not that easy. Relationships need to be cultivated, nurtured, safeguarded, and cherished. We have to be intentional about spending good quality time talking and getting to know each other. It takes time for persons to get to know one another. There is no substitute for spending time together.

Another vivid image that comes to mind from our lesson is the often-intoxicating feelings of love that springtime arouses. Springtime is a wonderful time to fall in love, with the sight and smell of fresh flowers triggering the feelings of love. There is an aroma in the air of newly-blossomed flowers, figs, and vines. How good it is to take in a deep breath of air. There are animals frolicking about the countryside. Off in the distance there is the sound of birds singing their love songs: "The time of singing has come, and the voice of the turtledove is heard in our land," the woman remembers in

345

her love poem. Who hasn't enjoyed walking through the grass following a spring rain and feeling the cool grass on their feet? Our senses come alive in the spring.

There are those times when being in love causes us to do crazy things we might not normally do. The young man nears the house, looking over the wall or hedge to see his cherished one. He peers through the window hoping to catch a glimpse of her. He invites his love to "arise, my love, my fair one, and come away." Does she respond immediately? The loving couple join hands and waltz down the hill together.

Like the flowers of spring our relationship grows and blossoms into something beautiful. There are other times when a relationship requires patience and endurance, during which we hope and pray for resolution. This brings us to another important aspect of relationships, the commitment to stay together. There will be times when there are disagreements and differences of opinion. Being committed to each other means being willing to work things out finding a suitable compromise. While no one looks forward to such times, they are without a doubt times when we grow in our relationship.

In spending time together we also need to engage in activities that the other person truly enjoys. The temptation is selfishly to do what we enjoy and neglect the other person's wants and needs. We might be surprised to discover that our companion does not enjoy the same things we do. It takes courage to work out differences in acceptable ways.

Like many newlyweds, Deena and Carl struggled during their first years of marriage. Shortly before they were married Carl accepted a job 120 miles away, leaving Deena to attend to all the details of their wedding. She was upset that Carl did not involve her in the decision. The summer after the wedding Deena felt all alone, away from her family and friends, living in a new city. To further complicate things, Carl was working different shifts, which added to their struggles. At first Deena tried to adjust her schedule to her husband's, which only made her miserable. It was decided that Deena should not try to copy Carl's schedule. Once she was able to slip into a steady sleep cycle, she says she began to smile again.

One day the next spring, Carl told Deena that his company was restructuring. "Team player" and teamwork would be the order of the day. Later that day Deena wondered why Carl was being rewarded at work because he was a team player. "Why hadn't I seen him that way?" she asked herself. She began praying, seeking God's guidance. Then she began to wonder if maybe she was the one who was not a "team player."

"I started to look anew at how well Carl worked at being a good — no, a great — husband rather than focusing on his shortcomings," Deena reflected. She recognized her own preoccupation with independence, which was the opposite way a partner should act. "Carl and I had gotten married because we loved each other more than anything else in the world. We'd made a commitment to each other."

Needless to say, this was a turning point in their relationship. "We make a pretty good team." From that moment on she would include God in their marriage. "God and Carl and I," was the way Deena put it. "And we make our decisions together. There, within that commitment, is where I have found freedom."[3]

In the very first book of the Bible, Genesis, we discover that God desires to be in relationship with humans. God is viewed as entering into relationship with the first couple, Adam and Eve, even walking in the Garden of Eden. Later God would enter into covenant with Abraham and Sarah. Still later God would give Moses the Ten Commandments. Finally God would enter into relationship with humanity through our Lord Jesus Christ.

Knowing that God loves each of us and desires to be in relationship with us allows us to enter into meaningful relationships with other people. Some suggest that in order to love another person we must first experience love. The New Testament Book of First John reminds us of this truth, "We love because God first loved us" (1 John 4:19).

The Song of Solomon rekindles in us those special feelings of being in love. May we continue to grow in all our relationships.

1. *Chasing Grace*, Martha Manning, (San Francisco: Harper San Francisco, 1996), p. 184.

2. "Joy Ride," Annette LaPlaca, *Marriage Partnership*, Fall 1999, Vol. 16, No. 3, p. 26.

3. "True Commitment," Deena Clark Farris, *Guideposts*, October 1999, pp. 36-39.

Abundant Love

The pastor began his sermon by telling of an encounter earlier that week. A man entered the church, dripping wet from the rain, looking for help. The man had nowhere else to go for help. As he stood there, it was obvious just how dirty his hair and face were, as water continued to drip down his face. He explained to the pastor that he hadn't eaten anything since the day before. He had no money. Any help the church could give would be appreciated.

He explained how he was traveling, mostly on foot from somewhere upstate. Someone had told him that he might be able to find a job in another part of the state, so he set out hitchhiking but ended up mostly walking. It had been a long time or at least it seemed like a long time since he held a steady job. While he was looking for a fresh start in life, all he really wanted that day was something to eat.

The pastor made arrangements with a nearby restaurant to give this man a good meal. The pastor could not help but wonder how this man would be received at the restaurant. Would the hostess refuse to seat him? Would the waitress not want to serve him? What would the paying customers think? The pastor gave the man directions; the restaurant was on the next block.

About an hour later the same man came back to the church. He wanted to thank the pastor for the delicious meal. The pastor wished him well as he continued on his journey.

As the pastor shared this story with the congregation, it was obvious that some of the people sitting in the pews were uncomfortable. The pastor asked the congregation, "Why do people who are down on their luck or who have not had the same advantages as others make us feel uncomfortable?" While we might be able to list several reasons perhaps they are just excuses for not getting involved or trying to help in some way.

Our honest response might be to look down on people who struggle with issues that many of us take for granted, like food and shelter. We find in our lesson from Proverbs the following verse, "The rich and the poor have this in common: the Lord is the maker of them all." God is the creator of both the rich and the poor. When we are tempted to look down on other people we need to remember that God loves all people. When people are struggling and do not have anywhere else to turn, they can always turn to the God who created them and never stops loving them. If only we could see people for who they really are and not judge people in superficial ways, by the kind of clothes they wear or cars they drive or the jobs they hold.

What is important for us to remember is that we cannot be good Christians in isolation, we need each other, and we need to be with other people. Our attitude toward the poor needs to be grounded in our faith. As the wise author of Proverbs clearly stated, "A good name is to be chosen rather than great riches, and favor is better than silver or gold." To have a good name or reputation means that we view other people as beloved children of God and not by outward appearances. As God explained to the prophet Samuel, "Do not look on his appearance or on the height of his stature, because I have rejected him; for the Lord does not see as mortals see; they look on the outward appearances, but the Lord looks on the heart" (1 Samuel 16:7).

We also have a responsibility to help others in their time of need. We should not take unfair advantage of anyone, especially those with the greatest needs. We are outraged when we read about people who take unfair advantage of the poor and in the process make a profit. And rightly so.

Throughout the scriptures we discover that God is on the side of the poor and oppressed. "Do not rob the poor because they are poor, or crush the afflicted at the gate; for the Lord pleads their cause." God has a special place for the "least of these who are

350

members of my family" (Matthew 25:40). Because people who are lost or forgotten matter to God, they should matter to us as well.

The greatest compliment anyone could give us is that we have made a positive impact in his or her life. Perhaps all it took was our willingness to listen to another person's problems. Or maybe sitting with a friend in a hospital waiting room awaiting news of a loved one. Or even giving someone a good meal that might give them the confidence to turn their lives around. There might be other times when our words make an indelible impression on another person. Only God knows how our words and actions will impact another person. We might truly be the person to make a difference in another person's life.

It was nearly midnight when Richard's plane landed in Bangkok. He would have another lengthy layover before his next flight that would take him to his final destination, Calcutta. With the support of his church back home in New York City, Richard was going to spend two months as a volunteer at Mother Teresa's mission.

Forty hours earlier, at the start of his trip, Richard said it was like a dream come true. Awaiting his final flight, he wasn't as sure. "My nerves worn raw by sleeplessness," he explained, "I tried to absorb the information that somewhere between South Korea and Thailand my luggage had been 'misdirected.' " He was beginning to think his trip was a mistake. Maybe he should have stayed at home, instead of traveling halfway around the world, without his luggage. He admitted, "I felt as lost as my bags." As he waited, he noticed four clocks on the wall telling the time in various places in the world. He realized that back home it was noon on Sunday.

He remembered how the church that was sponsoring his trip promised to pray for him at their noon service. It struck him that there were people praying for him at that very moment halfway around the world. Richard says with that realization "a peaceful assurance burst over me, and I felt comforted. I wasn't alone."

Richard spent two months volunteering at a home for the destitute run by Mother Teresa and the missionaries of Charity. "It was a holy experience," Richard said.[1] When we reach out to help others, offering them an encouraging word, it becomes a holy moment in our lives because we realize that we have made a difference.

As people of faith we realize that God permeates all of life. We cannot separate certain aspects of our lives. The way we treat other people, especially people who might be different from us in some way, is a reflection of how we understand our faith. Do we treat everyone we come in contact with as a precious child of God? Some might be tempted to take advantage of those less fortunate, thinking they will get away with it and that no one will ever know. The people who have been taken advantage of do not have the means to fight their maltreatment and so are powerless. No one would take his or her word over ours, we might think to ourselves.

The wise writer of Proverbs believes differently. "Whoever sows injustice will reap calamity, and the rod of anger will fail." Therefore we should not treat other people badly, because one day we might find ourselves in a similar situation or worse. Someday someone will treat us in the same way we've treated others. The day might come when we need someone's help or assistance and we expect to be treated fairly. Anyone who exploits the weakness of another person for personal gain, whether to rob or cheat, will one day pay for it. One thing we can all be certain of is that God will have the last word for each one of us.

After the worship service a woman asked if she might speak to the pastor for a minute or two. The pastor's encounter with the person who needed assistance caused her to think. She remembered visiting her grandmother when she was a young girl. Her grandmother would often tell her how during the Great Depression of the 1930s people would stop by the house asking for food. Her kindhearted grandmother would always give the person a sandwich and a glass of water. She said her grandmother would never turn anyone away hungry.

The woman asked the pastor why the church could not help feed hungry people like the man who wandered in from the street. Certainly if this one man found his way to the church there must be other people who are hungry. The pastor encouraged her, telling her to develop a plan to provide meals for needy persons. The woman gladly accepted the challenge to start a new ministry in their community. She said she knew other people from church who would help her as well.

By the next Sunday she had researched the problem and discovered that there were people living near the church who could use help. There were elderly people living on limited incomes that would appreciate a meal now and then. She also discovered that there were also some single-parent families living nearby who she knew statistically must be living near or below the poverty line that might accept occasional help.

She proposed starting a Saturday morning breakfast once a month for anyone who would like to come from the neighborhood. There would be no forms to fill out, no paper work, just a good nutritious breakfast cooked by people from the church. She could hardly contain her enthusiasm. She saw so many benefits from her idea. For those who lived alone this would provide a time to be with other people. It would also bring people into the church who might not feel welcomed, thinking specifically of the single-parent families. "Isn't being involved in our community what you've been preaching to us?" she asked her pastor. A new ministry was born. The first Saturday morning breakfast twenty people attended; there were even more the next month. Before too long others wanted to be involved in this ministry, helping to cook or serve, while others gladly donated food.

The last Saturday of the month, rain or shine the church would be open to people from the neighborhood. Within six months over seventy persons ate breakfast in the church's fellowship hall.

The love of God fills our lives to the point that God's love simply overflows. That overabundance of love can then be shared with other people. As our lesson reminds us, "Those who are generous are blessed, for they share their bread with the poor."

The truly faithful person is the one whose love of God is so full that it overflows with love toward other people no matter what their status or condition.

---

1. *Guideposts.*

Solid Foundation

There was much excitement on the first night of Vacation Bible School as parents eagerly registered their children at the door. Some of the children could hardly wait, while others were less than enthusiastic about participating. Nine-year-old Kyle was a hold out. He stood on the grass ten feet from the registration table, arms folded across his chest. He did not want and would not attend Bible School, he told his mother in no uncertain terms. He stood there by himself frowning. When the pastor tried to encourage him, he replied that he did not like anything about Vacation Bible School and in particular he hated singing. As Vacation Bible School began Kyle was still standing in the grass outside, refusing to participate. Disappointed his mother eventually took him home.

We smile at this all too familiar story partly because we have all dealt with this situation at one time or another. Maybe we recognize ourselves at one point not wanting to participate in the life of the church. There might have been a time in our lives when we protested attending Sunday school or worship. Or maybe it was one of our children or even grandchildren who, like Kyle, refused to attend Sunday school or worship. It might have been a sister or brother who would fight to stay home, gladly accepting any punishment handed out if only he or she could remain home while the rest of the family went to church. Some children might even fake sickness on Sunday morning in an attempt to stay home.

Then there are other people, grown adults, who have a hard time accepting the faith that we cherish. Our best efforts have repeatedly failed to pique their interest in matters of faith. They are nice people but they simply do not seem interested. For some people it might take years of steadfast prayer and repeated invitations before they are receptive to what we have to say.

One thing is almost certain, however: there will come a time when we need a strong faith to weather a crisis, or illness, or even the death of someone we love dearly. There are some who get caught up in the whirlwind of crisis with very little understanding of faith and nowhere to turn for help. The wise teacher in our lesson states that when the unthinkable happens it will strike with the suddenness of a storm. "Your calamity comes like a whirlwind." Unfortunately we know how true that statement is; one minute we are enjoying life but the next we are faced with a life-threatening illness. You feel secure in your job and then unexpectedly your company merges with another and you are laid-off. For others it might be unexpected family or personal problems that come suddenly and throw them into a storm they never saw coming. Once persons are caught in the midst of life's storms it might seem that there is no escape, just as there is no way to stop the pounding rain and the fierce winds of a hurricane.

We need a faith that will get us through all the storms of life that come our way. Like the house built on a firm foundation that is able to withstand the fiercest storm, we too can weather any storm with our strong faith.

Connie Cameron decided it was time to go to the doctor after weeks of soreness in her breast. That time was very stressful for her and she said she had difficulty giving her fears to God. A few days before surgery, the realization hit her that she might not be around to watch her children grow into adulthood. Once again she was paralyzed with fear. It was at this point that she remembered crying out to God for help.

"Suddenly," Connie said, "I remembered a comforting verse hidden in my heart for such a time as this, 'For I know the plans I have for you ... plans to prosper you and not to harm you, plans to give you hope and a future' " (Jeremiah 29:11). Peace that only God could give filled her with new confidence.

During this time of uncertainty she realized that she had not read the Bible as she much as she would have liked to. Had she not remembered that verse she might not have recognized it as God's voice. "I might have missed the blessing that God longed to give me," Connie states. The truth is that we cannot recall scripture in our moment of need unless we become familiar with it ahead of time. "With renewed vigor," she said, "I resumed my daily Bible study — not just for the blessings it offers today but for the hope it can bring tomorrow." Not everyone is as fortunate as Connie is; all of her tests came back negative.[1]

The ongoing question is: How can we reach people who might be reluctant or uninterested in matters of faith? Creative individuals have employed various methods to reach uninterested people. In our lesson the wise teacher portrayed wisdom as a woman calling passersby from the busy marketplace. On a crowded street among merchants selling their wares was a provocatively dressed woman, certain to gain attention. She has something important to teach others but few paid attention. She asked, "How long, O simple ones, will you love being simple?"

We know the reaction of others when we try to speak of matters of faith with someone who is totally disinterested. They do not want to engage in conversation with us. Or they change the subject to some safe topic, like the weather. There might even have been times when they simply walk away saying nothing. When that happens we feel frustrated. We want to say something like, "Listen up, this is for your own good." Yet we realize that we have to be careful not to distance them any further from matters of faith.

Just as wisdom had a message, "I will pour out my thoughts to you; I will make my words known to you," she too was not taken seriously. We can sense Wisdom's frustration, "Because I have called and you refused, have stretched out my hand and no one heeded." We have a life-changing message but find people are more interested in other things.

The wise teacher knew that the day would come when those who scoffed would wish they had listened. Often when that day comes it will be too late. "Because you have ignored all my council and would have none of my reproof, I will laugh at your calamity," Wisdom states. That seems harsh to us, doesn't it? Perhaps this was a method of calling attention to the seriousness of the situation or yet another way of gaining the attention of disinterested persons. The wise teacher would stop at nothing, hoping the person would reconsider and listen to and accept the message.

For the people who stop and listen, the gospel message can change their lives. Those who build a solid foundation will experience the peace that only God can give. As the wise teacher explains, "For those who listen to me will be secure and will live at ease."

Ruth Newcomer is a woman with a mission — an 84-year-old woman — to whom age is no obstacle. She believes in doing worthwhile things that have eternal value. Once a week Ruth leads a Bible study for incarcerated teenagers. She is frequently asked why she bothers with troubled teenagers. Ruth will tell you that years ago after a rather convicting sermon, she concluded that she was wasting her life on "selfish pleasures." As a result of that life-changing message she says, "I dropped out of everything I was selfishly engaged in and started doing things that had meaning in life."

Nine teenagers were waiting as Ruth entered the juvenile detention center. Long hair, short hair with blond tips, beards, hard eyes, soft eyes, cocky faces, slumping shoulders, girls and boys of all backgrounds. All of them had been arrested. She began her lesson by telling them about investments. Investments they make with their lives. She told them the "Parable of Talents" about the farmer who entrusted each of his workers with money before leaving on a trip.

Ruth drove home the message to these teens; "You are worth something even though you made a mistake. You have to find that talent and increase it." Ruth told them how God watches out for them and quoted from Psalms how God knew them before they were even born. "The Lord doesn't give you that talent to waste or hurt other people," she said.

A fifteen-year-old boy jeered, "You gotta do what you gotta do." He told her how his parents didn't care about him, how he lived with other family members who ran afoul of the law. Ruth walked over to the boy, put her hands on his shoulders and looked compassionately deep into his eyes, "You haven't had a fair chance in life," she told him. As she left she asked one of the guards to let her know when this young man was released so she can make sure he's being taken care of and not on his own.

Ruth views her mission in life as helping people everywhere she goes, connecting them with the God who loves them.[2] Ruth is not unlike the wise teacher, who pours "out my thoughts to you; I will make my words known to you."

The truth is that it is never too late to accept Jesus as Lord. It's not too late to start building that solid foundation by reading God's word and listening for God's voice. We build a firm foundation by being with God's people, the community of faith. Extended times of prayer and meditation are yet other ways we shore up our foundation.

We too seek after wisdom, as the Apostle Paul proclaims, Jesus Christ is the wisdom of God. "Christ the power of God and the wisdom of God" (1 Corinthians 1:24b). In Jesus we discover true wisdom. With Jesus we can withstand any of life's storms.

---

1. *Upper Room*, July/August 2000, p. 22.

2. "Love reaches across the generation gap," Linda Esbenshade, *Intelligencer Journal*, Lancaster, Pennsylvania, August 31, 2000.

My Life Is In You, Lord

When we affirm that our life belongs to God, this affirmation includes every aspect of our lives. For the modern person living this way can be difficult at times. We wrestle with how we practice our faith on a daily basis, realizing that for our faith to be vital we need to live it out 24 hours a day, seven days a week. In all that we do, we give glory to God. Declaring our faith in this manner influences the way we interact with other people including our spouse, our children, our friends, our coworkers, our neighbors, and the clerk at the store, as well as a person we might encounter on the street.

Throughout the book of Proverbs there is no distinction or separation made between faith and ordinary everyday living. The wise sage or teacher believed that every aspect of our life belongs to God. We cannot divide or categorize our lives between the secular and sacred as we might be tempted to do, since our entire life belongs to God, including even the most routine and mundane tasks. It is impossible to separate our faith from our ordinary everyday lives.

Like all parents who want the very best for their children, King Lemuel's mother offered guidance in the king's search for a "capable wife" or "woman of worth." From her list of attributes we get the impression that the king's mother had very high and perhaps unrealistic expectations. "A capable wife who can find?" she asks. From her description the answer would have to be "no one" because no such person exists.

To help us in our understanding of this lesson, think for a moment of the American frontier in the nineteenth and early twentieth centuries where the family farm was the center of all activity. The "capable wife" had her hands in everything from raising her children, to helping plant and harvest crops, to sewing and mending all the clothing, to feeding the livestock, to buying and selling, as well as handling any emergencies that might arise. The frontier wife was very resourceful, making what little she had to work with stretch to meet the demanding needs of her family. Often times it was a life and death struggle out on the frontier. It's the stuff of legend. The description of the "capable wife" found in Proverbs could very easily fit the frontier wife, "she rises while it is still night and provides food for her household."

The modern equivalent wife and mother might run a business from her home, take her children to their various activities, as well as take care of her family. While she might not weave the fabrics, she is nonetheless a smart shopper who knows where to find a bargain. She might have a garden, but relies on the local supermarket to do her grocery shopping. She is active in the life of her church. She doesn't complain about her many tasks, but finds her fulfillment in knowing she does her best. She is dependable. She puts the needs of her family first. Such a person would make any mother happy, and is "far more precious than jewels."

Such a capable wife always makes her family her number one priority. Maria Shriver tells of the time she interviewed Cuban President Fidel Castro for a two-hour retrospective on the Cuban Missile Crisis. The television network sent a large team of producers and technicians to record the historic interview. Not everything went according to schedule as Maria remembers waiting and waiting for the Cuban President who postponed the interview several times. The weekend was fast approaching and Maria was beginning to get anxious. Monday was her daughter's first day of preschool. Maria had promised her daughter that nothing would keep her from taking her to school. Her first child's first day at school was a big deal. By late Friday afternoon word was that Castro was sick and couldn't be interviewed.

On Saturday Castro called to say he was sick and would not be able to do the interview until Monday. "I can't do that!" Maria blurted out. "I have to go back home to take my daughter to school!" There was silence in the room. Her boss kicked her under the table and asked her to step outside. "Are you nuts?" he asked her, telling her how long he had waited for the opportunity to interview Castro. Her boss shared with her the worst case scenario, telling her if they left they might not be allowed back in the country. There was no denying this was an important interview. Maria understood what was at stake but told her boss that she had to return home. She explained to Castro about her daughter's first day of preschool and how she needed to be there. She said she would immediately return for the interview.

Maria flew home, took her daughter to preschool, and returned to Cuba the same day to film one of the most fascinating interviews of her career. By the way, the first thing Castro asked her was, "How was the first day of school?"

Maria shares, "Even though you may think your job is your life and your identity, it's not and it shouldn't be." At work you are replaceable, but as a parent you are irreplaceable.[1]

We learn that the capable wife "opens her hand to the poor, and reaches out her hand to the needy." Not only were family members responsible for each other's well being they also had an obligation to help provide food, shelter, and clothing for those in need. When we claim that our life is in God, we will naturally want to reach out to people in need. If we desire to live out our faith, then we will help others in need. Not only do those we help benefit from our generosity, but also it contributes to our own sense of well being. Several recent studies reveal that men and women who volunteer time helping others are both happier and healthier. Reaching out to others allows us to focus on other people, which takes our minds off ourselves.

Sheryl is a young woman who last year earned $200,000. Even though she earned this considerable amount of money, she still felt empty inside. She thought counseling might help her. During one of the sessions she revealed that she had lost her passion for work. Another problem was identified: Sheryl was overly concerned about not being able to pay her bills. She earned six figures but was terrified of being unable to pay the bills — not next year's, next month's. She was so afraid of loss that she could no longer give and she was shriveling up inside. The counselor suggested that she volunteer at a shelter for battered women one night a week.

Three weeks later Sheryl told her counselor that she had taken her eight- and ten-year-old sons with her so they could play with the other children at the shelter. As she sat and listened to the stories of women who had given up everything just so they and their children could be safe, she began to realize how fortunate she was. Her sons were shocked to learn that there were actually children who had no toys. They began a toy drive at their school.

Those three hours a week Sheryl volunteered made her feel more fulfilled and realize her abundance more than any amount of time she could have spent trying to fill a bank account that would before never have been enough. Sheryl got rich by giving something away.[2]

The wise mother wanting the very best for her son advises, "Charm is deceitful, and beauty is vain, but a woman who fears the Lord is to be praised." The Psalmist reminds us that "the fear of the Lord is the beginning of wisdom" (Psalm 111:10). Such a person believes, like the sages of old, that the beginning of wisdom is the belief in God as Creator and Sustainer. Wisdom is not only lived out in the classroom but is also received by divine revelation. We place our lives in God's hands because we love the Lord.

The irony is that the qualities that draw our attention to another person, namely charm and beauty, do not necessarily matter all that much nor do they endure. "Charm is deceitful, and beauty is vain." Charm and intrigue can be deceiving, while beauty fades with the passing of time. But the person who invests his or her life in the Lord has rewards in heaven.

The capable wife "opens her mouth with wisdom, and the teaching of kindness is on her tongue." This wife and mother takes time from her busy schedule to read to her children. She daily affirms and encourages her children. We know from experience how much a word of kindness is appreciated, especially to children. At times when life is unsettled, just having another person listen to us can make a big difference.

With encouragement comes challenge. Myra always viewed herself as a Christian. She took her family to church and Sunday school on a regular basis. One day she received a telephone call that would forever call to question the way she lived her faith. "Mom, something's happened," her daughter Julena said, calling long distance from college. "It's too complicated to explain over the phone," she said. Julena told her mother that she was sending a letter home that would explain everything. Before she finished her conversation she assured her mother that she was okay. Myra did not know what to think. Her daughter was 500 miles from home, on her own for the first time, exposed to all the temptations every college student faces.

Several anxious days later Myra breathed a sigh of relief when she received the letter from her daughter. Julena wrote that she committed her life to Jesus Christ, was attending church, and reading her Bible. She stayed clear of the college "party scene" and joined a Christian student organization called "The Prodigals."

"Happy as her news made me," Myra stated, "I was faced with some disturbing questions." She wondered why her daughter would join a group called "The Prodigals" when she had grown up in a Christian home. She wondered why Julena was only now learning to know Christ when she had attended Sunday school and worship all her life. Her family had always professed the Christian faith.

This allowed Myra to reflect deeply about her own faith. She admitted that while she had never actually "walked out" on God, her words and actions have not always honored Christ. Candidly she said, "It took my daughter's bold admission of faith and visible, ongoing pursuit of a changed lifestyle to make me realize I, too, wanted to become a child of God in more than name only."

In those first several months after reading her daughter's letter, she committed herself to the daily practice of purposeful prayer, and a commitment to read the entire Bible. As she explains, "I realized an intimate relationship with my Lord is the only source of power for lasting change and strength for living the Christian life." Myra grew in her faith as she spent more time in daily prayer and reading her Bible.[3]

While our lesson from Proverbs applauds the "capable wife," its teachings apply to everyone who seeks honestly to live out his or her faith. May we affirm that all of our life belongs to God and pray that God can use each one of us to God's glory.

---

1. *Ten Things I Wish I'd Known*, Maria Shriver (New York: Warner Books, Inc, 2000), pp. 80-81.

2. *Jesus, Inc.*, Laurie Beth Jones (New York: Random House, 2001), p. 231.

3. "Reality Check," Myra Langley Johnson, *Today's Christian Women*, January/February 1999.

Proper 21
Pentecost 19
Ordinary Time 26
Esther 7:1-6, 9-10; 9:20-22

You Can Make It Happen

Some friends invited Brenda to go rock climbing with them. Even though Brenda was scared of heights, she reluctantly went along. They were going to climb the face of a tremendous granite cliff. Brenda put on the necessary gear, took hold of the rope, and started climbing the rock.

When they reached a ledge, they decided to take a break. As they were resting, the safety rope snapped against Brenda's face, knocking out her contact lens. With her sight blurry, Brenda frantically began searching for her missing lens. It was nowhere to be found. Brenda was sitting on a rock ledge with hundreds of feet below her and hundreds of feet above her, far from home, unable to see clearly.

Naturally she was upset, so she prayed, asking the Lord to help her find her missing lens. Brenda was still unable to find her lens. They decided to continue their climb. Once they reached the top, a friend examined her clothing, thinking that maybe the lens was on her clothing. It was not.

As she waited for the rest of the group to reach the top, she continued to pray; "Lord, you can see all these mountains, you know every stone and leaf, and you know exactly where my contact lens is. Please help me." The Bible verse, "For the eyes of the Lord range throughout the entire earth ..." (2 Chronicles 16:9) came to mind.

As they were walking back down the trail, another group of climbers just starting up the face of the cliff met them. One of them shouted out, "Anybody lose a contact lens?"

The climber told how he had found it; an ant was moving slowly across the face of the rock, carrying it. Brenda could hardly believe it.

Brenda later told her dad, who is a cartoonist. He drew a picture of an ant lugging that contact lens with the caption: "Lord, I don't know why you want me to carry this thing. I can't eat it and it's awfully heavy. But if this is what you want me to do, I'll carry it for you."[1]

God has a wonderful way of using us to God's own glory. God is able to take all of our unique life experiences and somehow or another use them. That was precisely what happened to Esther. As our lesson reveals, God is able to put the right people in the right place at the right time.

Our scripture lesson has all the makings of a blockbuster action thriller movie — the kind that keeps you on the edge of your seat. It is the story of a reversal of fortunes, of political intrigue, and ultimately, the triumph of good over evil. What makes the story of Esther so memorable is that it reminds us that God is always at work in our world, even at those times when we do not perceive God's presence. And more importantly Esther re-enforces how God is able to put the right people in the right place at the right time.

Our story opens with young Esther becoming queen. What the king did not realize at the time was that Esther was Jewish. "Esther did not reveal her people or kindred" (2:10). God placed Esther in the right place at the right time to carry out God's design. Esther would liberate her people much like Joseph saved his family from famine back in Genesis. She would rescue her people from certain destruction in much the same way as Moses led the people from slavery to the Promised Land. As queen, Esther would have the king's attention and would be kept informed of what was happening in the kingdom.

Esther's relative, Mordecai, was also in the right place at the right time. One day he overheard two of the king's trusted guards plotting to assassinate the king. Mordecai told Esther who informed the king at just the right time. An investigation was launched that ended with the two guards hanging on the gallows. Mordecai won the favor of the king for uncovering this plot and saving the king's life.

The next character who enters the story is quickly identified as the enemy. His name was Haman. He had devised a devious plot to kill all the Jews throughout the kingdom. As an advisor to the king, Haman was able to secure the king's approval without the king knowing exactly what he was signing. Haman tricked the king in order to gain his consent. As word reached the people of Haman's deed, they might have felt that there was nothing they could do to prevent the impending doom. "Wherever the king's decree came, there was great mourning among the Jews, with fasting and weeping and lamenting, and most of them lay in sackcloth and ashes" (4:3).

When Esther heard about this plot, she called for a three-day fast in the hopes of receiving divine guidance in this most serious life and death struggle. In a time of national crisis it is wise to call upon God, seeking God's will and direction. Even at those times when our lives seem out of control, it is helpful to step back and seek out the Lord's guidance. That's exactly what Esther had the people do — pray with all their might, seeking God's direction.

To add to the intrigue, Haman developed such a strong dislike for Mordecai that he wanted to see him hanged. Haman began secretly plotting against the Jews and Mordecai while the king continued to praise Mordecai for uncovering the plot to assassinate him. Esther's hope was somehow to convince the king of Haman's evil intention. If only she could expose him for what he truly was, perhaps then she could save her people. From the very beginning she was well aware of the risk involved, "After that I will go to the king, though it is against the law; and if I perish, I perish," she said (4:16). There was a risk involved going to see the king and Esther knew it. So she decided to host several banquets, just hoping for an opportunity to expose Haman's plot and save her life and those of her people.

On the second day of the banquet, the king again asked Esther, "What is your petition, Queen Esther? It shall be granted you." After a little too much wine, the king was willing to grant Esther "half of my kingdom." This was Esther's moment. This was what she was hoping for — a chance to speak freely about Haman's evil scheme.

Even though there was a risk involved that the whole thing might backfire, Esther knew it was worth it to save the lives of her people, as well as her own life. In one daring move she requested, "Let my life be given me — that is my petition — and the lives of my people."

The long-held secret would now be told. The king was unprepared for what she would tell him, "For we have been sold, I and my people, to be destroyed, to be killed, and to be annihilated." The king was shocked; he knew nothing about it and asked, "Who is he, and where is he, who has presumed to do this?" The person responsible was nearby listening to every word. Esther told the king, "A foe and enemy, this wicked Haman!" The king had trusted his royal adviser to protect his interests and act accordingly. Haman must have felt uneasy as he stood there listening intently to the conversation. What Esther told the king would send him into a rage. Haman was guilty, no question about it. The king left in a fury while in a complete reversal of fortunes, Haman begged for mercy from Queen Esther. Haman was now fearful of his very life.

In a movie-like twist of fate, Haman was hung on the very gallows he had constructed for Mordecai. Esther had saved her people; they would not die. Esther was locked in a life and death struggle and took the necessary risks to win the release of her people. It was a moment of triumph that would be remembered for all time.

God has a wonderful way of placing the right people in the right place at the right time. We discover throughout the pages of the Bible how God has raised up the right people for the task at hand. Even at those times when it appears that God is absent, God is still at work behind the scenes to bring about God's own purposes.

God has brought us to this place at this time in the first decade of a new century and Christianity's third millennium — for a reason. How might God use each one of us in this time and place? God expects something from us as we blaze a pathway for others to follow.

There are times when our faith requires that we take risks. We might risk friendships when we feel compelled to confront someone who is acting in destructive ways. When we take a stand that might be viewed as unpopular by others, by standing firm we risk being labeled a fanatic or worse. When we feel called to start new ministries within our church and reach out to others, we place ourselves at risk.

One morning before school, twelve-year-old Craig Kielburger saw a picture in the newspaper of a boy about his age smiling. As he read the article he learned that the boy's name was Iqbal Masih. He had worked in a carpet factory in Pakistan for most of his life. The article reported that the boy had been shot dead by an unknown assailant. Craig was horrified, wondering how such a thing could happen. And why did the boy work in a factory?

That day at school Craig went to the library to find information on child labor. He wondered if there was anything he could do to prevent such abuse. The next morning in homeroom he passed around copies of the article and told the class what he learned from his research. The students were just as shocked as he had been the day before. That evening a group of interested students met at Craig's house. They searched the Internet for firsthand accounts of child labor from children all over the world. They decided to try to prevent child labor and named their effort, "Free the Children."

Not everyone shared Craig's enthusiasm. That summer his parents told him with the start of a new school year it was time to stop. When school started some fellow students resented his opposition to brand name sneakers and jeans made by child laborers. But Craig continued, believing that through his efforts he could make a difference.

A couple of months later, after some successful fund raisers, Craig had the opportunity to travel first to Bangladesh and then India. "I talked to ten-year-old boys who had quit school to work fifteen-hour days to help support their families," Craig explained, "and realize how frivolous my hours spent playing ball would seem." On that two-month trip Craig saw firsthand much injustice, but he also saw ways to change it. Through his efforts he knew he could make a difference. "It starts with me — with each one of us," he says, "with what we can do to make things better." While he realized that he cannot solve all the world's problems by himself, he and others can work to solve some — with the help of God.[2]

When we stop to examine our own lives, could the risks we have taken or in some cases failed to take be the reason our life has gone the way it has? That's a powerful question that only we can answer.

Esther risked everything including her own life to save her people. She was the right person at the right place at the right time. Only God is able to take our experiences and use them in ways we cannot even imagine. Remember that God does not call the qualified, God qualifies the called.

Jesus has called us to be his followers and that call demands our very best and often involves some degree of risk. Only God can take all of our experiences and weave them with other persons' to accomplish God's will. We are here for a reason; we have a purpose.

---

1. "The Ant and the Contact Lens," a true story by Josh and Karen Zarandona, via e-mail.

2. "It Starts With Me," Craig Kielburger, *Guideposts*, November 1999, pp. 2-6.

God Is Good All The Time

Imagine a person standing in the rain without an umbrella. All alone, soaking wet, in the middle of the night, the person cries out to no one in particular, "Why, God?" It's hard to distinguish the difference between the tears and the rain running down the person's cheek. Tragedy has struck as it usually does at a time when it is least expected. Everything seems fine, a regular day, and then comes that call in the middle of the night informing you that someone you love and care about has been involved in a serious accident. "Why has this happened?" we want to know. "Why has it happened in this way?" we ask almost in disbelief. It just doesn't seem fair. The person had everything to live for, and has been cut down in the prime of life, for no apparent reason. We have to admit that we struggle with that same question, "Why?"

Job was a deeply religious man who had the best of everything life had to offer. He owned more land, which produced more crops, than any of his neighbors; he had more livestock also. Job was blessed with a wonderful family, seven sons and three daughters. As scripture attests, Job "was the greatest of all the people of the east." Job was the type of person that you would envy, at least in your private thoughts. He had everything, a large family, wealth and fame. His luxurious home might even have been featured on "Lifestyles of the Rich and Famous" had there been television.

To the cynical it seemed that he was happy because he had so much. Some of us think that way today. We see someone with a nice house or new car or large bank account or children who never get into trouble, and we wish we would have it so good. "If only

373

we had ..." we convince ourselves, then we would be happy. While part of us might believe this is true, another part of us realizes that this notion is false. More possessions or prestige will not make us happy. There are an equal number of television programs, which portray someone who has it all, money or wealth, or power, who is miserable. Still, it was easy for the critics to charge that Job loved God because God had blessed him in so many ways.

Then Satan entered the picture, proposing a challenge. Satan thought that the reason Job was so faithful was because he had so much. What might happen, Satan pondered, if Job lost everything he had? Would Job still place his trust in God? Would this godly individual lose his religion along with everything he had? Or would he remain faithful and steadfast in his relationship with God? There was only one way to find out.

One day a messenger informed Job that an enemy came and stole all his livestock. And that was not all — the heartless scoundrels killed his workers. Not only would this cause financial setback but also heartache over losing all his employees in such a manner. The messenger just barely escaped and was the only one left. How could such a thing have happened, Job must have wondered. While Job was still grieving, another messenger came to tell him that fire destroyed all of his sheep, and another enemy seized his camels, and so it went until Job lost all of his animals. With this news the source of his livelihood had been wiped out in one afternoon. We've seen farmers in the Midwest who lost all their crops in a storm or drought tell how they do not know what they are going to do next. It promised to be a good crop and then the unexpected happened and destroyed it, and left them with nothing. Without a doubt Job was heavyhearted that day with all the bad news. Why was all this happening to him?

As if that were not enough, then came the most devastating news of all. While his grown children were dining at one of their homes, a storm blew the house down, killing all of them. How could such a thing happen? Didn't any of them hear the approaching storm and know enough to take cover? Job stood there among the ruins in utter disbelief. He was numb in his grief. How could this happen? It would be difficult for us to find the right words to say to such a person who in a very short time lost everything, including his livelihood and his family.

There was one thing that Job did not lose and that was his relationship with God. Job believed in God with all his heart. He believed that God is good all the time, not just some of the time. In the midst of his unimaginable grief Job could still manage to proclaim, "Blessed be the name of the Lord." Chapter 1 ends with these words, "In all this Job did not sin or charge God with wrongdoing."

If God entered into a wager with the devil it was obvious that God won the bet. Job lost everything he had yet still retained his integrity. Job still had a strong faith and believed that somehow God would see him through those dark days. Unfortunately for Job, the outcome of the wager did not convince the devil. The devil always pushes to the very limits, always wanting more until persons fall. Satan wondered what would happen to Job if he lost his health in addition to all his other losses. Would he still cling to his relationship with God? With his health gone, Satan was certain that Job would curse God and die.

Job had been through much and now was inflicted with painful sores from the bottom of his feet to the top of his head. It's not hard to imagine the pain he must have felt. Sitting on an ash heap, still mourning all his catastrophic losses, Job took a broken piece of pottery and began scraping his sores, seeking minimal relief.

While it might be possible to hide some of our hurt from others, it would be impossible to hide a skin disease. When we encounter another person, the first thing we see is the person's face or hands. Inflicting Job with sores all over his body would certainly cause embarrassment and social alienation. Either Job would not want to be around people or people would be so repulsed that they would stay away from him.

Job's wife found him sitting in ashes out in the middle of nowhere, scraping his sores with broken pottery. He must have been a sorry sight. "Do you still persist in your integrity?" she asked him in disbelief and then offered the following advice, "Curse God and die." Seeing her husband in such obvious pain all she wanted to do was put him out of his misery.

If Job had taken his wife's advice, then Satan would have won the wager. Although Job had lost everything he had, even his health, he still clung to the one thing he did not and would not lose and that was his relationship with God. The Lord God had been his friend in the past and Job would not for a moment compromise that relationship. Job dismissed his wife's advice, telling her, "You speak as any foolish woman would speak. Shall we receive the good at the hand of God, and not receive the bad?" Even though it might have appeared to others that God had deserted him, Job knew in his heart that God still loved him. Job held on to his belief that God would see him through. Deep down Job believed that God is good — all the time!

Anne and Jonas were married in 1968 and moved into a trailer on Jonas' family's farm. Jonas had his own body shop where Anne also worked. At night they would share their dreams of having children someday and both of their desires to grow closer to God. This young couple got together weekly with other couples at church for a prayer meeting. Life was good for all of them.

Three years into their marriage they were blessed with a daughter, LaWonna. A couple of years later Angela Joy was born. Anne says that her middle name, "Joy," was what she was feeling at that time. She thanked God for all her blessings; she described her life as a dream come true.

That dream was shattered one September morning in 1975. As twenty-month-old Angie scampered across the yard to visit her grandma and aunt, Anne heard an anguished scream. She ran out of the house only to be met by her father holding her lifeless baby daughter in his arms. Angie was killed instantly when Anne's sister accidentally backed the tractor onto her daughter.

After the funeral Anne and Jonas tried to bury their grief by working harder and they became more involved at their church. There was still a deep-seated pain in her life. "No matter how much I devoted myself to church work," Anne says, "the doubts, the emptiness inside me wouldn't go away." Like other parents in similar situations, she kept wondering if her daughter would still be alive if only she had kept a closer watch over her.

During this time Anne and Jonas' marriage started to suffer as the lines of communication were shut down. Jonas did not want to talk about his daughter's death. "It hurts too much to talk about it," was all he said. Problems continued. Soon the family moved to another state. In their new community they again became involved in church activities, but their marriage continued to crumble.

Their new church sponsored a marriage seminar which both Anne and Jonas attended. This was the first step in their healing. Next they sought professional help. It was then that Jonas felt God speaking to him. He had a real passion to help others who were experiencing difficulties similar to those he and Anne had. "I know there are families out there who need the help we've received," he said, "but they don't know where or how to find it." Jonas dreamed of starting a center where people could receive free counseling.

The family moved back home. Soon Jonas started counseling from their home while Anne got a job at a concession stand at a nearby farmer's market. Before too long a stand at another farmer's market was for sale, which they bought. Among the food items sold at the stand were hand rolled soft-pretzels which customers seemed really to enjoy. Soon the pretzels were selling better than anything else was; she sold over 2,000 pretzels a day. "Auntie Anne's Pretzels" was born in 1988. Just four years later with the profits they opened the Family Information Center which offers free counseling to families and today employs ten counselors and has helped many families dealing with a variety of problems.

As Anne reflects over her journey, she says: "It took many years of working through our sometimes heart-breaking struggles, but Jonas and I have succeeded in building a marriage and a life beyond what we ever dreamed — a partnership based on the love that brought and kept us together — God's love, the truest of all."[1]

God is good all the time! Job clung to his relationship with God. Even though he suffered great losses, he still placed his trust in God. He knew that God would not desert him in his hour of need. His wife was ready to give up; "Curse God and die" was her only advice. Later Job's friends came to offer advice that wasn't particularly helpful. Through it all Job held onto his faith. Through it all he held on to the only thing that mattered in his life — his relationship with God — and at the end of his life God blessed him. Job like another Old Testament character, Jacob, held on until God blessed him.

---

1. "Lasting Partnership," Anne F. Beiler, *Guideposts*, October 2000, pp. 11-15.

Sermons On The First Readings

For Sundays
After Pentecost
(Last Third)

H. Alan Stewart

Dedicated to the Reverend Dr. Robert H. Schuller
of the Crystal Cathedral in Garden Grove, California,
in appreciation for all his assistance
in helping me to bring "the Good News" to people in need.

Introduction

He will baptize you with the Holy Spirit and with fire.
His winnowing fork is in his hand, to clear his threshing floor
and to gather the wheat into his granary;
but the chaff he will burn with unquenchable fire.

John the Baptist; Luke 3:16b-17

The metaphor of the Spirit, or breath of God, separating the wheat from the chaff on the threshing floor is a powerful expression of God's creative spiritual influence in our human lives. While I am obviously not the first person to picture the dialogue of human and divine experience as a threshing floor, the notion speaks to the most basic, gut level, international, time irrelevant word for food and human survival: bread.

Not only is the bounty of the threshing floor revered in scripture, but we are surrounded by its presence to the point we no longer even notice the connection when a basket of bread is put in front of us at our restaurant table.

We struggle against the breath of God like a great storm's wind in our face at God's efforts in separating us from all that prevents communion: with ourselves, with our neighbor, and with God. Since God in Christ heals and our planet needs healing, our mission is to create that sacred space (the threshing floor) where the Spirit can separate the wheat from the chaff. When this happens, when the finest of wheat becomes the flour which is the bread of life for all who hunger, the realm of God flourishes.

These words are meant to be spoken in love to those assembled desiring the blessing of God in the Word of the Lord. You follow a noble, honored, and sacred tradition. Your words follow the manna from heaven that long ago fed the people in the wilderness. You serve the bread that echoes as a multiplication of five barley loaves that fed the hungry on a hillside 2,000 years ago. You symbolically break the bread in remembrance of the body broken on the cross.

May the breath of God blow away all of the chaff from your people as your love speaks these words: the chaff of shame, of self-hatred, of anger, of abuse, of fear, of longing, and of desire unfulfilled. May God's Spirit in your delivery be the leaven of the finest bread for the table of life. May your words be bread for the hungry.

For the bread of God is that which comes down from heaven
and gives life to the world.

Jesus of Nazareth, John 6:33

Rev. Alan Stewart

Proper 23
Pentecost 21
Ordinary Time 28
Job 23:1-9, 16-17

The Unanswered Question:
Will God Be Fair?

Ancient people were terrorized by the thought of God. We have to strain our minds and our imaginations to try to conceive of the confusion and fear that people of antiquity faced when trying to get to know and understand God. They looked at the weather, the storms and the peaceful days, their own lives, the times of the year, and the way nature unfolded and tried to understand God.

They did not have Jesus Christ and his teachings, so they looked upon bad things as tests and punishments by God for the behavior of their lives.

Rabbinical tradition concludes that the book of Job belongs to Moses and even one of the remnants from the Dead Sea Scrolls (dated from 225-150 B.C.E.) has the text in an ancient Hebrew script commonly used before the Babylonian exile (587-539 B.C.E.) This was probably retained to attest to its ancient origins.

Like many of us of today, Job was a man who had a lot and lost a lot. Job was a man from antiquity, and when we try to study and understand his ancient predicament, we have to come to Job with the mind of an archaeologist, looking backwards in trying to unearth his wisdom and his struggle in this speech to his friend, Eliphas. That being said, the beauty of the poetry of Job's struggle is, even today, God at work in antiquity as God is alive in our lives millenniums later.

Most of us know Job as a man of patience (James 5:11), but that is a superficial comment about the content of the book or the man.

383

Dr. Laura Schlessinger, the talk show host of great renown, says that the book of Job is about "character." Dealing with loss shows whether an individual has character or not.

Where on our list of priorities do we place "character"? How much effort do we spend with our children at home and with their education, and how much time and space do we see on television and in the newspapers dedicated to the issue of building "character"? Seems that beside fame, glamour, wealth, computer literacy, and youth, character is not important enough that we can call it worthy of the effort for "politically correct" discussion.

Today's reading has our heroic man of character in a place of deep darkness, frustration, and pain. The bottom line for us to understand is that this "man of character" feels abandoned by God: his complaint is bitter; he feels that the heavy hand of God is adding extra weight on his already heavy burden; he can't find God anywhere; God appears to be hiding and is therefore actively avoiding him; so he can't get God to listen as he pleads his case; he can't find out what it is that God understands that he doesn't; and he doesn't know if God doesn't speak to him perhaps because God is so much greater than he is.

The pain of this position has brought Job to the place where he feels that God has actually made him weak and fearful by his absence.

"If only I could vanish in darkness, and thick darkness would cover my face!" (23:17). This death wish sounds like Job is experiencing "clinical depression."

Job is not like our modern men. When they are depressed and you ask them what is wrong, they always say, "I don't want to talk about it!" Not our hero, Job! Talk about it he can and does, for page after page of eloquent poetry.

Maybe the first thing that Job has done for us is to give us a picture of the massive size of the silence concerning our own anguish. We can thank Job for that.

If we wish to discover "the word of the Lord" from this text for us, we are confronted by a problem that doesn't resolve; there is no conclusion; there is no story movement as we find in a parable of Jesus. We parachute into the middle of Job's dilemma, and all the text gives us is an unanswered question, an unresolved dilemma.

Where is God and why is he not helping this righteous man? Is God fair?

If we are good, then we are supposed to have God's ear, are we not? Is not our faithfulness and God's apparent inaction a pivotal issue for all humankind that cries for resolution?

You might say that there is an end to this story. We can look it up in chapter 42. Job does not know the conclusion at this point, and what is even more important, you and I can face the same dilemma in our own lives.

When we are in the middle of a mess, we can't look up chapter 42 either! There are simply times when we are in exactly the same place: we have an unanswered question ourselves, and God does not seem to be responding.

Why do good parents lose an innocent child? Why does an excellent person get fired from his or her job? Why do the good die young? Why does a good person suffer terribly from illness? Why does someone you love become an addict or exhibit other kinds of destructive behavior?

The deeper question is: Can we live with a question that has not been answered? Do we privately say to ourselves that if God doesn't answer this or that question the way I want, then I'll believe or not believe in God?

It is a human phenomenon that we want our questions answered. Our intelligence, our ability to reason and be rational, is a foundation of our humanity and our civility. We expect our politicians, our police, our physicians, our parents, our spouses, our children, our clergy, and why not our God to give us the answers we want and, especially, the answers we need.

There is no doubt that much of our activity in life is determined by the answers we receive for our questions.

But could we also be honest enough to admit that we often don't go by the answers we receive? We don't use the answers we do indeed have to make our choices: we still drink and drive, we take addictive drugs, we commit acts that lead to incarceration, we refuse to love our neighbor and forgive those close to us, we overeat, we overwork, we procrastinate, and we do all sort of things we know are not good, and yet we have the audacity to question God for some of the questions we feel are unanswered!

Is it not the height of arrogance for us to say, "I'm going to ignore all of the good information that I have for the betterment of my life, but I am going to have a real *snit* over this one question I feel is not answered"?

This is the point where we have to go back to Job, the eloquent, moral, suffering, tenacious man of character.

If there is one thing that the book of Job says to us, it is that "he honors the struggle." Job doesn't run away from the struggle, he doesn't go into denial, he doesn't act out, he doesn't give up, he keeps trying, and he keeps asking.

I can't speak for God; I can't make life anything other than what it is, but life is a struggle. There are unanswered questions and we can't make a case for good and bad that if you are good, you will have it easier. Surely the book of Job and his life tell us that the good may, and indeed do, struggle.

But what I can tell you for certain is that the struggle of living with unanswered questions does not stop life and happiness, personal growth and movement towards connection with the Creator and love of neighbor.

A missionary told a story about going to India during the monsoons. Hundreds of the hungry took refuge in the local railway station from the deluge. The resident church workers introduced the missionary to a particular woman whom they thought he might find interesting. He talked to her as the bread was distributed. She received hers as they were talking and she broke the bread and offered him a piece of her meager portion; the first bread she would have had for three days. He was stunned. Even though he had had breakfast before he came to the station, how could he reject this woman's opulent generosity in the midst of her poverty?

You want an unanswered question? Why did this hospitable woman offer a portion of her bread of life to this well-fed stranger?

The faithfulness to the principle of love is the answer Job, and this woman, lived in their lives thousands of years apart. It is the only answer you and I really need. Amen.

The Destination Of All Journeys

Today we encounter one of the most sacred moments for every single one of us. We encounter Job at the exact moment that the boy becomes the man. Each one of us has this one cathartic moment when we move from childhood to adulthood; girl to woman; boy to man.

There is what we might call a cosmic event inside of each of us when our inner universe shifts upside down at the same moment that the outward universe remains absolutely and exactly the same.

To your logic, it may seem confusing and silly to say that everything changes at the same moment that it remains the same, but that is the point: although the world remains the same, when we take off our child's glasses and put on our adult glasses, we see the same world with a new light, through a new set of lenses. We reinterpret the same reality in a different way than we observed one day, from what we recognized the next.

This passage, has God, himself calling Job out of his childhood and into his manhood: "Gird up your loins like a man. I will question you and you shall declare unto me."

A man who stopped his alcoholic drinking said, "I never used to believe in miracles, now I see them every day." He was walking down the same streets and going to work, seeing the same houses and people, but he was seeing them through a man's eyes instead of the boy's eyes, and he was grateful.

Children act and understand that they are God and want the world to be the way they want, when they want, and they want

387

their answers accommodated in their own way. Children see themselves at the center of the universe and basically want their own way. Adults move into a different perspective and see themselves as a part of the universe but accountable to God instead of the other way around.

At the moment of initiation, the man or the woman walks into the world of gratitude.

We meet Job when he is on the cusp of this transition into adulthood; we are meeting him during his initiation into manhood.

The character Job has traditionally been portrayed as the good and righteous man who lost it all and was always faithful to God in spite of his difficulties. With beautiful poetry he laments that God may have deserted him and even caused his pain to be worse because of his alleged absence and indifference.

But now we have a shift! After 37 chapters of absence, it is the voice of God himself out of the whirlwind that drags Job into the humility of the adult word with a strong litany of rebukes denouncing his childlike belief system and its resulting behavior.

> *Where were you when I laid the foundation of the earth?*
> *Tell me, if you have understanding*
> *Who determined its measurements — surely you know!*
> *Or who stretched the line upon it?*
> *On what were its bases sunk,*
> *or who laid its cornerstone*
> *when the morning stars sang together*
> *and all the heavenly beings shouted for joy?*

Job must have been experiencing some kind of reality check as the voice of God goes on ...

> *Can you lift up your voice to the clouds*
> *so that a flood of waters may cover you?*
> *Can you send forth lightning so that they might go*
> *and say to you, "Here we are"?*
> *Who has put wisdom in the inward parts,*
> *or given understanding to the minds?*
> *Who has the wisdom to number the clouds?*

The voice of Yahweh goes on and on and delineates the boundaries of the exclusively divine, so that there could be no mistake what Job's sin was: the presumption of playing God, the sin of humankind that stretched from the eating of the tree of the forbidden fruit in the garden, to those who wanted to make a name for themselves in building the tower of Babel, to the Roman soldiers who drove the nails through Jesus' body into the cross.

Who really is God here? In simple English, God was telling Job to "grow up"!

Like Job, we all have a difficult time trying to separate our wish that God shield us from adversity to God's theme that our faithfulness is what we use to cope with that very same adversity.

Each and every one of us is on a journey, a life's journey, "a once in a life time trip"! There's nothing like it! In the billions of years of eternity, God has given us the gift of experiencing life and love on this planet for a few years. Of course, we make choices here.

An integral part of our journey is growing from girl to woman, from boy to man; from child to adult. Like Job, we are all called to be adults: to be life-giving, generative, grateful mothers and fathers in our communities.

There are older males and females who are stuck in childhood: stuck in jail, stuck in addictive behaviors, stuck in feelings of anger or resentment, or, like Job, stuck in whining and complaining about why life is like it is.

We are all born, and somewhere (time and place unknown) down the road on that journey, we die.

Some people would want you to believe that your destination is simply "six feet under ground," and you can believe that if you want, but the other choice you can make is considering that your destination is the same voice from the whirlwind that spoke personally to Job: God!

Our choice of destination determines to a great extent our journey. If our destination is God and "God is love," then our preparations and the journey itself are sculpted by our choice of destination in exactly the same way that Job's journey was couched, guided, informed, and lead to God. If our destination is money and power, then our journey is determined by that choice: our rest stops along the way are places where we might grab a few more dollars, a little more power. If our destination is love, then our rest stops provide more opportunities to experience love to prepare us for the last stop at our destination.

If we were created by the God of love and our life's journey is love, then T. S. Elliot might have been talking about Job, or you and me, when he wrote:

> *We will not cease from exploration,*
> *And at the end of all our exploring*
> *Will be to arrive where we started*
> *And know that place for the first time.*

The destination of all journeys is God!
All aboard! Amen.

Proper 25
Pentecost 23
Ordinary Time 30
Job 42:1-6, 10-17

What Changes And What Doesn't?

(Before speaking, the speaker puts on a pair of "cool shades" [dark sunglasses] and takes them off when it seems the point has been made.)

The character Job is "a cool dude." What is "a cool dude"? A cool dude is one who can tell a story and thousands of years later we are still talking about what he said.

In matters of faith, Job confronts us with gut-wrenching reality. In a world where we face many superficial people and issues, Job drags us to "the bottom of the well," to the core issues that define who we are in relationship with God, and how we know God: Who is God? Does God test and reward the good and punish the bad? What does God require of us? How does suffering relate to the meaning of life and our positioning with God? Is God fair and consistent, following a considered and deliberate path, or is God whimsical and arbitrary? Is God indifferent to our situations, or does God intervene?

The most wonderful thing about the Bible, written by many individuals over thousands of years, is that it is full of contradictions! We human beings are then obligated to the task of finding God in the contradictions, and those contradictions are where God and life become both exciting and interesting.

We find some of these contradictions right in the book of Job! The poet who wrote most of the body of the book seems to present a different character than the narrator who begins and finishes the book. The poet writes as one who is talking about himself. The narrator writes as if he is talking about someone else. The narrator shows Job as being innocent; the poet shows him as being a blasphemer, a doubter, a frenzied rebel, and a proud giant (42:6).

We didn't read the verses 42:7-10 where the narrator is found to be severe about Job's friends, but the poet is not so. The narrator moves us in an inspirational way; the poet asks us to probe the bowels of our understanding. The narrator evokes a thrilling response in us, while the poet almost embarrasses us with the compelling grip of existential communication.

The fact that the ancient poet of the sixth century B.C.E. is different in style and presentation than the later narrator is not a problem. Do we not always say that "there are two sides to every story"? We need both the pull of the poet and the tug of the narrator to deal with the issues of Job, his goodness and virtue, as it impacts his suffering and loss, along with God's place in Job's story. Job is "us."

The reading today is partly written by the poet and partly by the narrator. We see the repentance of Job, and the return and restoration of his life with friends, family, and wealth. In fact the reading tells us that he has twice as much as he had before his great losses. In his repentance, Job is abundantly blessed with sheep, camels, oxen, and donkeys. Seven sons and three daughters complemented his fortune. His daughters were more than beautiful; "there were no women so beautiful as Job's daughters." We can only wonder what the sons looked like. We do know that they all benefitted from Job's restoration. The wellness of one member of the family benefits the entire family.

To top it all off, Job also received a long life. He lived to be 140 years old, so there were three generations of his family: his children and his children's children. "And Job died, old and full of days" — a happy ending to the story.

Did you notice that his wife didn't even get "an honorable mention"? She must have had something to do with his good fortune; even bearing ten children should be at least worthy of a footnote! There is always more to the story, is there not?

We see Job go through a lot of change in this story, from the beginning to the end: he had a lot, he lost a lot, he suffered a lot, he encountered God, he got it all back, and more. We see him grow up in this story: the boy becomes a man. There is a lot of change for our hero Job and his life.

We would do well to remember that Job lost more than his worldly goods in this story: he lost his ego, and he lost his false pride, and yet he found restoration and trust when he lost his slavery to himself.

When our future prospects look dim, we might remember that Job actually received what he earlier thought was impossible — "for all things are possible with God."

With all the changes that transformed Job, we don't get much information on how God changed from the beginning of the story to the end of the story.

In fact, Job seems like he just makes a full circle, and comes back to the same place:

> *I know that you can do all things,*
> *and that no purpose of yours can be thwarted ...*
> *I had heard of you by the hearing of the ear,*
> *but now my eye sees you;*
> *therefore I despise myself,*
> *and repent in dust and ashes.*

Job is really saying that "my eye has now seen what my ear had heard in the first place; sorry for the error; I now know you are who you are."

God, did not essentially change in this story.

You and I have lots of changes in our lives: we grow up, we have children, we get sick, and experience death, we have disappointments, we personally change, we have betrayals, we change jobs, and we are affected by the changes in other people's lives.

We need to know, as Job found out, that the reality of the presence of God and God's kingdom of loving acceptance, restoration, peace, and healing does *not* change. The one thing that did not change with Job himself was his faithfulness to God. Considering all of the changes that Job experienced, the two things that did not change in this story were God, and Job's faithfulness to God.

Every one of us has experienced changes in our lives, just like the Job of 2,600 years ago, but the one thing we need to know is that in 2,600 years, or a millennium from now, God will still be there, unchanged.

Another poet, Henry Francis Lyte (1793-1847), wrote some words on the same theme:

> *Swift to its close ebbs out life's little day;*
> *Earth's joys grow dim, its glories pass away;*
> *Change and decay in all around I see;*
> *O Thou Who changest not, abide with me.*

You can describe life in either of two ways: you can say that there is always change in life, or you can say, that one thing that never changes, is that there is always change.

Job in his faithfulness to God was anchored in his faith, to the one thing that never changes, and that is what sustained Job in the change and decay he experienced.

Job was more than a good man, he was a man of virtue. Virtue is a level of goodness that is victorious through trial. Virtue is considered a positive human characteristic; we don't ascribe virtue to God. As it was for Job, virtue is a life goal for us to achieve.

The secret of life is not found in what happens to us, even though we usually focus on ourselves, but that is not the issue.

Whatever happens to us in life, we would do well not to take it personally. We were not singled out to get sick or have a car accident; life just happens, and changes will and do occur.

Like Job, if we have faith in God, then we are anchored to the immovable and unchangeable source of all creation, the compass that always points in a true direction so that we will not lose our way.

The secret of life is realized by our faithfulness to God, in what we *do,* with what *ever* happens to us. Amen.

Blessing Revealed

"Trouble comes in threes," so many people say. Every time something goes wrong, those people expectantly look for numbers two and three to hit them, full force, taking a huge sigh of relief after number three. "Pessimists" we sometimes call them.

In our story, Naomi and Elimelech experience a famine in their homeland Judah. The couple goes to Moab, a neighboring country east of the Dead Sea, with their two sons, Mahlon and Chilion. Elimelech dies in Moab. The two sons each marry Moabite women, Orpah and our heroine, Ruth, and then the two sons both die.

Added to the famine (disaster number one), we now have to add the death of Naomi's husband and both of her sons. One plus three equals four. Ruining a perfectly good jingle; for Naomi, trouble came in "fours."

After sustaining four massive blows to her life, Naomi hears that things are going well back home in Judah, and she decides to return there so she can eat (so that she can continue to live). Her two daughters-in-law start out with her, but she seems to feel that this is selfish, so she tells them to go back to their mothers, so that they could have a chance to get new husbands. All Naomi had left were her two daughters-in-law. Even though this is painful, Orpah decides to go back, but Ruth (*Ruth* means: the "compassionate" one) clings to her mother-in-law, and is adamant about staying with her and adopting the life, country, customs, and God of her late husband.

> *"Where you go, I will go;*
> *Where you lodge, I will lodge;*
> *Your people shall be my people,*
> *and your God my God."* — Ruth 1:16

This is no simple, superficial, short-lived, ill-considered, flippant choice that Ruth makes. She goes on to say:

> *"Where you die, I will die —*
> *there will I be buried.*
> *May the Lord do thus and so to me,*
> *and more as well,*
> *if even death parts me from you!"* — Ruth 1:17

Rarely is there seen a more beautiful, powerful, touching, and loving devotion of one person for another in biblical literature. When Naomi sees the love and devotion that Ruth has for her, she accepts the love and they return to Judah.

When you look at this story, you will see that it is "famine driven." What set the whole story in motion was famine. Famine drove Naomi and Elimelech from their homeland Judah to Moab. Famine was a big issue back then. When you didn't have food, you died! There were no food stamps, social assistance, welfare systems, or food banks. You would be at the mercy of friends or relatives, hoping that they had some extra and were willing to share it, or you just starved and died. If crops failed, it took a long time to plant, grow, and harvest more. There were no overstocked supermarkets, with clerks filling the shelves as fast as shoppers could empty them.

This was a different world.

As different as it was, there are still times when we can experience the total lostness that drove Naomi and Elimelech to Moab, or the devastation that comes from losing three breadwinners with nowhere to turn. There are monuments to sons and fathers lost to war all over our country; 200 million people in the world died in the last century to war; there are monuments erected near the ocean to honor fishermen who gave their lives to the sea to bring in fish for our tables; there are monuments to thousands who died in the mines and at the workplace to avoid modern-day famines for their families.

We also have "famines of the heart"; experiences of starvation of the heart that drive us to places outside of the familiar: our personal Moabs; the places where we seek refuge to survive the fears that we face. There are places of loneliness, estrangement, and addictions where we go to survive, and like Naomi, Orpah, and Ruth, we may even face more tragedy and pain.

We have the luxury of standing back and looking at this ancient story from a distance and seeing how things were to develop. Don't overlook the significance of the details: "... a certain man of Bethlehem in Judah...."

Bethlehem is the place where King David and later, Jesus, was born. We know that Ruth, the Moabitess, eventually married another man of Judah, Boaz, and Naomi would become the great-grandmother of King David.

Consider if it was "famine driven" that Naomi would find the blessings of solace, love, family, comfort, and food so that she would not starve, all arising from the connection of her daughter-in-law, Ruth, and that tearful event on the road home. Was it "famine driven" that Ruth, a Moabitess, would be blessed in becoming the great-grandmother of a king?

Even though Naomi had tragically lost her husband and two sons, she was blessed with the love and devotion of her daughter-in-law, Ruth. And blessing was revealed for the Jewish people in the continuance of the royal line of David.

Even though Ruth lost her husband and the relative comfort of her own country, life lead her to the blessing of becoming the wife of Boaz and the great-grandmother of a king. For both of these women, blessing was, indeed, revealed.

What is the point for us?

Are we to say when bad things happen to people, as we know they will, "There is a silver lining in this cloud. God will bless you in your pain"?

No. There are no examples of anything like this in the scripture we have just studied. We are not called to make people feel worse by ignoring or minimizing their pain. But we do need to know that at any time in our lives, blessings from God are waiting to be revealed, just as blessings eventually became revealed to Naomi and Ruth!

The scripture tells us several things that are helpful. When Elimelech and Naomi were having difficult times in Judah, they took the initiative to move outside of their local comfort zones and do what they needed to do, even if it meant challenge and change. All of the characters in this story got on with their lives. They didn't sit and mope. They moved on as best they could. Ruth, our heroine, treated her mother-in-law with absolute respect, love, and devotion. Naomi accepted the love that Ruth offered her. All of these people were people of faith; their lives were grounded in faith in God. The language is laced with references to God's presence in their lives.

The message for us today is that by being faithful to God and, like Ruth, treating others with great love, reverence, and respect, and taking actions as we are able, we will be guaranteed that the blessings of God will be revealed to us in our lives. We are not promised eternal good times, but we are promised that the glory and blessings of God will be revealed in our faithfulness to God, no matter what. Amen.

Proper 27
Pentecost 25
Ordinary Time 32
Ruth 3:1-5; 4:13-17

The Threshing Floor

We so casually go to the supermarket and pick up a loaf of bread. The task is so easy; it defies comment. In our world, every corner store, every food warehouse has shelves of bread: white, whole wheat, multi-grain, rye, barley, cornbread, egg bread, pita bread, sliced, unsliced, plastic wrapped, paper bagged, and unwrapped. The bread comes in loaves of all shapes and sizes: long bread sticks, round loaves, brick shaped, or loaf shaped as the dough determines. All we have to do is choose the one we want.

Unlike most of the people of history, we do not know the farmer who planted the seeds that made the grain to make the bread. We do not know the farmer's name. We do not know where, nor do we know how, to find the place where the wheat was threshed to get the grain to make the flour to make the bread. Nor do we know who took the trouble to bake the bread and transport it to us. Nor do we care.

In ancient times, you and I would have lived or died if the seeds were not planted, if the rain did not come, if the wheat was not harvested, if the grain was not threshed, the flour ground, and the bread baked. There was nothing casual about a loaf of bread!

Everybody was quite aware of the fact that the seeds needed to be planted, rain was needed for there to be a harvest, the grain needed to be threshed, and the ground flour was needed to have the bread of life so that one would not die. One picked up a loaf of bread with sacred reverence.

Between the planting of the seeds and the making of the bread was a pivotal ritual: the grain needed to be threshed — the wheat needs to be separated from the chaff before you can make the flour that you need for the bread.

We may have a question for Naomi's motives when we read the opening of chapter 3 when she was giving Ruth instructions on how to connect with her well-to-do kinsman, Boaz. We might question whether Naomi was self-interested or whether she was really concerned about getting her daughter-in-law, Ruth, a home and a husband. This question is one for us, but not for the people of the time. They were too close to the soil, too close to life and death, to be able to be phony.

Our story lives or dies on the principle that Naomi, Ruth, and Boaz were all people of sterling character. The actions of the text, the interchanges, the connections made, the consequences, and the resulting marriage of Ruth and Boaz, all hang on the genuine integrity of these individuals.

It goes without saying that Naomi predates feminism. She was a woman living in a man's world, but we would be in error to think that she did not have power. Naomi used her wisdom, her position in the community, and her knowledge of custom, culture, and men to instruct Ruth in how to connect positively with Boaz.

Ruth was fortunate because she had a mentor in her mother-in-law, Naomi. Ruth had someone she could confide in and trust implicitly. Naomi was one who had "been there, done that, and had the video." The two women were powerfully joined by love, trust and integrity. They acted powerfully by the fact that they were not only women of character, but their relationship moved and flowed with the impulse of absolute trust.

Naomi chose a man of character, in the person of Boaz, for the best interests of her beloved Ruth.

Then Naomi instructs Ruth in the best way to connect with Boaz. She tells Ruth to wash and anoint herself, put on her best clothes, and wait until Boaz has had his meal. Then she is to uncover his feet, lie down at his feet, and do as he says. Her coaching has the desired effect as the closing verses have Ruth marrying Boaz and conceiving a son, Obed, who was to become the father of Jesse, the father of David.

The women of the community affirm that the love of Ruth is more important to Naomi than having seven sons. They affirm that God has blessed Naomi in restoring her family status and she becomes a nurse for the baby boy, Obed.

The story came together on the threshing floor, the place where the late afternoon breeze separated the chaff from the barley for the bread to be made. In this case it was not only the bread to be eaten but the bread of relationship: the chaff was separated from the grain. In all the possibilities of all of the variables of men and women who could have connected, the chaff was separated from the grain and Ruth became married to Boaz; thus the royal line of David went on. The spiritual thread that weaves its way through this story is the sterling character of these God-fearing people, Ruth, Naomi, and Boaz. The rightness of it all is confirmed by the wisdom and blessing of the women of the community.

Where are the threshing floors of our lives? Where is it that we can separate the chaff from the grain of the people we meet? Where is it that we can connect with the women and men of character to whom we might join our lives and live in blessedness? The threshing floor is and must be a place of nurture and character development and discernment. My friends, in the absence of places to take the grain, our entire lives have become our threshing floors!

Because we casually pick up our loaves of bread, and we don't have any threshing floors anymore, we need to forge our characters in our homes and our families and our churches. We need to teach our children how to discern character in the people they meet and in whom they choose to marry if we are to establish royal lines of character in our families. We need to honor the grief and pain of our lives on the threshing floors that exist.

When we treat the chaff in people we meet like they were wheat, we and our children get into destructive and dangerous trouble in our relationships. We need to be able to separate the chaff from the wheat.

The bread is on the shelf, but we still need to separate the chaff from the grain in our lives, and we still need to build character, because that is what makes it work. Real character is what makes life come together in positive and blessed ways.

Character is a principle. The character of Naomi connecting with Ruth and on to the man of character in Boaz is what moved the story on. The scripture is telling us that character connecting with character is what life is all about.

May God give us the grace to discern that our families and our churches are the threshing floors where we might build character and discern it in those with whom we choose to share our lives. Amen.

Humble Beginnings

Small town folk will often ask a person on first meeting, "Who was your mother?" What they mean is: "What was your mother's last name before she was married?" By being introduced with first and last name, the father's family connection has been disclosed, but another question is needed to clarify the individual's beginnings from the other side of the family: "Who was your mother?"

We human beings are strongly interested in a person's beginnings. We have many ways of asking people where they were before they were here. In a big city, we ask, "Where are you from, originally?" When we apply for a job, we must present information that tells our prospective employer who we are and where we started. When a couple wants to get married, the clergy will ask, "Have you been married before? How did you meet?" We can also do reference checks, police checks, and credit checks, and we hire private investigators to find out the rest. We do all kinds of things to find out any particular person's beginnings, humble or otherwise.

The way we use the information regarding a person's beginnings is confusing. A prospective spouse doesn't seem to think that a partner's three failed marriages won't lead to a fourth. There is no evidence that greatness has anything to do with where you come from; great people can come from tiny insignificant places. ("Can anything good come out of Nazareth?") Failing mathematics did not stop Albert Einstein from becoming a great scientist. Ludwig van Beethoven's abuse at the hands of his father, eventually leading to total deafness, did not stop him from becoming one of the world's greatest composers.

403

In spite of all of the evidence to the contrary, we still often think that a person's beginnings determine where he or she is going to go or who he or she is going to be in one's life or employment.

Samuel, the son of Elkanah and Hannah, was a giant of the Bible. During his life, he carried the identity of the people of Israel through a time of transition from pre-monarchy to monarchy, and defined their future. He was known as a military and judicial judge. He was known as a nazarite, although we usually think of him as a prophet. Yet Samuel came from humble beginnings that are best described as barren.

Samuel's mother had to endure the pain of childlessness for many years. She was shamed by Elkanah's other wife, Peninnah who had been blessed to have many children. Even though Elkanah gave Hannah double portions to affirm his love for her, she still suffered the pain of Peninnah's persistent provocations.

A strong theme that emerges in this vignette is one we human beings do not like: waiting. The problem we have with waiting is that we never know if it is hopeless waiting or fruitful waiting. Until the waiting is over, we don't know which it is: helpful or wasteful.

We do know that Hannah's anguish at being childless overrides the lavish love that Elkanah has for her. The sad truth remains that Elkanah, with his great and noble past, has a barren wife and no hope of an heir from her. The family hopelessness mirrors the state of the nation which is confused and demoralized by the threat of the Philistines. They need a great king — and the great King David will eventually come and make right all that is wrong — but at this moment we find them stuck in a holding pattern of waiting. Everything hinges on a barren womb that the text tells us God has closed. Hannah is grief-stricken, depressed, and unable to eat.

This impasse is broken by worship. Hannah presents herself to God at Shiloh and the temple priest, Eli, witnesses her struggle. Just as many of us bargain with God, Hannah vows that if God gives her a son, she will give the son back to the service of God.

Hannah has to set the record straight with the priest Eli. When he sees her praying, he thinks that she is drunk. The priest does not recognize her desperation, grief, frustration, and her intense piety. To this very day, those of us who are desperate look compromised to the ones who observe us from the comfort of viewing anguish from the outside.

The priest Eli gives his benediction to her prayer: "Go in peace; may the God of Israel grant the petition you have made to him" (v. 17). The passage speaks of a deep faith: Hannah is in need, the priest mediates, God answers. The waiting is over, hope has returned, and the sovereign God has responded. There is no doubt.

"And she said, 'Let your servant find favor in your sight.' Then the woman went to her quarters, ate and drank with her husband and her countenance was sad no longer" (v. 18). Husband and wife rose early in the morning, they worshiped, they made love, "the Lord remembered her" and she bore a son and "... she named him Samuel, for she said, 'I have asked him of the Lord' " (v. 20).

There are times when things may look bleak and barren for us. We can articulate how bad things are in great detail and with great conviction, but we must always remember and never forget, that even though Hannah was barren, she was still a creature of God's sovereign universe, and she was still an agent for God's future plans in the world.

There are times of "bareness" for each of us: retirement leaves us with the feeling that we are no longer productive; the passion and vigor seems to have left our relationship; our hopes and dreams seem to be mistaken or unfulfilled; our child appears to be lost in an abyss of failure; our church seems to be going downhill; life seems to have lost its zest; a drug addict relapses yet again; the well has gone dry.

Maybe you think that the predicament in which you find yourself is much too humble beginnings where God is unlikely to do anything creative and wonderful. But that is exactly where we first found Hannah — humble beginnings from which God produced the great Samuel. Hannah was the personification of "humble beginnings."

When we feel that we are in hopeless despair like Hannah, we need to remember her solution. She took her problem to God: "Hannah rose and presented herself before the Lord" (v. 9).

In a spirit of communion, she continued to have faith in God when her options had been exhausted. She knew that Yahweh was more than she was and knew more than she did, therefore Hannah prayed sincerely. She was not in isolation; she had her spiritual advisor in the priest, Eli. She was not discouraged by other's misunderstanding of her and of her goal; she stood her ground (when Eli thought she was drunk). She continued to love her husband and abide in her faith.

You will notice that Hannah was not one of these phony self-help motivators, who pretend to be inexhaustible and have all of the answers. Hannah's source of energy and hope was in something outside of her being, but directly connected to her being. Her source of energy and hope was her faith in God.

When you and I, and Hannah and Elkanah and Peninnah, and other people (like your spouse, your friends, your boss) think a situation is barren, Yahweh, the Creator, the Life-Giver, the One who knows and continues to see beyond our horizons, says: "There is more! My kingdom is going on. I have more plans for your future and they are good!" With God, there are no barren wombs! Amen.

Covenant Of The Heart;
Sacred Signature

Marriage is a covenant. The marriage service speaks to the new couple with the words, "You are entering a covenantal relationship so profound that it will affect your entire life, your whole being."

A covenant is a type of promise that has multi-layered consequences and considerations. The breaking of a simple promise may or may not have significant implications. A salesperson may promise to phone or show up on a particular time and date, and if he doesn't, it may simply mean that someone else gets the sale. When a covenant is broken there are usually life altering, massive implications.

When a person hears that his/her spouse has been unfaithful, his/her universe often erupts like a gigantic volcano. Re-covenanting that relationship may or may not happen. A painful divorce may occur.

Four hundred years ago, people like John Calvin and Martin Luther believed that the Roman Catholic Church had broken its covenantal responsibility of being the dispensers of the Good News of the Gospel of Jesus Christ by means of false doctrines and blatant corruption. The Protestant Reformation was a massive shift in the journey of the church of Jesus Christ. Much work has been done by many Roman Catholics and Protestants to heal this rupture of the covenant. It is not too many years since Lutherans and Roman Catholics have finally spoken on theology together, healing a 400-year estrangement. Some of us may remember a number of years ago, when the Pope and the Archbishop of Canterbury walked together down the nave of Canterbury Cathedral and knelt together at the high altar and prayed the Lord's Prayer together.

Prior to the time of Jeremiah, the Jewish people had been living under the power and belief that they had several secure covenants holding them in a special place in God's world.

Each rainbow would remind them of the covenant with Noah that God would never destroy the world with another flood. The Jewish people had the covenant with Abraham establishing them as God's chosen people. They had the special covenant with Moses in leading them to the Promised Land and the Ark of the Covenant residing in God's temple in the heavenly city, Jerusalem. Nothing could stop them from being God's chosen people, secure in God's covenants with them.

The prophet Jeremiah spoke powerfully to the people that they were not keeping up their end of the agreement! A covenant is an agreement between two parties and each party has to keep his end of the deal. According to Jeremiah, the people were not keeping up their religious and political responsibilities, and he forecast doom and gloom for them.

In fact, we probably have the book of Jeremiah in the Bible today because his prophecies came true in the fall of Jerusalem and destruction of the Temple in 587 B.C.E.! The curtain had fallen for the last time on the kingdom of Judah. Not every prophecy from every prophet comes true. Jeremiah was a kind of Moses character to the ancient people, and after most of the cream of the Jewish society was taken into exile in Babylon, Jeremiah stayed behind to help those who remained.

We have to remember that this was a cataclysmic ordeal to the kingdom of Judah. The Jewish people suffered a destruction in 587 B.C.E. by the Babylonians that was not repaired until 1948 in the creation of the state of Israel! Try to get your head around the fact that in 587 they not only lost their country, but they also lost their "favored nation status" by God. And they effectively lost God, too. Or they thought that they lost God; they thought that God had abandoned them.

This covenant that we read today is highly significant because this was given by the same prophet to whom they failed to listen, who turned out to be correct in a big way!

In the book of Jeremiah, chapters 30, 31, and 33 are known as "the book of consolation." In spite of the destruction of the kingdom of Judah, in spite of the destruction of the sacred temple of God with the loss of the precious Ark of the Covenant, and in spite of the exile of the people, out of the pain of destruction we find the prophet giving the people a new covenant from God.

When a man of Mosaic stature and power issues new words from God, the people are all ears:

> "... this is the covenant that I will make with the house of Israel after those days, says the Lord: I will put my law within them, and I will write it on their hearts; and I will be their God, and they shall be my people. No longer shall they teach one another, or say to each other, 'Know the Lord,' for they shall all know me, from the least of them to the greatest, says the Lord; for I will forgive their inequity, and remember their sins no more."

The new covenant is one of a deeper kind. This covenant goes from the heart of God directly to the hearts of the people, "from the least of them to the greatest, says the Lord."

The implications are liberating. No longer is our relationship to God limited to our political well-being. No longer is the presence of God limited to the ark in a particular building, like a temple. No longer is God simply limited to our intelligence, thoughts, wisdom, and understanding.

According to the prophet Jeremiah, the Lord God is connecting heart to heart with each one of us, to the point that even the admonition to "know the Lord" is irrelevant! The love from the heart of God is the only love that could send us Jesus. The love that is written on our hearts is one that goes with us anywhere, anytime. The love that is written on our hearts is the only kind of love that can sustain us. It is a love that is totally inclusive and all-embracing to every single one of us, no matter what.

It is a love that dares to forgive our inequity and does not even remember our sins. It is a love that challenges us in all of our understandings, both of ourselves and our relationships. It is a love that seeks to give and heal in a time of national and personal trauma in Jeremiah's time, a love that we need for the devastation and trauma of our own times and lives.

We human beings have many ways to pass on our faith: we have Bibles, we have churches and massive cathedrals, we have the faith of the people, we have clergy, we have crosses, we have sermons, testimonials, and books, we have councils, assemblies, presbyteries, and conventions, and we have bishops, archbishops and popes. But they all pale beside the words of the prophet from God telling us that God's love is individually written on our hearts, from the least of us to the greatest of us.

God has written on the heart of each of us, "My child, I love you."

But there is a question we must answer. Are we willing — are we willing to go there?

We are willing to go to many places. We are willing to travel around the world, we are willing to visit friends, we are willing to go on holidays, and we are willing to go places for other people. We are willing to go into marriage. We are willing to go to the mall, to bars, to hockey games, baseball games, football games, basketball games, to crack houses, funeral homes, and brothels. But, are we willing to go on the sacred journey inward to the place of God, the holy place where God has written his love, the place where that love is inscribed on our hearts, "I will put my law *within* them," God said?

Are you willing to go to the place of total equality with all of your brothers and sisters, the place of forgiveness, the place of love, the place lovingly touched by the Creator, the place of God? To the place where love is written and signed with your name on it; signed, sealed, and delivered by the sacrament of baptism? Are you willing to accept what God has written on your hearts? Are you willing to embrace the love put "within" you by God?

This prophet, the one speaking to you now, is telling you, the journey inward, the journey to the center of yourself, the journey towards God — the bottom line is: *that* journey is the *only one* worth taking. Amen.

All Saints' Sunday
Isaiah 25:6-9

The Moment Of Celebration

It is a known fact that most people like a party. However, strange as it might seem, most of the people don't want to be the center of attraction. Likewise, many adults, when presented with a thoughtful gift, often exclaim, "You *shouldn't* have!" Children, on the other hand, seem to enjoy the party whether it is theirs or someone else's party. Children relish the notion of celebration. They never say that they shouldn't have received a gift and they tear it open before they read the card!

Celebration is not an orgy of indulgence, but an occasion of honor, a time of refraining from ordinary tasks, a time to observe a notable occasion with festivities, a time of uplift. The person for whom the celebration is called is an honored person, and the people attending are also honored to be there.

Chapters 24 through 27 of Isaiah are sometimes known as the "Isaiah Apocalypse"; that is to say an Isaiah version of what the prophet says God is revealing to humankind; a revelation from God. The vignette we read today is a description of an eschatological banquet; a great celebratory banquet at the end of time, a feast hosted by the Lord of Creation, to which all peoples of the world are invited and which is held at a holy place, the mountain of the Lord: the place where God dwells, Mount Zion, the city of God.

We might think that, unlike us, Isaiah did not have any of the threats under which we live: AIDS, nuclear war, high rates of marital distress, and personal illness. Such was not the case. His country lived under the reality of the destruction by the Babylonians, exile, famine, high infant mortality, personal illness, and low life expectancy. Isaiah's litany of the banquet of joy means all the more if we remember that it was conceived and born in time of peril, anguish, and fear.

In our constant quest to make "the word of God" available and accessible to all people, we find that Isaiah was not a small provincial thinker with tunnel vision. Isaiah's description of this heavenly feast of celebration was one of a vast inclusion for all people. "On this mountain the Lord of hosts will make for all peoples a feast of rich food, a feast of well-aged wines, of rich food filled with marrow, of well-aged wines strained clear" (v. 6).

Do we ever consider *why* we celebrate? Why do we celebrate the sacraments, Easter, Christmas, thanksgiving, birthdays, baptisms, marriages, anniversaries, retirements, and all kinds of occasions? Do we party just to party? Do we celebrate just to feel good, just for its own sake?

According to verse 7, the answer is, "No." According to verse 7, there is more to the party than the party. According to verse 7, there is a significance to the celebration that is beyond the celebration itself: "And he will destroy on this mountain the shroud that is cast over all peoples, the sheet that is spread over all nations; he will swallow up death forever" (v. 7).

Isaiah is telling us that there is more to that moment of celebration than that which meets our eye or our understanding. The prophet is telling us that something else is going on: this rich feast of celebration is precipitating an action of God; the blessing of this divine banquet given to the guests by the host is the destruction of "the shroud that is cast over all peoples, the sheet that is spread over all nations; he will swallow up death forever."

The moment of divine celebration at this banquet of banquets is also the destruction of death: the elimination of our greatest fear, the calming of our worst anxiety, the healing of our worst nightmare, the destruction of the greatest obstacle to our growth and freedom.

The moment of divine celebration is one where all our veils are removed, all of the things that enslave us are lifted. This banquet is a supreme act of love and compassion by God on behalf of

412

God's beloved: "Then the Lord will wipe away the tears from all faces, and the disgrace of his people he will take away from all the earth, for the Lord has spoken" (v. 8).

God is personally embracing each of us like a loving parent and offering unconditional, unqualified, totally compassionate, grief healing, forgiving, redemptive acceptance.

And our response to the transforming, restorative joy of this event: "It will be said on that day, 'Lo, this is our God; we have waited for him, so that he might save us. This is the Lord for whom we have waited; let us be glad and rejoice in his salvation.' "

We are not to say for this magnanimous, magnificent gift, "O God, you *shouldn't* have!"

How can God love you without making you occasionally, the center of attention?

This is the God whom we loved, and he did come and love as he promised and as we expected, and we are now both together, and we have been saved by the Savior.

Hallelujah!

We need all the moments of celebration we can get. Friends, we need celebrations in our lives, because those very moments of celebration *define* our lives: the moments of celebration alter our course and set our coordinates in new directions, the moments of celebration give us energy to go on, the moments of celebration renew our lives, these moments nourish our lives and bring us back from exile, and the moments of celebration give us rest — they cause us to stop, pause, and gain insight as to who we are and where we are going.

Without the moments of celebration we are just "busy" all of the time without thinking about who we are and where we are going. Every time you and I have an opportunity to go to a celebration, we need to go and feed on that moment of celebration for the betterment of our lives.

Every time we worship, we celebrate our kinship with God. That experience serves to refocus, redefine, re-covenant, and reinvigorate our lives. True celebration creates holy, sacred space: safe space. The sacrament of Holy Communion connects us with the communion of all the millions of the Saints of Christendom. Communion is a powerful experience in feeling connected; a great antidote for loneliness, lostness, and loss of identity. We are creatures of communion created by our Maker to live at our best when we are in harmony with other people, *especially at the moment of celebration.*

The celebration of Baptism is another moment that serves to remind us that we exist as people saved by grace as a gift from God, not based on our merit, but that our salvation is based on our value as God's beloved daughters and sons.

Let us speak, with joy and utter trust to the Lord of history, the words of the prophet, that within each service of worship, we might be filled with the spirit of God and affirm in our hearts: "This is the Lord for whom we have waited; let us be glad and rejoice in his salvation!" (v. 9b). Amen.

Christ The King
2 Samuel 23:1-7

What Is Your Legacy?

Maybe you have had the experience of being mentioned in the last will and testament of someone who has died. As you listen during this poignant experience to the reading of a deceased person's last wishes, a legacy is being passed on. Both as we live and as we die, we pass on a legacy to the rest of the world.

If you think because you haven't been mentioned in someone's will that you are existing on your own, you will have to think again, because we all enter and continue to live in a world created by the legacy of the past: each one of us lives with the DNA of our parents; each one of us was born in a town and country that someone else built; we are born into the freedom or the tyranny that was handed to us by our ancestors; we were born in hospitals, attended schools, and lived in homes built by someone else; each one of us studied books and learned from the body of knowledge that was passed on to us; each one of us lived and fared, for better or for worse, in whatever state in which we found ourselves.

We may vary in our intelligence and our human gifts, we may move to other cities or countries, we may choose jobs or partners that our parents don't want, but we are greatly influenced by the legacy of what was passed on to us.

On this day, we celebrate as the Sunday of Christ the King, we read the last words, the legacy, of an earlier king, another man, a complex man: David, who at one point was King over all Israel. King David's legacy comes to us today as an oracle of David: a divinely inspired, wise, and authoritative utterance.

There are people who might describe themselves as being anti-monarchy, but we have to realize that the power of the king is not the king's power; the king was chosen by God as a vehicle to dispense God's power on his behalf, for the betterment of the common good of the people, and especially for those who are weak and vulnerable and need the king's blessing.

"... the oracle of the man whom God exalted, the anointed of the God of Jacob, the favorite of the Strong One of Israel." In other words, the king is not there because of his own personal greatness, but because of a calling. The king is there because he was chosen as God's chief servant. The king is accountable to a higher power, an honor more than a privilege.

David says that God is speaking through him: "The spirit of the Lord speaks through me," he says. Therefore what he does must be done with justice and with a deep connection founded on a relationship with God: "One who rules over people justly, ruling in the fear of God."

The king is to act with justice towards the people on God's behalf, with the king himself being a subject to God in a relationship of love and mutual respect with God. The king is not to rule as a despot or a dictator, or by his own whims and fantasies. He is to rule as an instrument of God's justice, with a deep sense of God's righteousness for all creation. The purpose is clear and positive. The reign and power of the king is to be "like the light of morning, like the sun rising on a cloudless morning, gleaming from the rain on the grassy land."

The image of the reign of the king is one that is fresh and uplifting, healthy, lush and exuberant; it is an image grounded in the Bible's eternal echo of mutual covenant with its implied responsibilities and benefits.

David says, "Is not my house like this with God? For he has made with me an everlasting covenant, ordered in all things and secure. Will he not cause to prosper all my help and my desire?"

King David's last words affirm God's sovereign power, with the accompanying moral expectations, and God's fidelity to his people, in spite of the historical humanity of a character like David. These words also give understanding to our notion of Jesus as King.

416

King David has given a legacy that was as good for his people then as it is for us now: as King David was the son of Jessie, we are all a product of our heritage; as David was the anointed of God, we are the baptized; we are each called into vocation on planet earth. As David was the sweet psalmist of Israel, we all have our gifts and we need to identity and express those gifts; as David spoke for the Lord, each of us speaks with a spirit, positive or negative, healing or destructive, peaceful or challenging. The health of our leaders is a reflection of the health of the nation; we identify with our leaders; our leaders are subject to a higher power. Part of our identity is that we all belong to God, and when we live in God, we pass along that "God lifeness" to others; the power of living in a covenantal relationship with God has a powerful benefit in the mutual connection of that relationship.

The anointed king's legacy is passed on in the ancient scriptures, through the anointed King Jesus, and through our baptism, and as we live, and pass on, our legacy is passed on to our children, our family, and to our world.

What is your legacy? As sure as you live, you are going to pass on *something*. What is your legacy? For what do you stand?

Can you confront evil? Can you say, "I am a Christian? This is where I stand." You may not go to speak at the UN. It may be over a meal with so called "friends" where you pound out your legacy. You may speak for the protection of your neighbor's child.

Do you stand for God? As God is love, do you stand for love or do you not? In your life, are you leaving a legacy of love by the actions of your life? Do you dare to love? Do you dare to love with a freedom that loves without asking for repayment?

If you do not love then what is the point of living, without love? You were created to love. Without love, all of the covenants, all of the anointing, all of the blessings, all of the words, all of the outpourings of the Spirit, they all come to nothing!

Surely, when the time comes and we stand before God and we are asked what we have done, we need only to reply:

"I loved.
With what you gave me, I loved.

I loved children.

I loved my family.

I loved my friends.

I loved people in need, as I was able.

I loved myself, so that Your Spirit would flow though me.

I loved you, dear God, in how I loved others.

I planted flowers. I celebrated birthdays to show people
that I loved and honored them.

When evil appeared, I loudly said, 'No!'

When an opportunity to love came along, I said, 'Yes.'

I tried to let go of the bad and hold on to the good; as I
opened my eyes, I saw there was lots of good you sent
my way to save me from the bad.

I realized that you were sending me each and every day
opportunities to love.

I tried very hard not to lose time from loving with wasting
time and energy in hating.

I loved music, I loved looking at the sky and the ocean, I
loved beautiful pictures, and all of the ways that you
awaken beauty in life on planet earth.

But most of all, dear Lord, I loved seeing your face in the
faces of all the people that I met each and every day of
my life, and I thank you for this great opportunity that
you have given me to love, in what some people call
'life.'

I joyfully and gladly pass on to others the wonderful legacy
that was passed on to me.

I thank you that I was able to understand for so many years
that life was meant to be called Love."

Amen.

The God Who Never Lets Go Of Us

The prophets of antiquity faced problems no different from the soothsayers of today: what language can you use and what power can you muster to call people into harmonious living with God and neighbor?

When we observe Catholics and Protestants fighting in Northern Ireland, when we observe wives and husbands fighting, when we observe Jews and Arabs fighting, when we see desperately poor, famine-ravaged countries in Africa fighting with their neighbors, when we observe children smoking and taking Ecstasy, when we observe our politicians fighting, when we read of acts of abuse and murder, the prophet in all of us screams: STOP!

For God's sake, STOP!

A prophet like Joel was in the same sort of position. He saw the people participating in self-destructive behavior, and he used all the power that he could muster in his words to get the people to come to a new way of thinking, to come to a resolution of the estrangement from themselves, from their neighbors, and from their God. The prophet desired peace, harmony, and fidelity to God.

We look at our planet in a different way than we used to 2,400 years ago, when this text was written. There is a description of a locust plague in the first part of the book of Joel. We don't know if Joel is referring to a recent plague or if he is referring to former events to illustrate God's call to repentance. The wisdom back then and what Joel implied was that God sent the plague. Today, when we listen to the weather, the television announcer doesn't say that God is going to send a horrific storm up the east coast to cause millions of dollars of damage and loss of life. We say that the satellites tells us a warm front is colliding with a cold front and it's going to cause a storm and we'd better take shelter. We don't take the storm and national calamity as personal attacks by God.

When we look at ancient texts, we have to open up our modern thinking so that we might hear "the word of the Lord" speak to us from the heart of the prophet uttered so many years ago. We have to go deeper than where the rationale of our present logic might take us.

In our text today, Joel is giving us God's response to his people when they turn to God — a picture of God's desire of what can happen between God and his people when both desire relationship. "Do not fear, O soil; be glad and rejoice, for the Lord has done great things. Do not fear, you animals of the field, for the pastures of the wilderness are green; the tree bears its fruit, the fig tree and vine give their full yield" (vv. 21, 22).

Joel opens both verses telling us, as he did the people of antiquity, not to be afraid. Did you know that the phrase, "Do not be afraid," is found 365 times in the Bible? Not only the prophet Joel, but the whole Bible is telling us that the God of peace and comfort does not want us to be afraid!

What is it that we fear?

These two verses tell us to "be glad and rejoice for the Lord has done great things." The passage even tells the animals of the field not to worry because they will have green pastures and there will be a full harvest.

In plain English these verses are telling us that God will be there for us, God will be present, and there will be plenty of food, water, oil, and wine. The abundance relayed in his prophecy is evidence of God's presence.

By deduction, what we must fear then, is the loss of God's presence: abandonment. We fear loneliness. We fear estrangement. We fear being alone. We fear being rejected by other people and by God. We fear being by ourselves.

The Bible and our own lives are full of experiences of our rejection of God and God's Word, whether it is Adam and Eve rejecting God's admonition not to eat of the tree of the forbidden

420

fruit in the Garden, the people at the time of Noah prior to the flood, the people who constructed the tower of Babel, the people to whom the prophet Joel was speaking, the warmongers who caused the deaths of 200 million people in the last century, or the crowd 2,000 years ago that cried, "Crucify him!"

In spite of our human rejection of God, the prophet Joel speaks to us of a God who, in spite of our constant rejection, *absolutely refuses to let us go!*

Joel speaks to us of a God who "vindicates" our transgressions, a God who pours down the rain both for our thirst and so our crops might grow, a God who promises that our "threshing floors will be full of grain," and our "vats shall overflow with wine and oil."

It has to confound our senses and challenge our petty "tit for tat" kind of thinking to comprehend a God who, faced with the massive rejection of humanity, overlooks our rejection and in turn promises us so much abundant love and prosperity.

How are we to figure this out? God's generous love is beyond our comprehension, so how can we understand it?

Maybe what we have to do is just accept it; embrace the love of God in our hearts and in our lives, with gratitude, on this special day of thanks, for all of the blessings that we receive from God.

Joel goes on to stretch our minds about the love of God. He goes on to say that God will repay us for the losses we have suffered (the losses eaten by the destroying locusts), furthermore: "You shall eat plenty and be satisfied, and praise the name of the Lord your God, who has dealt wondrously with you. And my people shall never again be put to shame. You shall know that I am in the midst of Israel, and that I, the Lord, am your God and there is no other. And my people shall never again be put to shame" (vv. 26, 27).

Twice in these two verses, we have God saying that he will destroy the shame of the people. Shame is a great destroyer. Shame destroys people's self-esteem, their spirit to live and love and do well in their lives. Shame obscures a person's ability to see the gifts one has been given by God to live one's life and to love other people.

What does a shamed person look like? A person who has been shamed is one who has a painful sense of having done something wrong. Shamed people often look happy and wear masks so that other people will not know the pain they carry, because they are ashamed. Shamed people's lives are determined by the secret pain they carry; they medicate it with drugs and alcohol, and all kinds of compulsive behaviors. Children are shamed when their parents divorce because they think they caused the divorce. (If only I had been a better boy or girl, Mommy and Daddy would still be together.) Shamed people think they are undeserving and unlovable and deserve to be alone.

Looks like "shame" and "abandonment" are connected, does it not?

If the prophet Joel was standing here today, and we said, "Cut to the chase! Tell us what you have to say in one sentence!" What would he say? I think he might say: "Folks, if you accepted the love of God into your lives, nobody would ever be able to shame you!"

"... if you accepted the love of God into your lives, nobody would be able to shame you!"

You would have to accept the moral and ethical imperative of your existence: since you were created by love, you are lovable. You would have to accept the fact that you are lovable.

The words of the prophet have more impact if you realize that the word "Joel" means "the Lord (Yahweh) is God." Joel is truly speaking for and as God's prophet, when he says: "And my people shall never again be put to shame."

I am going to leave you with a commandment for a successful life.

Being created by God and as "God is love," you were created for love and were never meant to be alone. You have God's promise that you will never be abandoned. And if you truly want to go in life where you were created to go, the choice is yours for an authentic life that will be all it is meant to be, so then you only need to believe in the God who believes in you and will never desert you! Amen.

Lectionary Preaching After Pentecost

The following index will aid the user of this book in matching the correct Sunday with the appropriate text during Pentecost. All texts in this book are from the series for the First Readings, Revised Common Lectionary. (Note that the ELCA division of Lutheranism is now following the Revised Common Lectionary.) The Lutheran designations indicate days comparable to Sundays on which Revised Common Lectionary Propers or Ordinary Time designations are used.

(Fixed dates do not pertain to Lutheran Lectionary)

Fixed Date Lectionaries *Revised Common (including ELCA)* *and Roman Catholic*	**Lutheran Lectionary** *Lutheran*
The Day of Pentecost	The Day of Pentecost
The Holy Trinity	The Holy Trinity
May 29-June 4 — Proper 4, Ordinary Time 9	Pentecost 2
June 5-11 — Proper 5, Ordinary Time 10	Pentecost 3
June 12-18 — Proper 6, Ordinary Time 11	Pentecost 4
June 19-25 — Proper 7, Ordinary Time 12	Pentecost 5
June 26-July 2 — Proper 8, Ordinary Time 13	Pentecost 6
July 3-9 — Proper 9, Ordinary Time 14	Pentecost 7
July 10-16 — Proper 10, Ordinary Time 15	Pentecost 8
July 17-23 — Proper 11, Ordinary Time 16	Pentecost 9
July 24-30 — Proper 12, Ordinary Time 17	Pentecost 10
July 31-Aug. 6 — Proper 13, Ordinary Time 18	Pentecost 11
Aug. 7-13 — Proper 14, Ordinary Time 19	Pentecost 12
Aug. 14-20 — Proper 15, Ordinary Time 20	Pentecost 13
Aug. 21-27 — Proper 16, Ordinary Time 21	Pentecost 14
Aug. 28-Sept. 3 — Proper 17, Ordinary Time 22	Pentecost 15
Sept. 4-10 — Proper 18, Ordinary Time 23	Pentecost 16
Sept. 11-17 — Proper 19, Ordinary Time 24	Pentecost 17
Sept. 18-24 — Proper 20, Ordinary Time 25	Pentecost 18

Sept. 25-Oct. 1 — Proper 21, Ordinary Time 26	Pentecost 19
Oct. 2-8 — Proper 22, Ordinary Time 27	Pentecost 20
Oct. 9-15 — Proper 23, Ordinary Time 28	Pentecost 21
Oct. 16-22 — Proper 24, Ordinary Time 29	Pentecost 22
Oct. 23-29 — Proper 25, Ordinary Time 30	Pentecost 23
Oct. 30-Nov. 5 — Proper 26, Ordinary Time 31	Pentecost 24
Nov. 6-12 — Proper 27, Ordinary Time 32	Pentecost 25
Nov. 13-19 — Proper 28, Ordinary Time 33	Pentecost 26
	Pentecost 27
Nov. 20-26 — Christ The King	Christ The King

Reformation Day (or last Sunday in October) is October 31 (Revised Common, Lutheran)

All Saints' Day (or first Sunday in November) is November 1 (Revised Common, Lutheran, Roman Catholic)

U.S. / Canadian Lectionary Comparison

The following index shows the correlation between the Sundays and special days of the church year as they are titled or labeled in the Revised Common Lectionary published by the Consultation On Common Texts and used in the United States (the reference used for this book) and the Sundays and special days of the church year as they are titled or labeled in the Revised Common Lectionary used in Canada.

Revised Common Lectionary	Canadian Revised Common Lectionary
Advent 1	Advent 1
Advent 2	Advent 2
Advent 3	Advent 3
Advent 4	Advent 4
Christmas Eve	Christmas Eve
Nativity Of The Lord/Christmas Day	The Nativity Of Our Lord
Christmas 1	Christmas 1
January 1 / Holy Name of Jesus	January 1 / The Name Of Jesus
Christmas 2	Christmas 2
Epiphany Of The Lord	The Epiphany Of Our Lord
Baptism Of The Lord / Epiphany 1	The Baptism Of Our Lord / Proper 1
Epiphany 2 / Ordinary Time 2	Epiphany 2 / Proper 2
Epiphany 3 / Ordinary Time 3	Epiphany 3 / Proper 3
Epiphany 4 / Ordinary Time 4	Epiphany 4 / Proper 4
Epiphany 5 / Ordinary Time 5	Epiphany 5 / Proper 5
Epiphany 6 / Ordinary Time 6	Epiphany 6 / Proper 6
Epiphany 7 / Ordinary Time 7	Epiphany 7 / Proper 7
Epiphany 8 / Ordinary Time 8	Epiphany 8 / Proper 8
Transfiguration Of The Lord / Last Sunday After Epiphany	The Transfiguration Of Our Lord / Last Sunday After Epiphany
Ash Wednesday	Ash Wednesday
Lent 1	Lent 1
Lent 2	Lent 2
Lent 3	Lent 3
Lent 4	Lent 4
Lent 5	Lent 5
Passion/Palm Sunday (Lent 6)	Passion/Palm Sunday
Holy/Maundy Thursday	Holy/Maundy Thursday
Good Friday	Good Friday
Resurrection Of The Lord / Easter	The Resurrection Of Our Lord

Easter 2	Easter 2
Easter 3	Easter 3
Easter 4	Easter 4
Easter 5	Easter 5
Easter 6	Easter 6
Ascension Of The Lord	The Ascension Of Our Lord
Easter 7	Easter 7
Day Of Pentecost	The Day Of Pentecost
Trinity Sunday	The Holy Trinity
Proper 4 / Pentecost 2 / O T 9*	Proper 9
Proper 5 / Pent 3 / O T 10	Proper 10
Proper 6 / Pent 4 / O T 11	Proper 11
Proper 7 / Pent 5 / O T 12	Proper 12
Proper 8 / Pent 6 / O T 13	Proper 13
Proper 9 / Pent 7 / O T 14	Proper 14
Proper 10 / Pent 8 / O T 15	Proper 15
Proper 11 / Pent 9 / O T 16	Proper 16
Proper 12 / Pent 10 / O T 17	Proper 17
Proper 13 / Pent 11 / O T 18	Proper 18
Proper 14 / Pent 12 / O T 19	Proper 19
Proper 15 / Pent 13 / O T 20	Proper 20
Proper 16 / Pent 14 / O T 21	Proper 21
Proper 17 / Pent 15 / O T 22	Proper 22
Proper 18 / Pent 16 / O T 23	Proper 23
Proper 19 / Pent 17 / O T 24	Proper 24
Proper 20 / Pent 18 / O T 25	Proper 25
Proper 21 / Pent 19 / O T 26	Proper 26
Proper 22 / Pent 20 / O T 27	Proper 27
Proper 23 / Pent 21 / O T 28	Proper 28
Proper 24 / Pent 22 / O T 29	Proper 29
Proper 25 / Pent 23 / O T 30	Proper 30
Proper 26 / Pent 24 / O T 31	Proper 31
Proper 27 / Pent 25 / O T 32	Proper 32
Proper 28 / Pent 26 / O T 33	Proper 33
Christ The King (Proper 29 / O T 34)	Proper 34 / Christ The King/ Reign Of Christ
Reformation Day (October 31)	Reformation Day (October 31)
All Saints' Day (November 1 or 1st Sunday in November)	All Saints' Day (November 1)
Thanksgiving Day (4th Thursday of November)	Thanksgiving Day (2nd Monday of October)

*O T = Ordinary Time

426

About The Authors

Curtis Lewis has served in the Church of the Nazarene as a parish pastor and college professor, where he has taught preaching and pastoral theology. He received his M.Div. degree from Nazarene Theological Seminary and his D.Min. degree from Trinity Lutheran Seminary. Since 1997 Lewis has been the District Superintendent of the Church of the Nazarene's Northern Michigan District.

Richard E. Gribble, CSC, the author of fourteen books and over 100 articles, currently teaches at Stonehill College in North Easton, Massachusetts. A graduate of the United States Naval Academy, Father Gribble served for five years on nuclear submarines before entering the priesthood. Gribble earned his Ph.D. from The Catholic University of America, and has also earned degrees from the University of Southern California and the Jesuit School of Theology at Berkeley. He is the former rector/superior of Moreau Seminary at the University of Notre Dame. Among his previous CSS publications is a three-volume series on *The Parables Of Jesus.*

Linda R. Forsberg is the senior pastor at First Evangelical Lutheran Church in East Greenwich, Rhode Island, and also serves as the chaplain for the East Greenwich Fire Department. She is a graduate of Brown University (B.A. in Religious Studies) and Harvard University (M.Div.).

Timothy J. Smith, currently the pastor of Ironville United Methodist Church in Columbia, Pennsylvania, has served several congregations in Eastern Pennsylvania during the past eighteen years. Over 100 of Smith's sermons have been published in the periodical *Dynamic Preaching*, and he is the author of the CSS titles *No Particular Place To Go* and *Lectionary Tales For The Pulpit* (Series II, Cycle A). Smith received his M.Div. degree with an emphasis on preaching and worship from United Theological Seminary and his B.A. degree in American History from Millersburg University.

H. Alan Stewart has been the pastor at Westview Presbyterian Church in Toronto, Ontario, Canada, since 1990. He is a frequent speaker on men's issues and a resource person for men's healing groups. Prior to entering the ministry, Stewart pursued careers in hotel management, music, and real estate. Stewart is a graduate of the University of Prince Edward Island (B.A.), McGill University (B.Mus.), and Knox College of the University of Toronto (M.Div.).